SELF-REGULATION
AND
HUMAN PROGRESS

SELF-REGULATION AND HUMAN PROGRESS

HOW SOCIETY GAINS WHEN WE GOVERN LESS

Evan Osborne

STANFORD ECONOMICS AND FINANCE

An Imprint of Stanford University Press

Stanford, California

Stanford University Press
Stanford, California

Special discounts for bulk quantities of titles in the Stanford Economics
and Finance imprint are available to corporations, professional
associations, and other organizations. For details and discount information,
contact the special sales department of Stanford University Press.
Tel: (650) 725-0820, Fax: (650) 725-3457

Printed in the United States of America on acid-free, archival-quality paper

Library of Congress Cataloging-in-Publication Data

Names: Osborne, Evan, author.
Title: Self-regulation and human progress : how society gains when we govern
less / Evan Osborne.
Description: Stanford, California : Stanford Economics and Finance, an
imprint of Stanford University Press, 2018. | Includes bibliographical
references and index.
Identifiers: LCCN 2017032094 (print) | LCCN 2017035283 (ebook) |
ISBN 9781503604247 (e-book) | ISBN 9780804796446 (cloth : alk. paper)
Subjects: LCSH: Free enterprise. | Liberty. | Economic policy. | Political
science. | Progress.
Classification: LCC HB95 (ebook) | LCC HB95 .O83 2017 (print) |
DDC 330.12/2--dc23
LC record available at https://lccn.loc.gov/2017032094

Typeset by Bruce Lundquist in 10/15 Sabon
Cover design: Rob Ehle
Cover photograph: iStock

To Victoria, who can usually work it out on her own

Contents

List of Tables and Figures

Preface and Acknowledgments

As I was editing this book, a horrifying story hit the front pages involving Flint, Michigan, once a hub of the auto industry but now struggling. Placed under emergency state management in 2013, the new managers decided, with the approval of the elected city council, to save money by taking drinking water from Lake Huron instead of continuing to buy it from the city of Detroit. But the project would take time to complete, and the Detroit Water and Sewage Department in April 2013 provided the required one-year notice to terminate the contract. The authorities (elected officials and appointed emergency managers disagree on the particulars) then elected to take water from the Flint River beginning in April 2014.

Flint's water pipes had not been properly treated to prevent corrosion from the river water, and as a result, lead and other toxins leached into the drinking water. Monitoring for lead and copper in the water began in July, and in September city officials told residents to boil water (which kills microorganisms but is useless against metals). In January 2015, Detroit water authorities offered to let Flint reconnect without charge, but no one accepted the offer. In May 2015, federal and state authorities began to trade e-mails about the problem. Concerns were raised at the federal Environmental Protection Agency in May 2015 over lead in the water, but amid disagreement about whether it was a state or federal responsibility, little was done. Various citizens began to speak out about lead specifically in September 2015, but not until September 25 did city authorities issue an advisory about lead in the water.

It is safe to say that not a single public official at any level in any way wanted residents to drink leaded water. And yet it happened. Why? The broader answer to that question is what this book is about. Note that General Motors, with both a direct incentive to closely monitor water quality and the capacity to do something about it, ceased using Flint River water at its engine plant in that city in October 2014. Note also that after the crisis emerged in late 2015, private companies such as Walmart quickly geared up to provide bottled water, something that has drawn some criticism from those who believe this encroaches on government's proper tasks.[1]

At no point had it been a closely held secret that untreated river water posed a threat if it passed through the pipes in Flint and the potential dangers of lead in water were widely known. But the incentives in political contexts, even democratic ones, are often primitive. The local authorities faced little competition to provide water to individual consumers. The process through which public authorities could get feedback about the quality of their decisions was similarly stinted.

Much of the public commentary since the revelation of these events has turned on whose fault it was. That is important in a political context, because generally fault is allocated to our side or theirs, and rewards to politicians depend on what voters decide. But assigning blame does not get lead out of the water any faster; indeed the incentives of democratic politics did not prevent it from getting into the water in the first place. Such sustained disasters are the hallmark of processes where feedback is weak. The argument is not that the private sector could have more effectively and cheaply provided water to Flint residents from the beginning, although that's probably true. (In fairness, such catastrophes happen in commercial environments as well. For example, a chemical plant owned by the private firm Union Carbide leaked toxic chemicals in Bhopal, India, in 1984, and thousands died.) Rather, it is an invitation to think about how decisions get made in environments where humans organize. As you proceed into this book, you may wish to consider also the U.S. income tax code, which no one would design in its present form from scratch, and yet which appears difficult, if not impossible, to significantly alter. You may also wish to think about how we travel, communicate, work, and otherwise live—umbrella topics that pose challenges far more complex than redoing the tax code.

At the most basic level, this book is about what happens when we just let people work it out. It sketches the rise and wane of the idea that people's intrinsic motivations are often sufficient to govern their collective choices and lead them to the best ones available. In thinking about economics, this idea is well known and long disputed. But it turns out that laissez-faire in economics was the culmination of thinking in other realms that had been going on for well over a century. It's a story that begins in the

1500s and echoes through the subsequent centuries. It connects disparate realms of science, free speech, and socioeconomics. And along the way, it argues for the virtues of leaving well enough alone to solve problems like the crisis in Flint.

Long before thinking of the idea for this book, I had been exposed to many other ideas that put me in a position to tell this tale. And so I thank Steven Landsburg, Deirdre McCloskey, Thomas Sowell, and Don Boudreaux for unknowingly preparing me so nicely through their own work in a variety of media. I also thank Russ Roberts, at least in his EconTalk incarnation, for providing the very model of a forum where people can contend intellectually—not to win but purely with the goal of getting to the truth. I have never met any of these people, but that doesn't mean I haven't learned from them. As always, I thank above all my students, on whom I try to impress the value of reasoned disagreement and from whom I always learn so much. Comments from readers are always welcome, at evan.osborne@wright.edu.

SELF-REGULATION
AND
HUMAN PROGRESS

CHAPTER I

Problems and Responses

I maintain that Liberty is the chief cause of excellence.

EDWARD BAINES JR. (1800–1890)[1]

Consider the following situations, and how best to address them:

1. A major media figure claims that eating a certain kind of food may cause the (literal) consumer to incur a fatal disease. Sellers of the food, maybe believing the charge false and certainly worried about damage to their sales, wish to prevent the claim from gaining acceptance and to prevent future similar claims from being made.

2. A property developer wishes to build single-family homes on undeveloped land, plus roads to service them. If he does so, people have more housing choices, but traffic, and crowding more generally, increase there.

3. People with certain types of autoimmune problems become convinced that ingesting parasitic worms, ordinarily a dangerous thing to do, will reset their immune systems, restoring their health. The government, worried about the unproven efficacy and unknown danger of such treatment, then prohibits it.

4. A scientist publishes a paper the truth of whose data come into question. The scientist asserts they are accurate.

5. The central square of a European city laid out before the invention of the internal combustion engine now has many automobile accidents.

All of these situations are based on actual events, and in each, there is expected harm to be traded against potential gain no matter what we do. The first is based on a case involving Oprah Winfrey, who allowed people on her television show to make claims about the danger of consuming beef. These claims generated a lawsuit (which Ms. Winfrey ultimately won) by Texas cattle ranchers worried about "defamation" of their product. If people wrongly believe a false claim about the danger of consuming beef, it does indeed damage the livelihood of those ranchers, but to punish the person who made the claim will deter other people from publicly raising what they see as other serious problems for fear of incurring similar, misplaced (if the claim is true) punishment.

The trade-offs of urbanization and exurbanization have generated a movement known as "smart growth" (the phrase is telling) that proposes to contain "unplanned" development by creating more zoning rules to channel it in desirable directions. The third story, about the worms, is told in a book by Moisés Velasquez-Manoff on new thinking about why auto-immune diseases happen.[2] The Americans he describes resort to visits to Mexico or subterranean markets in the United States to obtain treatment that is prohibited by U.S. authorities. As for the fourth example, disputed scientific papers, whose value depends on their authenticity, are of course far from rare. And finally, it is always possible to try to improve traffic safety by more tightly controlling driving behavior, but the more copious traffic regulations are, the more difficult it is to get where you wish to go. Despite predictions that without traffic regulations drivers will be heedless of other drivers, several European cities in recent years have ended all traffic rules concerning their central squares, and there is evidence that accident rates have subsequently gone down.[3]

In thinking about the best choice in situations such as these, people will have different views about what ought to be done. So how to decide? In advocating for a nonpolitical way of addressing situations such as these, where everyone is partly right and partly wrong, there are two factors I ask readers to accept as true:

1. We live in a world of limits, and information is one of the most important of these limits.
2. The human condition has improved over time, and dramatically so in the past several centuries.

The first factor means that people make mistakes, and the second that despite this, some of these mistakes have been dealt with. I suggest that making those mistakes is part of learning how to take care of social problems. It is common when thinking about the generation of such responses to speak of regulated versus unregulated processes. More precisely, it is common to describe a lack of *political* regulation as equivalent to an unregulated process. When the comparison is made in these terms, generally the conclusion drawn is unflattering to the latter. But this is a mistake. All human interactions are regulated in some way. The contest over how to more often elicit better choices is not between regulated and unregulated processes, but among different kinds of regulation.

Each of the cases I set out has at least two means of regulating the problem, and the contrast between those two is the subject of this book. In one case, something intrinsic to the process allows it to satisfactorily, even optimally (given the limits of what we can know), self-regulate. In the other, people either do not even conceive of or doubt the efficacy of whatever self-regulating processes exist. Thus, regulation has to be accomplished externally. Of course, from the broadest possible perspective, there is only one human system, and any regulatory processes, including political ones, are thus internal to that system. And there are many systems that can be characterized as externally regulated, yet not by the political system. Examples include hierarchical religions, where leadership reserves the right to interfere in the self-governance of local congregations (external regulation), versus denominations where each congregation has almost complete freedom of action, subject only to maintaining a sufficiently large number of members to persist (self-regulation). And there are also systems that contain a subsidiary self-regulating process and an external entity that can regulate it—for example, the family as the self-regulating entity, but in fact one that receives external rewards and punishment from political or religious authorities. Such relations that do not implicate the state are also interesting, but I do not discuss them here. Rather, this is a book about the intersection of politics with self-regulating processes.

The question of interest then involves human systems that might, but need not (and often do not), rely extensively for regulation on application of state power (which is how I use *politics* throughout). To modern readers, accustomed to believing that political regulation of a system, especially an economic system, can improve its performance, the idea of a self-regulating system is increasingly implausible as a society becomes more complex. There is, however, substantial historical reason to believe, as I seek to demonstrate, that as society becomes more complex, the inadequacies of political regulation, and therefore the need for self-regulation, actually grow. But if instead it is political regulation that grows, existing problems fail to be addressed effectively, generating more anger and in turn *more* political regulation. Opportunities for human advancement thus shrink.

We shall see in Chapter 2 that for much of human history, such regulation by the state, which often thoroughly controlled the economic, political, and social system through nothing more than rulers' possession of sufficient military force to deter challengers for power, was accepted as the natural order of things. (The role of order is important throughout the book.) But even in that world, self-regulating social processes existed. The clearest example is language. The English that the average, say, Canadian or Briton speaks now is somewhat different from the English of the late eighteenth century, quite different from the English of Shakespeare's time, and worlds apart from the English of the era of *Beowulf*. But no central authority has designed the evolution of English. People invent new words to describe phenomena that cannot be efficiently described by the existing vocabulary, and words that lose their informative value fall out of use. And yet lacking central direction, grammar and vocabulary nonetheless evolve to meet the needs of contemporary users.[4] In short, language regulates itself. That the economy is important while language is not is no objection. Language is essential to human communication; it is difficult to imagine there being much in the way of commerce, science, or ideas without it.

What we eat largely self-regulates too. Although governments regulate food safety and require the publication of certain nutritional information, it would strike most people as preposterous if the government were not just to forbid the consumption of some foods but require the consumption of others. Indeed, even a limited version of such a system, like that of the mandatory communal dining in much of China during the first decades of the communist era, seems to readers used to autonomy in such matters to demonstrate the remarkable reach of communist totalitarianism: the government told Chinese what to eat and where and when to eat it.[5] Instead, our diets have become ever more diverse as wealth and improved global transportation allow us not just to sample, and fall in love with, cuisines from distant places but to combine and recombine ingredients and styles from different places to create a constant flow of food innovations. An example is the "Chinese Mexican" cuisine that is found along the California-Mexico border; depending on whether it appeals to large numbers of people in other places, it may soon spread and be subject to further mutation.[6] Cuisine, like language, even while essential to human survival, manages to do just fine without much in the way of political regulation.

The significant amount of socioeconomic political regulation today is widely accepted in many countries. But the arguments for socioeconomic self-regulation were radical in their day. This book tells that story in the context of the development of the broader idea of self-regulation, of which socioeconomic self-regulation is only a part. These ideas were generated between the seventeenth and nineteenth centuries in Europe. The argument for unregulated markets came about after very similar arguments were made for self-regulation in both science and communication. Socioeconomic activity, and to an extent science and communication, are now more subject to political regulation, despite the argument for trusting self-regulation being the same then as now, and in each case. The book argues for greater confidence in self-regulating social systems, particularly in the socioeconomic context.

DEFINITIONS

Any argument for the superiority of self-regulating processes must ultimately appeal to utilitarian considerations. While one can certainly appeal to a right to be left alone by the state, a major impetus for the partial repeal of the liberal consensus of the late nineteenth century was based on, first, pointing out deficiencies in the operation of an "unregulated" economy, and, second, an immediate resort to politics as the proper way to remedy these deficiencies. It was, and is, too seldom asked whether the consequences of politics *as they are actually practiced* are likely to be better or worse than those that will result when participants in the system attempt to work out problems within that system. It is common enough, not least among economists, to assert that the market in particular "fails" in this or that realm in deciding how resources will be used and the resulting production "distributed" among the citizenry. But given the political system as we find it rather than as we would like it to be, it is precisely the feedback embedded within it that promotes the desired reactions from its participants, a property lacked by political regulation. In making this argument, I use a number of terms that I now set out.

Systems

What properties should a properly self-regulating social system possess? At a minimum, a *system* is a set of components with a specified, if perhaps subject to alteration, set of *links* among them. We wish to describe both the components and the links, and upon doing so may be able to make some statements about the system as a whole. In the solar system, for example, each planet and moon has characteristics such as mass, nature of the atmosphere, and so on. Once Newtonian laws of motion were sufficiently well understood, the properties of the links and thus the system as a whole could be stated: the planets revolve around the sun and the moons around their nearest planets with certain frequencies, for example. The biological system also has components in the forms of its many species. In varying combinations, they consume sunlight, atmospheric gases, and nutrients found in other species. It is the links generated among these various species, cooperative in some cases and predatory in others, that allow us to speak of a "system." Within the Darwinian system writ large, many biologists now also like to speak of discrete subsystems, food webs or ecosystems, that can plausibly be partitioned from the rest of the larger system for analysis. We may thus speak of changes in one ecosystem brought about by, for example, the entry (perhaps human-enabled) of "invasive" species from other ecosystems.

Biologists think of species (and, more recently, genes) as the fundamental components of the Darwinian system. Depending on the purpose one has in analyzing the system elements, their atoms or subatomic particles can be usefully thought of similarly for the natural world. But in the sort of comparison among social systems envisioned here, humans must be the fundamental unit because they are the ones who interact with other humans in every social system. Analogous to the distinction drawn between an ecosystem and the global biological system, this is not to say that the system must encompass the entire human population. We may speak of the "French socioeconomy" or the system of artistic expression we call music. (Throughout I use the term *socioeconomy* where appropriate in lieu of *economy* to describe the full spectrum of potentially self-regulating human activities, not all of them involving monetary commerce.) But even in such subsystems, humans are what species and atoms often are in natural systems. We predict how a social system works based on some belief about how humans will react with each other given the system's institutional structure.

And yet, for an analysis of social systems, this is not enough. There are no moral statements to be made about the operation of the Darwinian system. Living things cooperate, free-ride, and devour or are devoured, and given the natural environment, some species flourish and some disappear. But to correctly observe that over the long term, single-celled organisms become multicellular organisms of ever greater complexity or some species emerge and others die out cannot be to make any moral claims about how the Darwinian system *should* operate. The biological system is constantly changing, and such change operates according to understandable principles. But unless one has a special place in one's heart for the human species (as I do), this increasing complexity has no *moral* purpose; it is merely the empty one of propagating genes. No one can say that the global ecosystem of 100 million years ago was "better" than that of 50 million years ago or of today. That trilobites died out and were replaced by cephalopods, crustaceans, and other invertebrates of greater complexity is not a triumph, a tragedy, or a crime; it just *is*.[7]

If we are to judge human social systems, in contrast, moral criteria are essential. This book takes the utilitarian perspective, broadly defined. The purpose of a socioeconomic system is to promote a better way of life; the purpose of a scientific system is to promote the accumulation of scientific knowledge; the purpose of human communication is to promote more insight into the natural and human worlds. The concept of insight encompasses all claims that might be made by artists or moral or other philosophers through their work, as well as other insights that the accumulated commentary by readers or other "consumers," including readers who are paid to render such judgments, might lend. To emphasize this purpose, unless discussing information traveling in only one direction, I refer to "communication" rather than "expression" or "speech," emphasizing that the information flows usefully in multiple directions.

A System's Components

Every social system has certain parts. The *agents* of a social system are those who participate in it. I choose this term specifically because of the philosophical idea of agency—the power to make things happen through one's own choices. Second, a social system needs a *goal*. The three mentioned in the previous paragraph are the ones by which the systems in this book are judged. They are not further justified, even though it is possible to imagine alternatives. For example, one could judge a scientific system by the extent to which it preserves support for the existing religious hierarchy, or a socioeconomic system by the extent to which it generates equality in consumption. In theory, there may be multiple goals that can be in conflict or pursued together.

Agents will choose their goals based on the *feedback* they get, that is, information about the consequences that (may) occur from various choices. Feedback generates the *incentives* agents receive based on the *rules* of the system. While rules are often thought of as a set of what is and is not "allowable," ultimately this is not a precise definition. To do something not "allowed" is usually not to violate the laws of physics but merely to court a set of negative consequences—fines, imprisonment, or worse in the case of a criminal justice system, for example. It will be very rare for the full set of consequences of the various choices available to an agent to be certain. But some feedback is more useful than others. If profits and losses, for example, are handed out randomly regardless of whether the product sold is high or low quality, or if criminal sanctions are handed out independent of whether the person receiving the sanctions committed the criminal act in question, then feedback is useless. We would be surprised if such a rule had any success in furthering the goal of eliciting socially valuable products or the avoidance of crimes. Alternatively, an omnipotent and omniscient system designer—the perfect "social planner" so beloved in much economics scholarship—would always impose whatever combination of feedback and incentives was required to achieve completely whatever goal that planner had. The "only" requirement for optimal system performance would then be that the planner's goal was agreeable—that he be more like Plato or Buddha and less like Stalin. Presumably the incentives available to frail humanity are imperfect with regard to achieving the desired goals. Finally, *networks* refers to agents and the links among them in a self-regulating system.

EVALUATING A SYSTEM'S PERFORMANCE

The fact that we live in an all-too-flawed world means that social systems ought to be required to repair errors, or at least the consequences of those errors, once they are made. And so whether this system is homeostatic—

in other words, whether deviations from choices that promote the goal are quickly corrected (not merely changed, but changed in a desirable direction)—is crucial in evaluating the system's performance. A thermostat is a good example of a homeostatic system. If the temperature becomes too high or too low by some predetermined margin, a well-functioning thermostat will adjust so that the temperature returns to its programmed level. The goal of the homeostatic system is maintenance of a particular temperature range.

But errors are also addressed in other ways than periodic correction of deviation from some defined norm, a return to what I will call *static equilibrium*. Instead, the system can continuously improve. In science, flawed hypotheses can be abandoned and new ones adopted. In public contention among ideas about what society is and ought to be, mistaken views can be discarded. In an economy, the standard of living may rise as poor resource-use decisions are abandoned and better ones adopted. Such innovation results not just in new opportunities to use property in different ways for personal gain but for others to reap the corresponding benefits—better ways to promote health and more opportunities to travel and learn, for example. All of this will involve varying combinations of competition and cooperation among agents. This is not simply restoration of previous, optimal conditions (as in the thermostat setting), but dynamic progress in furthering the goal.

Effective error correction of either sort can be beset by difficulties, however. The success in achieving our postulated goal for the system as a whole may not be related to, or may be negatively related to, the particular goals of its individual members, who might give little thought to the performance of the system as a whole, as opposed to the achievement of their own goals. While many individual scientists care about scientific advancement writ large along with their own fame or career success, individual businesspeople generally do not think much about overall social progress when they make decisions about how to run their particular businesses. Participants in the public conversation on the great issues of the day, whether they are artists, journalists, or bloggers, probably do usually want to promote a better society, but they act primarily out of a conviction that what they say is true. They often mean to win the debates in which they engage—to persuade others that they possess Truth and that humanity is best served if they can get others to believe it. But the efficacy of the larger process by which we try to get at the truth is little on their mind.

In fact, to the extent that individual agents have incentives that conflict with the system's overall goal, its error-correction attributes become all the more important. If a writer can make an extravagant, controversial claim that leads many people to agree with him when they buy and read the book he writes, his incentives to investigate carefully and thoroughly before making claims are correspondingly relatively diminished. If the advocate *knows* a claim is false but feedback incents him to make people think it is true (either because he believes some broader claim that this little white lie supports *is* true or because he has material or other interests furthered when many people think it is true), the costs of false claims are all the greater. Similarly, a business owner may not actively wish to sell a dangerous or otherwise inferior product, but if the monetary stake is large enough, he may persuade himself to neglect contrary evidence or even actively deceive potential buyers. So the error-detection process must effectively counteract these tendencies. To minimize the cost of such errors, the incentives should be structured so as to induce agents to do what, from society's point of view, they ought to do, including making productive (i.e., instructive) mistakes.

This is, then, a condition for a self-regulating process to be effective. But political regulation of such processes, from a utilitarian perspective, also requires that two conditions be met. First, the political process must be able to effectively harvest knowledge about the problems generated by the operation of the self-regulating process. Second, political actors must on the whole use this information to craft solutions that will effectively address these deficiencies. It is important to remember these minimum requirements in comparing self-regulating and politically regulated processes.

A GUIDE TO THE REMAINDER OF THE BOOK

Fundamentally, this is a book about people figuring things out on their own. When they do, free of commands from outside the system, the results are often better. Whereas politics is rigid and monolithic, self-regulation is flexible and competitive. Self-regulation does not per se respect existing institutions, although people may use them in the course of creating new institutions and techniques. In a self-regulating system, there is a greater flow of things that might work, and things that don't work are exposed and discarded more quickly. For a time from the seventeenth to the late nineteenth centuries, this thinking was consistently applied across a wide spectrum of human endeavor. The book documents this rise and (especially socioeconomically) its retreat. In doing so, it draws on several distinct scholarly traditions, especially study of the evolution of social institutions that bring out the best in us and mitigate our worst instincts in a variety of environments.[8] The story begins with a discussion in Chapter 2 on the progress from hierarchical regimentation to the very idea of self-regulation. Humans are wired for competition as the occasion calls for, violent if need be, and most of human history is one in which might made right, and the mightiest thought it perfectly normal to regiment the rest of society. Chapter 2 tells this story, as well as of the rise in belief in self-regulating alternatives, based on the realization that some forms of competition can serve human purposes. The first comprehensive arguments for institutions based on self-regulation were made for science, as outlined in Chapter 3. Chapters 4 and 5 tell the story of the resulting development of similar arguments in the area of communication and socioeconomic activity. We will see that, especially in the latter case, arguments based on both discovered scientific principles and the operation of the scientific system itself were transferred to these spheres.

There are existing, albeit limited, versions of this type of analysis. For science, Michael Polanyi (1891–1976) explicitly used Adam Smith's phrase "invisible hand" to describe the workings of the scientific process. He even argued that the rules of this process incent individual scientists to work on the "right" problem, given the goal of advancing scientific knowledge given individual scientists' strengths and weaknesses. He also noted the importance of uncoordinated, dynamic self-regulation, although without using this term. Jonathan Rauch has also described the commonality of the two parts of what he calls "Liberal Science," likening traditional scientific exploration to the search for ethical truth.[9]

Subsequent to the substitution of self-regulation for political regulation, the state of scientific knowledge, the span of human ideas, and our life possibilities all improved substantially. But self-regulation often requires tolerance of dramatic change, and such change is often resisted. So too it was with socioeconomic self-regulation in particular. Chapter 6 traces the development of the idea that socioeconomic self-regulation can malfunction. Chapter 7 describes the development of ideas about its fundamental flaws: that we should default, if not outright surrender, to political regulation as the proper form of organization for the socioeconomic system. The ideas in these two chapters amount to counterreactions to the claims of eighteenth-century Enlightenment thinking, which saw great moral purpose in lessening the grip of the state on individuals, who, when free to succeed and, critically, to fail were seen as the prime movers of social progress. Chapter 8 documents the growth of this counterreaction. In concluding, Chapter 9 offers some evidence on the negative effect of the partial retreat from self-regulation. It also speculates on the future of self-regulation in all three arenas and provides some advice about how to best take advantage of its extraordinary properties.

CHAPTER 2

Getting There

The Long Road to Self-Regulation

The [Inca] did not have to do any thinking for himself. The government thought and acted for him, and if its action was suspended, social life would stop short. Under the rule of the Incas this inertia expressed itself in the stagnation of commerce that we have already noted, in the lack of vitality and the absence of originality in the arts, in dogmatism in science and in the rareness of even the simplest inventions.

LOUIS BAUDIN (1887-1964)[1]

Since the dawn of sophisticated political thought over two thousand years ago, one of the favorite themes of intellectuals has been how to organize society. It turns out, according to the current thinking of evolutionary psychologists, that the roots of human behavior, including social behavior, can substantially be found in our genes. At the same time, it would be foolish to reduce all or even most observed behavior to biological processes, although as we will see, there have been repeated attempts to do just that since the seventeenth century. Humanity has had over two thousand years to generate ideas about how we should live individually and collectively, based on abstract moral reasoning and from observation. This chapter traces the long journey to the idea that self-regulation can produce superior outcomes in a variety of human processes.

EVOLUTION'S MIXED GIFTS

Psalm 8 asks what the nature of man is, and part of the answer given is that the Lord "hast made him a little lower than the angels."[2] Humanity collectively is neither savage nor saintly and is capable of both appalling cruelty and inspiring benevolence. Overall, a sometimes grudging agathism is probably the default modern sensibility about human nature—morally and materially, we take two steps forward and one step back. But this on-balance optimistic view was rejected outright by many ancient traditions and is rejected by modern conservatives who believe in preserving them.

In biological taxonomy, humans are great apes. Our closest living relatives are chimpanzees and bonobos. The behavior of these close cousins is sometimes cooperative and sometimes combative, the latter including violence both within and among groups. Both species display empathy for victims of suffering, including that brought on by violence. Both live together in groups of perhaps several dozen. These groups have parties that forage together and have leaders and followers.

To be sure, there are differences of degree between the two species. Chimpanzees are thought to be somewhat more prone to intragroup violence and warfare among groups. The term *alpha male* is used to indicate which male in the group dominates in terms of access to desired goods, such as food and females. Higher-ranking males receive visual signs of submission from lower-ranking males and females. But uneasy lies the head that wears a crown. Male chimpanzees, particularly younger ones, frequently scheme to challenge and then usurp the highest-ranking male.

Yet cooperative activities, such as defending the group from outsiders and gathering food, are common. And for all the trappings of hierarchy and dominance that can readily be observed in chimpanzee "society," individual chimpanzees also have a significant degree of autonomy. They frequently go out alone to forage, and individuals, particularly males, are free to leave the group at any time; once they do so, however, they are extremely vulnerable to attack by members of other groups whose territory they have the misfortune to enter. So while groups of chimpanzees have alpha males, what they do not have it is outright despotism of the sort that has become all too common in more complex human societies.

In contrast, ever since they were first designated as a separate species in 1933, bonobos have been thought to be somewhat less prone to violence and to be a species in which females play a less subservient role. Among bonobos, females frequently organize single-sex coalitions to rein in and even dominate particular males. Indeed research on this less well-known great ape has become popular among nonprimatologists eager to make points about the nature of human society. It is true that the comforting image of bonobos as our nonviolent ancestors—the "hippy chimpanzee"—has diminished because of recent research. But it is safe to say that the research to this point indicates that of the two species, bonobos on the whole are more sociable and less violent.[3]

But no matter the particulars, our closest living cousins demonstrate cooperative and violent tendencies, albeit in very small "societies." While there were other differences between humans and other great apes that eventually manifested themselves, such as walking upright and possessing less physical strength, humans' incremental evolution primarily involved a tremendous increase in intellectual ability. One way that this intellectual ability has promoted evolutionary fitness is through its ability to enable humans to form complex social groups.[4]

HUMAN PREHISTORY

While the taxonomical terms may differ, anthropologists agree that human groups-cum-societies may be crudely described by their differing levels of complexity. The anthropologist Elman Rogers Service in 1962 created a classification system that is still widely used. In his description, humans divide themselves into, in increasing order of complexity, bands, tribes, chiefdoms, and states.[5] The classification system is not precise, but it is sufficiently rigorous to allow some general statements to be made. Table 2.1 presents a simplified version of it.

TABLE 2.1. *Levels of social complexity.*

Bands	Individuals specialize in solving social problems Freedom to leave limits hierarchical authority
Tribes	Structures of leadership involving more than one person Specialization in warfare, religion, sometimes primitive agriculture Consistent but gradual and unrecorded evolution in culture and technology
Chiefdoms	Permanent, often hereditary leadership classes, often supported by religious beliefs but designed in part to control socially costly activities; onset of continuous political regulation Parallel development of permanent military/police class, often in partnership with ruling class Direction of productive activities by this leadership
States	Facilitated by agricultural revolution More extensive and thorough control than chiefdoms; institutionalized control by leadership (religious and political) of most human activity through formal legal codes

Source: Service (1962).

Bands

The band most resembles the chimpanzee and bonobo groups, with most members being extended kin and nutrition coming from hunting animals and harvesting the produce of wild plants. Bands are mobile, and smaller groups can split off and go their own way. There is leadership but no slavery in the modern sense. And while there is violence, even warfare, there is also cooperation and great effort expended both individually and collectively to shepherd the young to adulthood. There is significant sexual division of labor, presumably due to physical differences between males and females.

Bands are complex enough to have problems to address after reflection. Any limiting of self-regulating processes must be imposed by a leadership with a strong ability to impose obedience on followers. In hunter-gatherer bands, such leadership capacity was not much stronger than it is in chimpanzee or bonobo society. As with the great apes, individual leaders are not capable of directing the entire society, since individuals and whole families can leave. Anthropologists are divided on the extent to which foraging bands are dominated by hierarchy or cooperation, commands or negotiation. But they do agree that numerous mechanisms exist to mitigate conflicts, including those arising from struggles over dominance. In particular, individuals can form coalitions to check socially costly struggles, and indeed some groups of individuals may acquire a reputation for wisdom in conflict resolution. This can be seen as an early manifestation of self-regulation, with the goal being to limit costly in-group struggle.

Even now, such behavior is common in complex human organizations, when members of the group—mutual friends, a company, a civic organization—collectively make it plain to one or more other members of the group that his or their behavior is damaging. Another example of an innate self-regulating propensity is the respect recorded in many modern societies to the elderly, whose right to scold the more physically robust young for misbehavior is generally respected and who are often even due a substantial amount of deference from younger people. This norm allows the elderly to remain safe and the young to benefit from their wisdom.

Greater Complexity: Tribes and Chiefdoms

This tendency for people to regulate outside the context of formal politics, whether spontaneously expressed or inscribed in social custom, is known to be long-standing. Many such prepolitical or subpolitical practices have been described by anthropologists.[6] But at higher levels of organization, societies develop structures of leadership. Tribes frequently have leadership circles drawn from one or a few family groups; similar groups may be formed to specialize in carrying out religious activities or warfare. (Note that this specification of "tribe" is unrelated to the modern use, applied only to aboriginal people in places like the Western Hemisphere and groups in Africa, who would be called "ethnic groups" otherwise.)

As social organization becomes more complex, the taxonomy becomes somewhat less precise. Whereas bands have the common trait of foraging and therefore mobility, as societies became further removed geographically and temporally from their Rift Valley predecessors, the forms those societies took became more varied and complex. Some humans moved completely out of Africa in several waves starting perhaps 130,000 years ago.[7] Both groups developed what anthropologists call behavioral modernity, which includes "creative and innovative culture, language, art, religious beliefs, and complex technologies."[8] Among the practical manifestations of this improvement in human capacity were the invention of tools of increasing sophistication and the ability to use symbols to communicate.

We also learned to do other things. Tribes developed an increasing capacity to turn biota into nutrients beyond directly harvesting animals or plants found in the wild—through cooking, for example. In addition, there arose a growing desire to keep records, though not yet in writing, which was not invented until perhaps 3000 B.C., although it appeared independently in several locations. Oral transmission of information about the tribe's founding, customs, and rules had already become possible with the invention of language, so there was more systematic specialization in the tribe than in the band. There was sometimes domestication of animals for both their meat and dairy products, as well as for assistance in hunting. But generally the band's pattern of a nonsettled lifestyle, migrating either randomly or in a regular pattern back and forth, was maintained. The increasing complexity of tribes relative to bands meant that the problem of social organization now became a substantial one, especially if members of a tribe were more reluctant to leave than members of a band. There might be more danger outside and possibly more shame to be borne by oneself and one's family from the feeling of having violated a taboo; moreover, there could be more to lose from permanent separation from the fruits of the tribe's division of labor.

At some point, according to Service, tribes began to be replaced by chiefdoms. They were now organizations with permanent leaders who generally inherited their post, rather than earned it because of some skill in social problem solving, warfare, or something more prosaic. With his focus on creating a precise taxonomy and based on European records of initial contact with Polynesians, Service devoted much attention to the details of ritual such as gift giving. Colin Renfrew even goes so far as to outline the twenty characteristics commonly found in chiefdoms, as opposed to tribes or states.[9] For our purposes, the increasingly permanent character of social leadership, along with the concomitant establishment of a growing bureaucracy to serve it, is what matters.

The reason it matters is that in larger societies, the more extensive and permanent ruling class started to "find" that the new more hierarchical structures they headed were their hammers and every interaction within society was a nail (i.e., a problem to be solved). These leaders, who, following anthropological custom, can be called chiefs, now supervised the organization of many activities. If hierarchy with a fair amount of independence for individuals was the truth for much of human history, it now began to be replaced by organization by those to the manor born. The power to impose order by giving orders had to await the formation of states for its complete fulfillment, but the trend was clear.

Among the problems the leadership might have wanted to solve were crime and potential crime, obviously, and warfare. Lawrence H. Keeley has extensively documented both the prevalence and the savagery of war at levels of complexity below the nation-state. At least partly, his aim was to criticize what he felt to be a naive tendency among anthropologists to suppose that violence itself was mostly a product of social complexity—civilization as the abandonment of our bonobo heritage, if you like.[10] In his view, the scale of violence only grew with such complexity. By this time, societies had sufficiently increased in complexity that there was a class of professional soldiers who nominally served the group as a whole, usually served the interests of current leaders in particular, and occasionally served their own interests against those of their leaders. Division of labor sufficient to politically regulate society was now in place. The combination of the ability to solve problems through politics and the will to power was a critical juncture in human history. Rulers had to be obeyed; otherwise society would fall apart.

But there was still an interest in minimizing social conflict generally, not just because it threatened to devolve into violence but because it was displeasing to the gods. Religion was a force that would often prop up the existing ruling class, strengthening its ability to preserve the status quo rather than tolerate decentralized social change. At other times, it was also a force for resolving conflicts. The origins of religious belief far predate writing and even archaeological evidence, but in summarizing the scholarship, Robert Wright describes the consensus belief that the human brain is disposed to accept supernatural explanations for things that are observed.

It is known that smaller-scale societies had shamans—individuals with particular expertise in or connections to the supernatural life that determined the workings of the natural world but were not detectable by the five senses. These spirits often intervened in human affairs, and their favorable intervention could be sought through gifts or sacrifices, the same sorts of offerings already being made at those stages of human history to political leaders.[11] The job of religious figures was initially not to pray to the divine to make certain things happen, but to divine the knowledge these spirits had about what would happen—events about which humans could do nothing.[12]

The function of religion was not just personal gain, although it was sometimes that for these human intermediaries to the spirit world and for rulers. It was also to restore order. At one point, Wright quotes William James that religion "consists of the belief that there is an unseen order, and that our supreme good lies in harmoniously adjusting ourselves thereto"—one of the merits of self-regulating systems in general.[13] Of course, unlike the examples discussed later, we do not know the extent to which religion was *created* to give people ways to limit the consequences of disruptive behavior. (Disruption is often part of effective dynamic self-regulation.) And later, when many religions became exclusive in the sense of being coterminous with a unique metaphysical Truth, the throwing together of different religions in the same space became a disruptive rather than a harmonizing force.

And yet religion was a tool of self-regulation as well; it was used to motivate harder work when more fish had to be caught or crops had to be harvested (the shortfalls often seen as reflecting divine displeasure) and, especially, as justification to be relied on when the chief crossed some line. By this time, chiefs themselves were increasingly taking on the trappings of divinity, but new priestly classes were able to be somewhat independent. As the next stage of human society, the state, began to consolidate and then evolve, however, the role of religion became more destructive than supportive of self-regulation.

THE STATE AS A CENTRALIZING, PRESERVATIONIST FORCE

The urge to strive for and then use power became more consequential with the development of large-scale sedentary farming as a source of nutrition, which happened in many places over several thousand years. The application of human cognition to the problem of how to eat better—presumably from the point of view of both nutritional reliability and taste—resulted in the independent discovery of the benefits of planting and then patiently waiting in lieu of (and, early on, in addition to) foraging. This took place not just in the Fertile Crescent, but in Central America, China, and a number of islands in the Pacific. In each case, the fertile soil of rivers or lakes probably served as a creative stimulant in the senses of both generating the idea of farming and the nourishment of the seeds planted.

There were two dramatic immediate effects. The first was to substantially increase the population density that could be supported on a given amount of land, other things equal. In addition, the idea of how to use a fixed plot of productive land, a question that did not arise in a foraging or pastoral society, was suddenly fundamental.[14] Agriculture also increased the importance of patience. The need to wait for the passage of time between effort exerted and food produced made the questions of what to grow, who should get it, and how to ensure those who produced stayed on task instead of leaving or shirking became critical questions for agriculture-dependent leaders. They defaulted to an essentially slavelike mode of production, where a few gave orders that most took. In so doing, the order-givers extracted every last possible grain from peasants. In the words of Patricia Crone, the authorities were induced to "take everything they could without destroying agriculture altogether."[15]

I refer to the organization directly trying to control this process as an early "state." Although it was organized and claimed a unique right to rule, it is distinct from the more thoroughly organized nation, discussed in chapter 6. The surpluses that agriculture generated appealed to the hierarchical instincts in humanity, with the result that the first states were born. Some became large enough to leave written records, with writing itself being at least partly created to keep track of the agricultural surpluses generated and how they were disposed of, as well as to keep track of resources, including human resources, available to be commandeered by rulers. Invariably these larger groups were drawn not toward consultative "democracy" of either the modern or the chiefdom type, but of the absolute dominance of one or at most a small circle of men who claimed to be representatives of the gods or divine themselves. Records from literate civilizations in the Middle East, China, and, to a lesser extent, India all contain examples.

The Babylonian ruler Hammurabi described himself in the famous code that bears his name as the man the god Marduk sent to "bring about the rule of her righteousness in the land, to destroy the wicked and the evildoers" and "to rule over men."[16] (Perhaps it is not too surprising in this light that of the 282 laws in his code, 35 of them called for capital punishment.) In China, the ancient character for "emperor" (帝) had divine connotations, as it does now. A frequent desire of the Chinese emperor, or even a mere local king, was to settle newly acquired territory, with their peasants ordered to do so because the population increase enabled more food to be produced. This level of control is particularly striking because China, unlike most other advanced ancient civilizations, had no extremely powerful, willful, and supernatural gods that they worshiped; rather, they mainly invoked the spirits associated with particular deceased ancestors, natural phenomena, and inanimate objects. From the time the Qin dynasty unified the country in 221 B.C., the emperor was considered divine.[17] (The Chinese did believe in the idea of "heaven" (天, *tiān*), but this was a distant entity, with no emotional attachment to humans of the sort seen in theistic religions.) Individuals too were to be placed where they *belonged* in the Chinese worldview. Suggestively in this regard, in Chinese painting, the standard was scenes in which "man fits inconspicuously, even obscurely."[18] Order—everything in its proper place—was the ideal: its presence was credited to the imperial leadership, and its absence signaled that the leader should be replaced.

In Egypt the pharaoh was seen as a divine intermediary between his subjects and the gods. Prior to European contact, the leaders of several major civilizations in what was later known as Latin America were also seen as gods. As representatives of the divine or as divine themselves, leaders of early states had by modern standards the authority to order society at will—not just to organize agriculture but to start or end wars, transfer resources among subjects, order mass enslavement or the release of slaves, and commandeer labor for public works or religious temples. (In the eyes of peoples where the fate of humans was largely seen as being in the hands of gods, temples *were* public works.)

The only highly organized ancient civilizations that have left extensive archaeological records where the ruler may not have exercised this kind of smothering control were found in South Asia. The Harappan civilization was established in the valley of the Indus River in perhaps 3300 B.C., and traces of it survived to perhaps 1900 B.C. We know little about the particulars of its political history because its language has yet to be deciphered, although it is thought that there was less hierarchy compared to other contemporaneous states. Those societies were probably already in decline by the time the invading Indo-Europeans or Aryans arrived from the Eurasian steppes between 1800 B.C. and 1500 B.C.

The spread and mixture of Indo-European customs and technology throughout the region coincided with the presumed origins of some of the ancient subcontinental epics. The political legacy of these epics was multifaceted. While there was much in them that served to legitimize monarchy, especially the *Ramayana*, committed to paper in 400 B.C. but orally transmitted from as far back as 1500 B.C., it was also true that during the Vedic age (1700 B.C.–500 B.C.), some areas of the subcontinent became traditional monarchical states, and some became what John Keay calls "republics."[19] The religious hierarchy also acquired a distinctive level of power. This hierarchy was close to the top of the social pyramid in most ancient societies from the Maya to the Romans to the Egyptians (and hence, in a time when access to food was the most compelling issue for people everywhere, most likely to produce many offspring). In much of the Indian peninsula and Southeast Asia, however, the priestly classes (Brahmans) had authority independent of the warrior classes (Kshatriya) and even kings. Collectively, it is unlikely that any subcontinental leader during this time had the kind of power that was available to a Babylonian leader or, centuries later, an Incan emperor.

So India aside, if we stipulate that a common feature of sophisticated ancient civilizations was a leadership class based on lineage, and perhaps a single hereditary leader, with near-absolute power over the lives of most subjects, how was that power exercised? Perhaps the most striking manifestation to the modern mind is in the socioeconomic sphere. In a pattern that faded away in many places long before the modern era began, only to reappear in twentieth-century communist totalitarianism, management of the provision and distribution of essential goods, food in particular, soon came to be seen as a natural task of the single leader and his designated underlings. The Harappan civilization, for example, has been described as one "in which the state controlled many facets of daily living—milling grain, manufacturing bricks and mass producing pottery, obtaining firewood, and building residences."[20] Robert Sharer had this to say on the Maya: "Ultimately, the power of kings depended on their ability to control resources. Maya rulers managed the production and distribution of status goods used to enhance their prestige and power. They also controlled some critical (non-local) commodities that included critical everyday resources each family needed, like salt."[21] In many such societies, the assigned division of labor was permanent and inheritable. The idea of agency hardly existed in ancient states (as opposed to in less complex societies). In the words of the historian J. Donald Hughes, "The vast majority of ancient people regarded themselves primarily as part of their societies, and only secondarily, if at all, as individuals. Each person had a place in the social hierarchy which was rigidly defined and rarely changed."[22]

By the middle of the first millennium B.C., several experiments in more collective governance were simultaneously unfolding on opposite sides of the world. In the valleys of the Ganges River, landowning families sometimes governed themselves through assemblies. In classical Athens in the fourth century B.C., there were experiments in democratic governance, with all free males having the right to participate in public matters. As the Romans expanded from their ancestral territories throughout the Mediterranean basin, they continued to adhere, first in substance and later primarily in form, to the idea that all free Roman citizens had political rights and indeed political obligations. (Both Greece and Rome limited such rights substantially, not least for their large and, in the Roman case, growing over time populations of slaves.)

Progress Unthinkable, Order Essential

The newer societies were based on limited but real notions of civic rights shared with the highly centralized societies still common throughout the world. However, and very important for our purposes, government lacked the concept of unpredictable social progress, a condition for belief in dynamic self-regulating processes to even be useful.

A key element of static self-regulation did exist, in the sense that society had an ideal form, which it might currently conform to or not, much like the supply-and-demand equilibrium in economics. But it was the ruler(s) who needed to use force to restore any social disequilibrium or be replaced, as in the Chinese case. This was similar to the prevailing thinking about the nature of human health—that an external actor (e.g., a doctor) sometimes needed to restore the body's internal "order." Many ancient societies had a belief that human health required that various internal energies or ingredients be kept in balance. The ancient Greeks had their humors, Ayurvedic medicine its categorization of foods' characteristics (their tastes, their "hot" or "cold" properties) and the belief that a sick person should eat so as to restore the balance,[23] even to the extent of asserting that such balance required that all people remained in the place where they were born.[24] The Chinese believed sickness emanated from imbalances between yin and yang, a pattern of disharmony among various organs or sources of *qì*, energy (氣), for example. (Modern science-based medicine, while it does focus on disease as coming from external attack by pathogens or internal dysfunction perhaps brought about by aging, does not rely excessively on the idea of overall equilibrium in the human body that must be restored if symptoms appear.) In politics as in health, external, often outright divine regulation was required to cure what ailed people by restoring balance. For the individual, as for art and society as a whole, disorder was to be avoided or remedied.

Divinely Mandated Stability

A revealing feature of how premodern societies idealized order is found in ancient accounts of how things came to be. A useful summary of hundreds of such accounts is *Creation Myths of the World: An Encyclope-*

dia.[25] Many of these stories of creation and what comes after emphasize a single fall, usually related to moral degradation, and many others stress cyclical falls and restoration. Again, this is something that occurred in many states. The Vāyu Purāṇa, recorded at some point before 1000 A.D. in what is now South India, has the moral depreciation occurring this way (note the similarity to the first verses of Genesis):

In the beginning, people lived in perfect happiness, without class distinctions or property; all their needs were supplied by magic wishing trees. Then because of the great power of time and the changes it wrought upon them, they were overcome by passion and greed. It was from the influence of time, and no other cause, that their perfection vanished. Due to their greed, the wishing trees disappeared; the people felt heat and cold, built houses, and were close.[26]

It should be noted that the series of Sanskrit texts known as the Purāṇas are not precisely dated. And although they do not carry quite the religious authority that the Vedas do, they are nevertheless considered to be highly influential in Hindu belief.

Other examples include China (not yet a unified jurisdiction), where pre-Confucian texts tell of "sage kings" who ruled justly and with wisdom. Social chaos could result from the failure to obey legitimate authority, or the failure of those in authority to rule with the ancient virtue. Hesiod (birth and death dates not known, although thought to have lived sometime between 750 and 650 B.C.) is the first Greek thinker for whom we have any records, his poems having been attributed to him by later Greeks in written accounts. He talks in "Works and Days" of how society once was a sort of golden age from which humanity had descended. Plato (c. 428 B.C.–347 B.C.) in *Cratylus* (397E–398) has dialogue participants recalling Hesiod's likening of man in earlier times to gold, while the current age was one in which men were merely iron. Similar accounts appear in *one of Plato's later dialogues. Critias* (120E) described a world of nine thousand years before in which the earth was more bountiful and the people inhabiting it, descended from gods, had "gentleness joined with wisdom in dealing with the changes and chances of life and in their dealings with one another," before the vanishing of their divine origins manifested itself in increased corruption.[27] Thucydides (c. 460 B.C.–c. 400 B.C.) too, in his *History of the Peloponnesian War,* exhibited this naive backward myopia as he laments the war as having allowed corrupt moderns to destroy the ancient beliefs: "simplicity, the chief ingredient in a noble nature, was ridiculed and disappeared" (III:83).[28]

Many cyclical accounts assert that despite human corruption, through intelligent design of society (by the person with the power to design it, naturally), this corruption can be escaped at least for a time. A regime can be better or worse, and may even at points reach something close to the ideal (especially when young), but inevitably corruption sets in, the government becomes more oppressive of the common people, and things begin to fall apart. Perhaps after a period of chaos, order is restored, and then the cycle begins anew.

In Greek thought, at least the possibility of such degeneration is found in the writings of Plato, Polybius (c. 200–c. 118), and Aristotle (384 B.C.–322 B.C.). In Plato's (c. 438 B.C.–347 B.C.) *Republic* (written c. 380 B.C.) and Polybius's (c. 200 B.C.–c. 118 B.C.) *Histories* (c. 150 B.C., II.7), the cyclical process is explicitly discussed, with the former concerning itself also with the ideal state. The state can depreciate from its ideal past form and can never be improved beyond it. In Aristotle, especially in the second-century B.C. *Politics* (Book V) and the *Histories* (VI throughout), the contemporary danger (and, in the *Histories* VI.7–9, the final inevitability) of degeneration exists. The best way to prevent or at least defer it is to adopt elements of different kinds of government (democracy, oligarchy, and so on) so as to benefit from the strengths and limit the damage from the weaknesses of each type.[29] The Arab thinker Ibn Khaldun (1332–1406), in his *Muqaddimah* ("An Introduction to History"), presented the cyclical nature of history. Early on in any cycle, "Bedouins" living in the desert are satisfied with a simple system of authority in order to facilitate both cooperation and early-stage social organization. At some point, the need to restrain innate human aggressiveness requires the establishment of clearer authority and the building of cities. But the strength of group loyalty, still possessed by the desert Bedouins, allows them to conquer the city and, initially, rule it with justice. Eventually, corruption and repression come from city life and its luxury; rebellion is generated, and the city collapses. The cycle then repeats.

In short, whether we have fallen from the initial blissful state or are merely in a recurring stage of repeated social deterioration, there is a social ideal, a perfection to compare society against. The ruler's job, by whatever means necessary, is to repair the damage or prevent further deterioration caused by poor choices of corrupt agents.

THE INCONCEIVABILITY OF PERMANENT PROGRESS

All of the widespread ideas about politics and society noted in this chapter share a common feature: no belief in any kind of endless progress, let alone one achieved through trial and error. But this is precisely the kind of process that dynamic self-regulation depends on. The ancients around the world, with their beliefs that we must regain what has been lost or, at best, preserve the very fragile equilibrium of the present, were generally unable to conceive that continuous, gradual social improvement is something that people can be motivated to try to achieve. In fact, imperial greatness was frequently built by extending the existing imperial model by brute force. And so such progress as could be achieved happened when the civilized extended their civilization by conquering the barbarians, often in the name of racial, religious, or cultural superiority. The superior could certainly bring improvement to the inferior by conquering and assimilating them, but there was no moving beyond rendering the gift of the conquerors' perfection.

The claim of an absence of a thorough idea of continuous progress is in no way a claim of a lack of imagination or creativity among thinkers of ancient and medieval times. But technological progress was extremely slow for most of human history, and when it happened, no one was in a position to document it and certify it as an innovation because of the lack of widespread literacy and often writing itself. Progress was too scattershot and poorly recorded even to be conceived, let alone encouraged. The wheel was far from the only technology whose inventor will ever be unknown. In the premodern world, such innovations as occurred could usually travel only through migration, conquest, or the travels of merchants. Since most innovations were agricultural in any event, they were generally useful only in areas of approximately equal latitude where climatic conditions were similar.[30] When combined with the preference among the leaders of strongly hierarchical societies for stability, the inability to generate an ideology of self-sustaining progress or, conversely, the belief that "a society which is economically stagnant can only remain in harmony and stability if the status quo is basically unchanging," is not hard to understand.[31]

No wonder that it was common among people in all cultures to believe that the social order was given, and disruption could only cause society to deteriorate. Either stand still and obey your leaders, or go backward. People were perforce assumed to be born into the stratum where they belonged, an idea that would last until the early modern era. It was normal that they were living the lives their great-grandparents had lived and that, in turn their great-grandchildren would live after them. It seldom occurred to anyone to think otherwise.

Earlier eras did have useful things to say about social structure and governance more broadly. Recognizing that the only extant records are from societies that had writing, several ancient societies were unusually fruitful in this regard. As noted, the Greeks, with Plato at the head of the class, developed a philosophy of proper governance that is informative even now. The Romans added their own ideas about the rights of Roman citizens, although written more in regret for what was lost as their civil wars began in earnest in approximately 100 B.C. Chinese writers discussed the essence of good governance even before Confucius, and many of these ideas resonate in today's rapidly changing China. The most famous work in this regard in the Indian heritage is probably the *Arthashastra*, often attributed to Chanakya (also known as Kautilya, c. 350–c. 275 B.C.), and written one to three centuries before Christ. Considered eyes-wide-open advice to the Mauryan emperor about how to govern effectively, it is often likened to Machiavelli's (1469–1527) *The Prince* (1513). The *Muqaddimah* includes not just a theory of historical decay but a comprehensive look at religious, political, and economic organization around the known world; in its latter dimension, it presages Adam Smith's (1723–1790) analysis of the division of labor and the pro-growth effects of easy taxes. The text also includes what we would now call comparative ethnography. Such analysis of different peoples and societies and how they compared to the writer's own have a long history in Western thought as well, with the *Histories* of Herodotus (c. 484 B.C.–425 B.C., who had the advantage of having traveled to the places he wrote about) and the *Germania* of Tacitus (c. 56–c. 120, who did not) among the more notable early Western examples.

THE EMERGENCE OF SELF-REGULATED THINKING

Almost nothing in any of these cultural corpuses raises, let alone advocates, the idea of letting society improve itself by having the state leave well enough alone. This idea of possible progress began to take shape in Western European culture in the late Middle Ages. Note that individual human perfectibility had been advocated from a nonmonotheistic perspective in several cultures, such as in Buddhist thinking. But now *social* improvement was advocated, not least by Thomas Aquinas (1225–1274) in *Summa Theologica*, written over roughly a decade between 1265 and 1274. This text described humanity's ability to know God, the world he created, and the moral duties he requires of men. To Aquinas, knowledge about the world was not handed down ideally from the past, but could be sought in the present through human capacities.

In Western Europe, truly novel and penetrating investigations of the entire human experience began to appear in larger numbers as the Renaissance unfolded. While much of what made this era important was reconnection with ancient Greek wisdom, it also saw the spread of the idea that things could be better, so that humanity could move beyond mere adherence to the ancient wisdom. The invention in Europe by Johannes Gutenberg (c. 1398–1468) in approximately 1440 of movable type, itself spontaneously driven by the availability of ever-cheaper paper and the change to writing with punctuation and spaces between words, facilitated the construction of broader human networks for the propagation and spread of ideas. People wrote, and other people read and then wrote in reaction. Some of those ideas had earthshaking consequences. It is said that by the time Martin Luther got to the University of Wittenberg, he was able to benefit in formulating his theses from the fact that the library there already "groaned with the fruit of the Gutenberg revolution."[32]

The Renaissance was driven by some combination of new technology, rediscovery of old knowledge, and a spirit in the air. This was partly owing to the community of sometimes itinerant scholars established first among the universities of Europe that had been established in the late Middle Ages, and partly to thinkers who spurned the university system and made their names as members of royal courts or as outright independent scholars. By the modern typology of knowledge, Renaissance and then early-modern people invented an array of speculative genres. Examples are the essay, notably from Michel de Montaigne (1533–1592) and Blaise Pascal (1623–1662). Montaigne titled his works *Essais*, "Attempts" (1580), and Pascal's were posthumously published and known to moderns as *Pensées*, "Thoughts." There was also improvement in astronomy (the development and eventual triumph of the model of the solar system as heliocentric with elliptical orbits) and of the philosophy of science, particularly Francis Bacon's (1561–1626) *Novum Organon Scientarium* (1620), further discussed in Chapter 3. By the mid-eighteenth century, thinkers and, in conducting scientific experimentation, increasingly doers as well, had formed networks described even contemporaneously as the Invisible College and the Republic of Letters, terms popularized by Robert Boyle (1627–1691) and Pierre Bayle (1647–1706), respectively. These men of thought and action did their individual work in places like the laboratories of Oxford and at their desks in Amsterdam. Then, through the mail and discussion in the salons of Paris and elsewhere, they began to seek feedback from the other members of the networks that they were spontaneously constructing. For now, we look at two key thinkers, one a believer in static and one in dynamic self-regulation.

Montesquieu

During this time, and based on the Scientific Revolution discussed in the next chapter, comprehensive investigations of human society writ large now came with increasing frequency. Such accounts grew in popularity throughout eighteenth-century Europe.[33] While eponymously an investigation merely of law in various societies across time, the most provocative early depiction of the idea of self-regulation was that in the French nobleman baron de Montesquieu's (1689–1755) *Spirit of the Laws* (1748).[34] It investigated the relation between a society's culture and laws, and in so doing speculated on a wide variety of topics, including history, comparative anthropology, legal sociology, education, and the rights of women. In analyzing government as it functioned well or not, he was not just descriptive but prescriptive as well.

Critically, in distinguishing between well- and poorly run republics and monarchies, Montesquieu proposed for these types the *conditions* to maintain political stability and justice. In a "well-regulated democracy . . . men are equal only as citizens" and, not unequal, "as magistrates, as Senators, as judges, as fathers, as husbands, or as masters" (Book VIII, chap. III). By this, he appears to mean the limiting of the public will on public matters. The resulting disorder from failing to govern this way paves the way for despotism. For aristocracies, the thing to avoid is "the power of the nobles becom[ing] arbitrary" (VIII.V). The damage of hereditary nobility, and its attendant separation of authority from merit, can be limited by a constitution that "render[s] the Nobles more sensible of the perils and fatigue, than of the pleasure, of command" (VIII.V). Fear of a foreign invasion can also cultivate the appropriate caution. Monarchies are destroyed in turn when the monarch thinks he can ignore the traditional principles of order and strips groups of their traditional privileges to benefit him and his cronies. In both cases, there is a narrow path that, when walked faithfully, incents the governing authorities to rule justly and therefore preserve the government. Off that path, all is chaos and despotism. Monarchies are also contrasted with despotisms, with monarchs being rulers "who live under the fundamental laws of their country," while despots "have nothing to regulate, neither their own passions nor those of their subjects" (V.XI).[35] While despotisms have no redeeming features, both monarchies and republics do, and they also possess internal regulatory mechanisms.

In support of his claim, Montesquieu invoked the example of England, which achieves stability through a separation of powers. To preserve freedom, "power should be a check to power" (XI.IV). An attempt by any element of the government to accumulate excessive power, in other words, will, in a well-structured political system as found in England, elicit a self-interested counterreaction that preserves the balance. The ability to rely on self-interest makes the system self-regulating, with the "separate views and interests" (XI.VI) of each branch of the state sufficient to motivate them to do what from the point of view of the broader social goal they need to do. (This claim influenced the drafters of the U.S. Constitution.) The ancient Germans who ultimately conquered the Western Roman Empire also dispersed powers eventually, after much trial and error, across various governing entities, yielding "so perfect a harmony between the civil liberty of the people, the privileges of the nobility and clergy, and the prince's prerogative, that I really think there never was in the world a government so well tempered" (XI.VIII).[36] Montesquieu argued that politics itself could self-regulate. Although that is different from the claim here

about the merits of self- versus political regulation, it is testimony to the
fact that the idea of self-regulation was in the air by this time.

It is true that Montesquieu's thoughts in a few places were somewhat
eccentric. For example, he had unusual theories about the impact of climate on a people's temperament, politics, and even drinking habits; about
why Christians suffered so much in Japan in particular; and why Chinese
emperors were driven to avoid public displays of luxury. To modern eyes,
much of it reads as frankly racist, and yet he made arguments against both
ancient and contemporary slavery that anticipated later Enlightenment
thought. Most important, *The Spirit of the Laws* critically bequeathed the
idea of static self-regulation. Much of it was a discussion of self-regulating
politics, a paean to republics and monarchies as having built-in protection
against excess. But it was a thorough European crafting of the argument
that a properly designed social system could rely on homeostatic tendencies
to prevent disaster. The growing holistic nature of self-regulation in the
thinking of eighteenth-century writers can be gleaned from Montesquieu's
use of a Newtonian metaphor to describe a properly functioning polity:
"It is with this kind of government as with the system of the universe, in
which there is a power that constantly repels all bodies from the centre,
and a power of gravitation that attracts it."[37]

Hegel

Another author whose work merits special attention as representative of the
growth of self-regulation thinking, dynamic in this case, is Georg Wilhelm
Frederic Hegel (1770–1831). In a series of works with even now many different interpretations, notably *The Phenomenology of Mind* (1807), Hegel
investigated the entire human project—thought, achievement, and culture.[38]
He first rejected Plato's idea of static, objective, ideal forms unknowable
to most humans. Instead, he noted that things in isolation cannot have
definitions; there can be no idea, for example, that someone is tall unless
one also knows someone who is short. (Economists similarly emphasize
the importance of relative, not absolute, prices in motivating decision
making.) Concepts, broadly defined to include ideas and objects, in other
words, can exist only in contrast to other concepts. He then dramatically
extended the long-standing idea of dialectic reasoning. Socratic dialectic is
simply a way of asking questions to cast doubt on the speaker's assertion

in order to make progress toward the truth. But for Hegel, the dialectic is an eternal conversation, not just between individuals (although they can in the realm of ideas certainly introduce new perspectives) but between all elements of human thought as it is dispersed among people across space and time and across different human institutions and structures. Often summarized as thesis, antithesis, synthesis, it is perhaps better thought of as a repeated series of encounter, reflection, and reinterpretation, where each reinterpretation sets the stage for the next encounter.

Thus, Hegel's world is not a battle between mutually exclusive conceptions of reality or ethics, so that what today's thinker says annihilates what previous thinkers said, but is instead a process of innovative growth. So there is a dynamic process in human thought and achievement, full of trial and error, that yields progress. The evolution of human consciousness today is not Darwinian emptiness, but yields a civilization superior to that of yesterday. Knowledge cannot be destroyed, and adding new cognition to the existing stock of knowledge can only improve human consciousness. Human thinking is always in motion, and in the longer term, all such motion cannot help, perhaps after frequent detours and blind alleys, but be forward.

The Hegelian framework cannot be said to be comprehensively self-regulatory, in that there is no intrinsic incentive to expand and thus improve human consciousness; that the generation of more, better knowledge is natural, is simply and reasonably assumed. But the framework is dynamic, and progressive. There is a goal, and the broad human conversation, through dynamic self-regulation, facilitates it. Other differences exist between it and true dynamic self-regulation. Most notable, unlike the self-regulating systems outlined in subsequent chapters, there was for Hegel, as for the perfectionist thinkers of old, an ideal terminus of the process. Hegel scholars typically denote this as the Absolute (Hegel called the last chapter of *The Phenomenology of Spirit* "Absolute Knowledge," *Absolutes Wissen*), which is essentially when all knowledge, cognition, culture, and history knows itself. In the preface to *Phenomenology* he wrote:

The truth is the whole. The whole, however, is merely the essential nature reaching its completeness through the process of its own development. Of the Absolute it must be said that it is essentially a result, that only at the end is it what it is in very truth; and just in that consists its nature, which is to be actual, subject, or self-becoming, self-development.[39]

There must be a complete awareness not just of all knowledge but how it has come to be. So there is progress, albeit toward a destination, and there is a built-in mechanism for getting there. The idea of continuous, though not eternal, dynamic-regulating improvement is there.

Hegel, however, took a peculiar view of *the state* as the culmination of the human collective experience whose perfection is the goal in his philosophy. Just as all cognitive reflection yields insight and as a whole inevitably yields progress, the state is a perfection first of the family and later "civil society" (*bürgerliche gesellshaft*, burgher society), a term he used in the sense we use *state* today.[40] The state not only protects people's safety and property; it also is "an external organization for attaining their particular and common interests" and "is brought back to and welded into unity in the Constitution of the State which is the end and actuality of both the substantial universal order and the public life devoted thereto."[41] In the words of Stephen Houlgate, for Hegel the state's role is to "fully express the nature of social institutions in their most rational form" and represents "complete ethical actuality."[42] Hegel, who in his own lifetime saw two momentous revolutions and was a beneficiary of the legacy of the enlightened Prussian emperor Frederick the Great (1712–1786, ruled 1740–1786), saw government as the vehicle for perfecting each unique people's ethical and social life. In the words of Michael Alan Fox, Hegel had the "enlightened" view that "the state represents the presence of a rational principal in the world of impersonal affairs and why we are therefore incomplete, as human individuals, apart from it."[43]

Given the heavy hand that the powerful state will be shown to have played in frustrating established self-regulating processes beginning in the late nineteenth century, Hegel's legacy for the self-regulating idea is mixed. Nevertheless, his dynamic model of ethical and scientific progress of the human enterprise is a landmark in the acceptance of the self-regulating idea.

THE AGE OF SELF-REGULATION TAKES OFF

A striking picture that appeared in the July 1895 issue of *Harper's* magazine depicted the victorious Napoleon Bonaparte (1769–1821) riding in

October 1806 through the streets of Jena, Prussia, where he had just defeated the Prussian army and where the young Hegel was already a distinguished scholar. The author of the surrounding article, Poultney Bigelow (1855–1954), recounted the moment depicted in the picture, in which Hegel, returning from the post office having failed to deliver the manuscript of *Phenomenology of Spirit* because of the chaos after the Prussian army's defeat, sees Napoleon ride by. The bookish-looking professor watches with an expression suggesting his recognition that an old era has died of exhaustion.[44] Hegel supposedly later told friends it was "a most exalting moment."[45] In this view, he was not alone. According to the magazine account, in the view of many in the German states, Napoleon, having restored order in France, "seemed to have been sent by Heaven for the purpose of inaugurating a great European millennium" and his rule was "so manifestly of interest to art, literature, science, and human happiness."[46]

While the Corsican corporal-cum-emperor was primarily a bringer of death and destruction (several million dead in his wars, civilian and non-civilian is a widely accepted estimate), his admirers saw him as an avatar of modernity. To some degree, he governed accordingly: hidebound feudal institutions that were obstacles to self-regulation were swept away wherever his armies went; Prussia abolished serfdom, for example, in 1807. His soldiers brought the modern nation birthed by the French Revolution and its laws, with its meritocratically selected civil servants to administer them and a general belief in the triumph of modernity.

Lamentably, these changes provided the mechanism for implementing the ideas that would later go on, fueled by the different sort of competition that is politics, to restrain self-regulating processes. But for now, self-regulation was everywhere in the early and mid-nineteenth century. For Darwin, it was natural selection that drove changes in the composition of biota. Thus, if the environment changed, species that were more suited to the environment would be introduced and flourish. An ecosystem, in other words, operated without external control, yet predictably in response to stimuli within or outside the system. While lacking moral purpose, a central tenet of evolutionary theory is that evolution over the long term creates organisms that are more complex, which bears some resemblance to Hegel's claims about human knowledge becoming richer as humanity progresses toward complete self-awareness.

A little earlier, another prominent hypothesis of static self-regulation had actually offered a pessimistic account of the ability of human society to escape what was a predictable, self-regulating trap. This was the prediction of Thomas Malthus (1766–1834) offered in *An Essay on the Principle of Population* (1789). Given a fixed technology of agricultural production, people's desire to have children meant that in times of plenty, they had many, who then went on to overtax production capacity, resulting in famine. So salient were beliefs in Malthus's grim self-regulating process that a number of civic groups eventually sprang up to express fundamental pessimism about the ability of humanity, particularly in poor societies, to sustain itself. Indeed, this belief, even though it was being rendered obsolete even as Malthus was writing it by the early Industrial Revolution, arguably influences even now the widespread claim that population must be externally regulated due to the "unsustainability" of modern human activity. And by the late nineteenth century, what is now called sociology was engaging in far more complex analysis of social structure, finding human society becoming ever more complex and fragmenting into complex subsystems. Dynamic social change was for these thinkers front and center, although the self-regulatory mechanism sometimes made an appearance and sometimes did not.

On the ground, the increased building of networks of all sorts, in addition to those of intellectual communication, further enabled self-regulatory processes. The eighteenth and nineteenth centuries saw the building of extensive commercial and transportation networks—what we now call globalization.[47] Firms did business with more partner firms across greater distances, accelerating network construction. During these times, people were also liberated to move out of their villages, and indeed their countries, as never before, from places of poorer opportunities to those of greater ones. (To be fair, some of that movement was the product of Western military conquest. But not all of it, and in any event, the introduction of modern ideas of commerce and science was liberating in its own way for people who were still living in tradition-bound stasis.) If the movement of ideas, merchandise, and people across physical and intellectual space is the sine qua non of virtuous self-regulation, the latter could not but flower as never before during this time. If Montesquieu, Hegel, Darwin, and others were examples of the rising tide of self-regulation thinking, migration and commerce were self-regulation in action.

But such mobility, and its concomitant social change, was necessarily disruptive, and disruption brings resistance from those who benefit from the existing order. The decrease of belief in traditional, often divinely mandated, social hierarchies in the West, in the face of the epic social change of the nineteenth century, meant that some account of this fact of such continuous change was required. Thus, the question of whether to leave such change well enough alone or to manage or reverse it through the increasing capacity of the state would become an issue of pressing importance. This dispute will be taken up in Chapters 6 and 7, but first, we must go back in time a bit to the history of science to find the first explicit advocacy of progress through benign political neglect of a sufficiently self-regulating process, and at the results of that process's successes.

CHAPTER 3

Wrongs Make Rights

Self-Regulating Science

Scientists are human—they're as biased as any other group. But they do
have one great advantage in that science is a self-correcting process.
CYRIL PONNAMPERUMA (1923–1994), biologist[1]

Béla Schick (1877–1967) was a Hungarian-born pediatrician and researcher
of no small distinction. After spending time as a professor of medicine at the
University of Vienna, he came to the United States in 1923. At Columbia
University and Mount Sinai Hospital, he oversaw research on numerous
diseases that frequently struck and killed children. He also developed a
test for susceptibility to diphtheria that contributed mightily to essentially
eliminating the disease in the developed world.

Given these achievements, it is somewhat surprising to reflect on another incident in his career. According to an account by his own pen in
an Austrian medical journal, he had once asked a reluctant woman in his
employ to place flowers in a vase. It turned out that the reason for her several refusals was that she was menstruating, and every time this was happening, her touch was fatal to flowers. Schick designed and performed an
experiment in which he compared the outcome for flowers when handled
by women who were menstruating with those handled by women who
were not. The higher death rates among the flowers touched by the former
led him to posit that such women emitted "menotoxins."[2] Subsequent research reported mixed results, and eventually investigators came up with
a further hypothesis based on this idea. They posited that the toxicity of
menstrual blood increased when women were irradiated with ultraviolet
light, and that the same sort of deadly effect could emanate from the fin-
gers of men in the grip of infections of various kinds. The Soviet scientist
Olga Lepeshinskaya (1871–1963) hypothesized in the 1920s that when
an organism died, its dead cells should emit ultraviolet radiation.

Both of these hypotheses were widely believed by scientists and journalists for years after they were first proposed. Lepeshinskaya's "necro-biotic rays" were written of favorably in the early 1930s in *Science*, and there was debate going on about menotoxins in *The Lancet* as late as the 1970s, although they were in the letters portion rather than through referereed articles.[3] Like many other claims that seem *outré* now, this one was seriously entertained by serious thinkers at the time.

What on earth was going on with these claims, or the one that magnetic emissions from animals could cure mental disorders, or that a horse could solve arithmetic problems that humans asked it, or that sitting on chairs rather than on the floor caused the internal organs to sag, leading to changed skin color and unfortunate odors that bespoke graver ills? In a word, science—the foundation of subsequent self-regulating thought.[4]

HOW WE THINK

Humans are blessed with the power to figure out why things happen, why the world is the way it is and not some other way, and to use these results to predict what will happen. Early religious beliefs are now thought to be an attempt to do precisely this. These were certainly hypotheses, if not exactly science, in the modern sense. But as these religious beliefs got entangled with the powers that were in increasingly hierarchical societies, dissenting interpretations of why things happen became harder, since now they threatened to bring the wrath not just of the king but the supernatural world on the speaker. In that sense, it is perhaps a small miracle that certain thinkers in several societies had the freedom they did to think about other possibilities.

Science, tautologically, is anything done according to the scientific method. This method is now widely held to mean creating a testable hypothesis, conducting controlled experiments, and using the hypothesis to predict their outcomes. Any hypotheses whose predictions are not in agreement with the results of the experiment are "falsified" and discarded.[5] Any hypothesis whose predictions are not falsified is still in the running, and as more experiments in more environments continue to fail to falsify the hypothesis, the confidence of scientists that it usefully describes the world increases.

The modern scientific *system* also has certain characteristics. It is a network of both people and ideas. The people who are engaging in science can be found in almost every corner of the earth. They are linked together, typically in lower-level networks of specialists and subspecialists—theorists, empiricists, lepidopterists, cosmic ray physicists, and so on. Participants in the scientific enterprise agreeably play by the rules of the scientific game. Perhaps most important, science is a continuing and ongoing enterprise. Old ideas that continue to pass the falsification test are part of the training of new scientists, and each new generation uses that which is accepted as not yet falsified from the work of previous generations as the foundation for its own work. Each generation's ideas, in other words, draw on the ideas of others who came before them in extending or replacing existing hypotheses and in conducting falsifiable experiments. There is a clearly a Hegelian cast to the scientific enterprise.

But to systematically carry out "science" in this sense requires a certain frame of mind. In particular, there must be a belief that consistent, observable rules govern the behavior of the universe. These rules must also be detectable through the senses, including through the use of whatever instruments (e.g., telescopes) humans can bring to bear to collect the necessary sensory evidence. This way of thinking had to appear, take root as a significant phenomenon in the intellectual culture, and finally be accepted as the standard by which a community of "scientists" could define itself. Only then could a scientific system take shape and become sustainable.

Some of the necessary elements of the scientific way of thinking were extensively and independently developed long ago outside what became the West. Writers in the Indian subcontinent by 500 A.D. had already developed a sophisticated body of thought on questions of epistemology (what can be known) and ontology (thinking about the nature of reality). The Chinese by roughly 1000 A.D. had an extensive literature describing the systematic relations inherent in existence, which included both ethical and material dimensions; incorporation of both elements into the idea of the overall nature of all things (*dǎo*, 道) was a key innovation of Chinese thought.

But only in Western Europe would all of the seeds of the scientific method sprout. The idea that a consistent logic governed both natural phenomena and human behavior, especially ethical behavior, was already important in ancient Greek thinking. To know what is or what should be was to have deduced it. Aristotle, like Euclid (dates of birth, death unknown) and Archimedes (c. 287 B.C. –c. 212 B.C.) before him, at least granted that no matter how long a syllogism was, there was a premise at the beginning that had to be assumed. But he also insisted that there had to be an order governing the world, and the task was to use logic to figure out what it is. The primary alternative was the atomism of Democritus (c. 460 B.C. –c. 370 B.C.), which held that the essentially random movements of the elementary particles of the cosmos determined the form of the universe as a whole at any moment. Aristotle developed a way that the first-premise problem could be handled—in the words of Chunglin Kwa, by "frequent observation, guided by intuition."[6] Experience, in other words, could tell us what to assume as the starting point for any syllogism. Remembering that Aristotle was using syllogisms to get at the natural forms that constitute the universe, he argued explicitly, if briefly, in the *Posterior Analytics* (II.19.100b) that the senses "transmit" universally true but nondeducible phenomenon to the mind.[7]

Greek knowledge, in all its dimensions, was passed on and added to by the Romans. But this knowledge was essentially lost, outside of some of the Christian monasteries, to Western Europe after the Western Empire fell in the fifth century A.D. Part of Aristotle's corpus, along with the rest of this learning, returned to Western Europe during the Crusades and through Arab rule over and then Christian *reconquista* of Iberia. During these several centuries of conquest by Christian soldiers of Arab territory in what is now Spain, this knowledge came back to the West and was known to Aquinas, who used it in the course of creating the *Summa*.

The absence of a widely accepted scientific method did not mean that there was no science, or technological progress broadly defined. Inventions to improve human productivity, whether through water-generated power to enable tasks that human power alone could not achieve (medieval Europe), suspension bridges to facilitate goods transport (China), double-entry accounting (Florence), or lending and borrowing (polygenetic, but for which records exist from ancient Babylon), occurred everywhere. That the pace of such inventions outstripped that of scientific progress for many centuries suggests that sometimes the latter is overstated as a condition for the former to exist.[8] In addition, people in Europe, the Byzantine Empire, the Arab world, India, and China meticulously observed the skies with the goal of predicting future movements of heavenly bodies, although without an extensive networking and feedback process. The purpose was to predict human affairs through astrology and, in the Islamic case, to set prayer times, rather than to describe predictable rules of the behavior of the universe simply because that was itself a theological or other imperative. But each civilization's early science was limited by the failure to rigorously conceive of the role of experiments.[9]

The importance of such predictive activity in Western Europe was subsequently enhanced by the Black Death in the fourteenth century, widely thought to be caused by divine vengeance, which through God's will could be foretold by an ill-starred (as the saying still has it) planetary alignment. Contemporary astrologers predicted the next major alignment of this kind would occur in 1365, and some went so far as to conclude that God would take vengeance on the Arabs and later the Turks, who had long since conquered large stretches of Christian territory and were even then a threat to Constantinople.[10]

THE THEORY OF EXPERIMENTS

European astrologers were supposed to make predictions, although it is safe to say that systematically keeping track of them as a whole and how they worked out were not common practices. The situation was a little better with alchemy, widely practiced in late medieval and early modern Europe. This attempt to explore how to carry out the transmutation of substances, especially into gold, certainly gave its practitioners an interest in keeping track of what did (or, typically, didn't) work. But the immense value to ruling circles if one of their alchemists could pull it off (the analogue to scientific research related to national security in the modern era) meant that there was little incentive to share research methods or results or to seek constructive criticism from other alchemists. (If one king possessed the means to turn iron into gold, clearly there was no reason to share it with anyone.) There had been progress too in the technique of hypothesizing, including an acceptance of an idea often traced to William of Ockham's (c. 1287–1347) argument that, other things equal, the simpler hypothesis was the better one.

The primary steps in defining the scientific *method* and building the self-regulating scientific system were taken almost simultaneously on opposite sides of the North Sea. First, by just a few years, and on the English side, was the approach of Bacon in *Novum Organon Scientiarum* (1620). Translated roughly from the Latin as *The New Instrument of Knowledge*, it was a title perhaps mischievously chosen to invoke the collection of Aristotle's six major works on logic, named by his followers after he had compiled them as *Organon* ("Instrument"). On the cover of the original printed work, planned to be one of six volumes, although only four were completed, was a sailing ship on the ocean passing through the gates of knowledge, the implication being that knowledge was something that was created by the explorations of many. Bacon explicitly criticized Aristotelian deduction as the key to knowledge. Rather, he said, the task required traveling the road of repeated observation to distinguish circumstances where a natural phenomenon was present from where it wasn't, and developing from that an idea of the cause of the phenomenon. The Aristotelian method was, in his words "only strong for disputation and contentions, but barren of the production of works for the benefit of the life of man."[11] Only through *inductive* reasoning was it possible to productively understand the nature of things.

Outlining the importance of inductive versus deductive thinking in trying to solve problems (e.g., to understand the rules governing the universe) is critical. By its nature, inductive reasoning is tentative and not certain; it yields hypotheses, not dogma. Deductive reasoning always has definite beginnings and ends. One starts from an assumption and proceeds one logical step at a time to the fixed conclusion. Unless there is a logical error or the starting point is at least suspected to be false, there is no more work to be done once we get to this conclusion. It is perhaps for this reason that Aristotelian deduction about the nature of creation was so difficult to dislodge for so long. In contrast, testing hypotheses against what is observed always leaves open the possibility for new observations to overturn these hypotheses. So it is that at various times, cancer was thought to be caused by imbalances in the humors, mysterious elements between normal tissue called blastema, and later (especially after the discovery of microorganisms) to be purely an infectious disease. Now, cancer is often thought of as many diseases with many causes whose etiologies are often poorly understood. Its cause is not a thing to be deduced in the manner of a geometric proposition; hypotheses must instead be proposed and tested against the observed evidence.

Meanwhile, in 1637 in the relatively liberal Netherlands, a publishing company in Leiden published a work by the Frenchman René Descartes (1596–1650). In this *Discourse on the Method of Rightly Conducting One's Reason and of Seeking Truth in the Sciences*, Descartes, who chose to write in modern French rather than traditional Latin, started by admitting that human intelligence can always go wrong—in his implied example, the intelligence that had generated the ancient classics. Having been traditionally educated in the classically/religiously doctrinal Scholastic tradition, he found himself entertaining doubts about the received wisdom of the ancients, which in the sciences were a dead end, deciding "that no solid superstructures could be reared on foundations so infirm."[12] He sought to create a better "method" of getting at the truth of a complex world. He first argued that nothing other than first principles can be taken on faith. Everything else must be arrived at slowly, one reasoned step at a time. So far, the "method" resembles Aristotle's. Then Descartes added that any puzzle must be broken down into the smallest steps, so that each step can be definitively determined to be true or not. In the last section, he explicitly acknowledged on several occasions that acquiring knowledge about the natural world (at one point he invoked medicine in particular) is difficult and subject to error and that what we know pales in comparison to what we have yet to discover. Science, in other words, is an ongoing process of discovery and not something handed down in pristine form from the ancient world. He also invoked "experiments" (*expériences*) as the way to make scientific progress in conjunction with the efforts of others:

to communicate to the public all the little I might myself have found, and incite men of superior genius to strive to proceed farther, by contributing, each according to his inclination and ability, the experiments it would be necessary to make, and also by informing the public of all they might discover, so that, by the last beginning where those before them had left off, and thus *connecting the lives and labors of many*, we might collectively proceed much farther than each himself could do. [emphasis added]

He even criticized his own investigations into scientific questions as insufficient by virtue of being done by one man alone, and "request[s] all who may have any objections to make to them to take the trouble of forwarding these to my publisher, who will give me notice of them, that I may endeavor to subjoin at the same time my reply; and in this way readers seeing both at once will more easily determine where the truth lies."[13] Scientific progress, in other words, depends on effective feedback through a network that grows over time.

Some of Descartes' thinking was itself soon rejected due to the new scientific method—for example, his belief that the entire universe, even what we now know (think?) to be the vast empty spaces between celestial bodies, was filled with matter all moving on a predetermined track determined at the beginning of time. One supposes that had he lived to see it, he would have taken pleasure in this result.

NETWORKS AND STANDARDS

Although he did not coin it, U.S. Vice President Al Gore is famously associated with the phrase "information superhighway." A superhighway, of course, is nothing more than a performance-enhanced highway, and the construction of the first such information highways—a predecessor of the Internet if you like—is an important part of the rise of self-regulating science.

The arguments of Bacon and Descartes, and of Robert Hooke (1635–1703), whose belief in all-too-fallible humans led him to advocate the construction of mechanical instruments to measure experimental outcomes,[14] naturally implied a need, if science was to progress, for scientists to communicate their hypotheses and results with one another. Without much impetus from the state, these new "natural philosophers" simply constructed their own networks. It is true that some regimes, particularly that of France, exercised some control over the publication of anything that might represent a threat to royal authority or social stability, a problem that rulers had perceived since soon after the invention of the printing press. These censorious impulses were also directed against the new science. The climate in the Netherlands, in contrast, was distinctively more liberal.

But France's expurgatory enthusiasm did not stop the priest Marin Mersenne (1588–1648), who himself wrote about theology, the acoustics of stringed instruments, and mathematics and after whom Mersenne primes are named,[15] from becoming the clearinghouse for the growing number of scientific investigations across Western Europe. His correspondents included Descartes, Galileo, Thomas Hobbes (1588–1679), and Pierre de Fermat (1601–1665), and they extended to the Ottoman territories of Constantinople, Tunisia, and Syria.[16] His modest home in Paris constituted a significant node of the rapidly flowering network of scientific exploration and feedback. Through correspondence with his thinker friends, periodic meetings with some of them in his home or elsewhere in Paris, and several trips to the Netherlands, he was able to communicate with scientists and give them his own feedback and that of others on their work. All of this feedback was in the spirit of the pursuit of the goal of discovering truth. By the end of Mersenne's life, Boyle was referring in his correspondence to the "Invisible College," a similar network of scholars in England dedicated to hypothesizing, experimenting, and sharing the results of these activities. It is not clear to whom he was referring, but many now use the term to refer to the entire community of the curious that was growing in importance throughout the seventeenth century.[17]

And what a community it was! Over the course of what we might call the long seventeenth century, Isaac Newton (1643–1727) laid down many of the fundamentals of physics and astronomy. In his *Philosophiae Naturalis Principia Mathematica* (1687), he also advocated the use of mathematics to understand the natural world and the possibility that hypotheses could be continually revised in light of new observations.[18] His view of a self-regulating material world, where forces would be counteracted by other forces or move objects to their new equilibrium position, was later unusually influential in developing the hypothesis of a self-regulating socioeconomy (a topic presented in Chapter 5). Johannes Kepler (1571–1630) made the heliocentric model of the solar system consistent with the growing body of data by positing elliptical orbits, William Harvey (1578–1657) specified a highly fruitful model of the circulatory system, and Antonie von Leeuwenhoek (1632–1723) built a better microscope and used it to discover microorganisms (a discovery that would revolutionize medical theory and treatment). Boyle at least set the agenda for what became modern chemistry by asserting that there must be fundamental elements beyond earth, air, fire, and water. He also documented the proportional relationship between the volume and temperature of a gas in a closed system.

By the standards of the seventeenth century, let alone all the history that had come before it, this was extraordinary progress. It is probably true that for most new branches of science, the earliest discoveries come relatively quickly because the necessary experimental equipment could be designed and constructed at relatively low cost. (Think of magnifying lenses versus vast underground supercolliders.) But why now? Surely a big part of the story was the development of an international scientific network in constant communication. Mersenne's role has already been mentioned, but many social movements that depend on the energy of one person are vulnerable to that person's death. Fortunately, science had already reached the takeoff point. In the 1640s, groups of natural philosophers were meeting regularly in London and Oxford to discuss the latest questions. By 1662, a single group requested and received a charter from Charles II (1630–1685, ruled 1660–1685) as The President, Council, and Fellows of the Royal Society of London for Improving Natural Knowledge, today known informally as the Royal Society.

At the outset, they developed the fundamentals of the scientific method as guiding principles for conducting natural philosophy. Almost from the beginning there was a practice of requesting that experiments that had been conducted in private facilities, and the results of which had been reported to the society, be conducted in front of an audience of members and their guests. (The society's motto even now, *Nullius in Verba*, can be translated as "take nobody's word for it.") This practice had occurred in secret before the restoration of the monarchy in 1660 and now flowered into public experimentation, whose outcome, science being so young, was often difficult to predict, and vigorous, unfettered debate. These traditions became essential in the world's first permanent scientific institution. The initial concern may not have been so much dishonesty as the need to check to make sure the experiment itself was scientifically sound. At an experiment's conclusion, the witnesses could also discuss how to interpret it.[19] Under such conditions, experimentation became in the eyes of the scientific community as close to an unbiased feedback system as has so far been imagined.

The Royal Society also established the world's first scientific journal, *Philosophical Transactions of the Royal Society*, in 1665. Still published today, it looks quite different from the early issues. After a dedication to the king, the first volume had this brief introduction by the Bremen native Henry Oldenburg (c. 1619–1677), who also sat at the center of his own epistolary scientific network:

Whereas there is nothing more necessary for promoting the improvement of Philosophical Matters, than the communicating to such, as apply their Studies and Endeavours that way, such things as are discovered or put in practise by others;

it is therefore thought fit to employ the Press, as the most proper way to gratifie those, whose engagement in such Studies, and delight in the advancement of Learning and profitable Discoveries, doth entitle them to the knowledge of what this Kingdom, or other parts of the World, do, from time to time, afford, as well of the progress of the Studies, Labours, and attempts of the Curious and learned in things of this kind, as of their compleat Discoveries and performances: To the end, that such Productions being clearly and truly communicated, desires after solid and usefull knowledge may be further entertained, ingenious Endeavours and Undertakings cherished, and those, addicted to and conversant in such matters, may be invited and encouraged to search, try, and find out new things, impart their knowledge to one another, and contribute what they can to the Grand design of improving Natural Knowledge, and perfecting all Philosophical Arts, and Sciences, All for the Glory of God, the Honour and Advantage of these Kingdoms, and the Universal Good of Mankind.

All of the elements of the self-regulating system are there: the higher (unanimously agreed here) goal; the claim that the feedback from making accumulated information widely available is essential to this goal; a network of people to provide this feedback; and a competition among people free to offer better ideas for achieving the goal. For the first time in recorded history, a significant community of humans decided to establish a community that threw caution to the wind and resolved to go wherever self-regulated experimentation, both literal and intellectual, took them. The whole process had a Hegelian feel to it a century and a half before Hegel himself, testimony to the importance of the scientific revolution in generating respect for self-regulating processes.

Implicit in this introduction was the idea that a still relatively new technology—"the Press"—would best facilitate this sharing of information. The nature of the information conveyed in 1665 is rather different from that found in the *Transactions* now. Essentially, Oldenburg and Boyle simply relayed the results of investigations conveyed to them by mail or in person. Some of these investigations were from the twenty-first-century perspective somewhat eccentric. The contents included "an account of a very odd monstrous Calf," which had detailed descriptions of a seemingly deformed unborn cow observed inside the body of its mother, and a first-person account of harvesting whales in the West Indies. Already the first issue of the first scientific journal contained a comment on a prior report (presumably known to the readers), followed by a reply to the comment by the author of the report, a practice still followed today in many scholarly journals. (The topic of the exchange was the location in the sky of the orbit of a newly discovered comet.)

The motives of the new Royal Society and its journal, being as important to humanity as they were, were sufficient for its members to leave their political and religious divides at the door, a major concern just after the end of Oliver Cromwell's (1599–1658) Commonwealth. In fact, the members themselves were hopeful that their cooperative, reasoned approach to progress could serve as an example to the political classes. (It is left to the reader's judgment how much this goal was subsequently achieved.) In its early years, it published papers submitted from Italy and Holland. The society's first official historian, Thomas Sprat (1635–1713), in his *History of the Royal Society of London* (1667), recounted the society's meetings in the early years:

Nor is it the least commendation the Royal Society deserves, that designing a union of men's hands and reasons, it has proceeded so far in uniting their affections. For there we behold an unusual sight to the English nation, that men of disagreeing parties, and ways of life, have forgotten to hate, and have met in the unanimous advancement of the same works. The soldier, the tradesman, the merchant, the scholar, the gentleman, the courtier, the divine, the Presbyterian, the Papist, the Independent, and those of Orthodox judgment, have laid aside their names of distinction, and calmly inspired in a mutual agreement of laborers and desires.[20]

Similar arguments would be made for communication, for commerce, to a lesser degree for art, and even for sports in subsequent centuries. The value of scientific networks is certainly suggested by the establishment of similar societies in other countries, though perhaps this enthusiasm should be discounted by a desire to succeed in an imagined national scientific rivalry.

Scientists realized after a time that standardization also facilitates feedback, allowing scientists to more easily communicate with one another. Think of the benefits of a common currency, for example, as a measure of costs, profits, and losses in a socioeconomy. Scientists in England, France, and the German states were each using local systems of measurement, when, as part of their rationalization of French society, the Revolutionary authorities in that country introduced the metric system in 1795. The new system was based on work done in the years after 1789 by a commission that suggested that science itself be the foundation of a universal measuring system. One could certainly quarrel with how useful every attempt at imposed social change by those authorities was; their reconfiguration of the Gregorian calendar on a decimal basis has been widely mocked, for example. But here they struck gold. So sensible were the units, both because they were based on units of 10 and because of their scientific basis (the original definition of the meter, for example, was the best estimate of one ten-millionth of the distance from the equator to the North Pole), that they spread quickly, admittedly first partly under the persuasive force of Napoleon's armies. By 1875, all of Europe except the United Kingdom and Russia used the system, and through colonialism, it spread to most of the world. For scientific and technological/industrial reasons, universal units of electricity were added in 1873. In addition, the practice of citation, not apparent in early editions of *Philosophical Transactions* yet long known from ancient Greek, rabbinical, and Islamic commentary, and long-standing in English common law, gradually took hold. This practice, which has the combined properties of relying on the authority of something already published and allowing the reader to trace back the history of a particular scientific idea, is universally accepted today.

As for language, during the early Scientific Revolution, Latin was already in eclipse and French in the ascendancy as the language of communication for elites of all sorts, including scientific elites, across national borders. The need to express new scientific ideas difficult to translate into the language of the ancient Romans accelerated the abandonment of Latin, a tactic begun by Descartes, as the common transnational language. It was replaced by scientific French, English, or German; one of the things that made Oldenburg so valuable was his fluency in numerous languages. Leeuwenhoek, who used his microscopes to investigate previously unknowable microorganisms, spoke only Dutch; this did not compromise his ability to contribute but did require someone to make his work more accessible to the scientific network. German became dominant in the second half of the nineteenth century, and English triumphed over the course of the twentieth century, becoming the global language not just of science but of business and, to a lesser extent, journalism.

Mathematics was a cleaner story. Mathematical expressions of claims about the world are unambiguous and easy to test experimentally; both Galileo and Boyle used mathematical expressions to describe their hypotheses. The development of calculus by Newton and Gottfried Leibniz (1646–1716) immensely facilitated the expression of hypotheses in mathematical notation and would have been unthinkable without the development of the standard of decimal notation as a replacement for fractional notation by Simon Stevin (1548–1620) and John Napier (1550–1617). These innovations in mathematical notation have at least two advantages, independent of the accuracy of hypotheses expressed in such notation instead of words. First, math can say so much that is testable with so little notation. Second, it can easily be understood across cultures. For example, when the Japanese desperately sought to master Western science after the Meiji restoration in 1868, they could have chosen to simply use their essentially adequate indigenous mathematical notation. But they chose instead to keep that system *and* adopt the Western notation all at once to enable them to learn faster.[21] Math, citation, common language: all products of dynamic self-regulation, internally generated rules to improve the system's ability to promote the goal of furthering scientific knowledge by making the network more productive.

PROFESSIONALIZATION OF THE NEW SELF-REGULATING SCIENCE

At first, scientists were generally born into relatively high-status families. Boyle, born in Ireland, was the son of the first earl of Cork, and Newton was the son of a well-to-do farmer. This is not surprising; the nascent science was already impossible to carry out without the tools of writing and mathematics, in addition to the ability to build still relatively simple experimental equipment. (This class bias would not be the case later with the inventions that powered the Industrial Revolution, many of which were conceived by people of modest backgrounds.) The upper-class dominance of science was still broadly true throughout the eighteenth century, but as scientific knowledge ramified, it became more difficult for any individual to know much of it personally and more reasonable therefore for the now greater number of people pursuing science not just to specialize in subfields of knowledge but to adopt science as a full-time profession.

UNIVERSITIES

Where to house these new scientists? The Royal Society could still serve as a clearinghouse for knowledge. So too could similar organizations established at about the same time in other countries. The French Académie des Sciences had been established under the patronage of Louis XIV (1638–1715, ruled 1643–1715) in 1666, following the unsuccessful Académie de Montmor, established in 1657 but essentially extinct by the end of 1664. But scattered as their members were, it was difficult for these organizations to directly organize and employ the new breed of career scientists. Place-bound institutions that could employ them and already specialized in dealing with knowledge would be obviously helpful, and such institutions already existed in the form of the European university, which had a long history in Europe, traceable back to Bologna and Paris in the eleventh and twelfth centuries, respectively.

If by "university" we mean "a place of the most advanced education," such institutions had already existed for centuries in India, Persia, and elsewhere. But the European university was different. Even its name suggests a transcendent range of knowledge. Since the early years, the European version had made disputation, that is, logical debate over various propositions, the heart of its curriculum. It also had a tradition of independence from the sovereign, in that most universities in the early centuries were affiliated with the Church. In 1158, the Holy Roman Emperor, Frederick Barbarossa (1112–1190, ruled 1155–1190), had issued the *Privilegium Scholasticum*, a document that granted members of the new universities (Bologna in particular) the right to travel freely and to be exempt from the common practice of seizing the property of people for crimes their countrymen had been convicted of. And so the idea that universities were islands of freedom was established. Of course, the Church's distant hierarchy frequently attempted to assert theological discipline. Each university operated as an independent community of students and often itinerant scholars. Its tradition almost from the beginning of promoting dialectic, debate-style inquiry, in which students were frequently required to make and defend propositions that violated prevailing Church interpretation in matters of theology, astronomy, and the like, gave it an atmosphere of open inquiry, although deductive rather than empirical/inductive, that its members vigorously defended.

And yet the Scientific Revolution had come from outside these centers of learning. This is not surprising, because the task of universities was to transmit classical wisdom rather than create new knowledge. Theology, medicine, and even astronomy were definite, circumscribed fields; all that needed to be known had been known since ancient times. The task was to get the young to learn this knowledge rather than encourage them to go out and discover more. When scientists begin to adopt their hypothesize/ experiment/rehypothesize-as-needed approach, the universities were not particularly friendly to it, although the new knowledge in medicine and astronomy that was discovered largely outside the academy quickly found a home within it. Nonetheless, as late as 1768, Johann David Michaelis (1717–1791), writing from inside the academy (the University of Göttingen in Hanover in particular), could write of German universities that "the betterment of sciences, and the making of new discoveries, is not really the duty of a school, whether they be lower or higher. It is instead the affair of gifted individuals, or . . . of scientific societies."[22]

Even the usefully contentious spirit of the medieval universities had been significantly dulled by the Wars of Religion that followed the onset of the Protestant Reformation. Universities became above all a means for promoting one or another side of the boiling denominational disputes. Luther himself was a theologian on the faculty of the University of Wittenberg when he proposed a disputation to be discussed by faculty and students. It was a long-standing form of theological debate, which included his ninety-five theses on perceived corruption in the Church. (The story that he posted them on the door of a church there is apocryphal.) So by the end of the eighteenth century, university faculty were welcome to specialize in and transmit the scientific knowledge largely being generated outside the university, although some scientists, including Newton, Boyle, and Hooke, did some of their work at universities. But overall university faculty were not yet in much of a position, even for reasons having nothing to do with theology, to create this knowledge themselves. (The University of Edinburgh was a conspicuous exception, especially in medicine.[23])

In France during the early Revolutionary period and especially in Prussia after its catastrophic defeat in 1806, efforts were made to turn the university into an instrument of evolutionary scientific progress. The modern research university was born. The École polytechnique, founded as the École centrale des travaux publics in 1794 to study the sciences, quickly fell under the thumb of Napoleon, who turned it into a military academy. But the ethos of creating and transmitting the most advanced scientific knowledge for the new Revolutionary authorities had already motivated its founding.

The flagship campus, as it were, of the new modern university system might well be the University of Berlin (today Humboldt University of Berlin, Humboldt-Universität zu Berlin), founded in 1810. Traditionally it had four schools: law, medicine, philosophy, and theology. But it quickly added specialists in chemistry, physics, mathematics, and medical science, something without precedent at the time. And while the new universities inherited the long-standing European university tradition of the freedom to teach, now freedom was justified as essential in both teaching and research, for the very practical goal of advancing scientific knowledge. In fact, Friedrich Paulsen (1846–1908), a philosophy professor at Berlin, in a passage indicating a necessary rule of the scientific game and the unending dynamism of proper science, in 1906 more or less overturned Michaelis's conception of what the university was about:

It is no longer, as formerly, the function of the university teacher to hand down a body of truth established by authorities, but to search after scientific knowledge by investigation, and to teach his hearers to do the same. Science, that is the fundamental principle, does not exist as a fixed and finished system. It possesses a stock of truth, but not only is this infinitely far from embracing the entire field of possible knowledge, but it is both possible and necessary to subject its title to constant criticism. In science there is no statute of limitations nor law of proscription, hence no absolute property right. It consists solely in the constant and new appropriation of old truths and the acquisition of new knowledge; it exists only as a constantly repeated attempt to solve an endless problem, in which every seemingly settled point can be again called in question by the presentation of new evidence. Hence it follows that truly scientific instruction, that is, instruction that shall lead to scientific thinking and investigation, can be conceived only as absolutely free.[24]

Admittedly, research universities were subject to political influence from the beginning. The administrators of the new universities were often chosen, or the choice was heavily influenced, by political authorities. And it is undeniable that the government was essential in creating this new university breed, as much to contribute to national power as to promote the discovery of scientific knowledge. The state also extensively influenced the curriculum, as it still does, including in the United States. But independence of inquiry was already seen as indispensable to the goal of identifying and rectifying scientific error, a key component of all self-regulating processes. The idea of good science being free science, perhaps in combination with the earlier European tradition of giving professors and students the rights to speak and think freely that other people did not have, meant that this operating principle extended quickly to fields of knowledge other than science, drawing substantially on the broader arguments for free communication discussed in Chapter 4.

PEER REVIEW

That scientific ideas should compete, and better ones (meaning nonfalsified given all that is currently known) should replace inferior ones in the thinking of scientists, and the general public to the extent possible, was already taken for granted by the late seventeenth century. The ability of scientists to report their results grew gradually, if modestly, with the spread of the new journals. But soon the growth of knowledge made the original approach, in which scientists simply accepted that debate of published ideas among the community of scientists was sufficient to self-regulate, so successful that scientific knowledge grew rapidly. By now, scientific discussion had outstripped the ability of such old institutions as the Royal Society to monitor whether a particular case of scientific argumentation actually furthered the debate, as opposed to simply repeating something already known or misstating or misusing generally accepted knowledge. New methods had to be found to keep science functioning as it was supposed to. But as the amount of accepted knowledge grew, it became impossible for any individual, even in consultation with scholars he knew personally, to know everything that needed to be known to render judgment on whether a particular submission to a journal constituted new knowledge. It is sometimes said that Aristotle was the last man who knew everything, and according to the philosopher Pierre Lévy, when Denis Diderot (1713–1784) and Jean le Rond d'Alembert (1717–1783) published their *Encyclopédie* between 1551 and 1772, it was worth doing because "until that time, a small group of men could hope to master all knowledge (or at least the principal knowledge, and propose to others the ideal of this mastery. Knowledge was still totalizable, integrable."[25]

Scientists who sought to transmit whatever new knowledge emerged faced a new challenge. In 1752, the Royal Society began sending items sent to it for publication to members who were particularly knowledgeable about the research in question. But truth be told, it may have been as much technological inadequacy as the inability to know everything an editor needed to know that delayed the spread of peer review. Until the late nineteenth century, the amount of space available in journals exceeded the amount of material available to fill it unless the editors made serious effort to fill that space. Only after the invention of the typewriter was it possible to make one or more copies, using carbon paper, for outside review, obviating the need to pass the one manuscript sequentially to personal acquaintances.

The increase in scientists led to an increase in research that had to be considered as possible scientific advance. The invention of the photocopier in the late 1950s further facilitated the process as it now exists: journal editors send manuscripts to reviewers who are seen as experts in the perhaps arcane subfield, to evaluate whether they are worth publishing.[26] Furthermore, scientists, and scholars generally, accepted that for reasons of corruption or bias, reviewers may not be able to evaluate submissions objectively. The fragmentation of scientific expertise and specialization, with its attendant increase in productivity from the division of labor, and the improvement of communications technology increased within any given field the problems of ignorance, bias, and hurt feelings. In response, reviews increasingly became double-blind, which in most fields is now standard practice.

SELF-REGULATING SELF-REGULATION

We thus have the remarkable circumstance in which even the process of self-regulation was subject to the self-regulation principle. And the domain of what constituted "science" also gradually began to expand. If the development of controlled experimentation marked the onset of the scientific process, questions about what and how to falsify extended its reach into ever-expanding definitions of the "natural world."

Alistair Crombie (1915–1996) delineated six kinds of scientific thinking: postulation, experimental, hypothetical modeling, taxonomy, probabilistic and statistical analysis, and historical derivation or the genetic method.[27] The first is the Aristotelian deductive style and is largely confined to mathematics. The experimental method is as described above and, along with modeling (e.g., the wave model of light), long dominated physics and chemistry. Taxonomy emerged in the mid-eighteenth century with the species classification system of Carl Linnaeus (1707–1778), and probability and statistics have become prominent in systems analysis, in which scientists investigate a network of species, humans, and human ethnotypes, for example. It has also made inroads into the oldest natural sciences. The final method is also used to analyze the behavior of systems, but it describes change in the system's behavior and structure rather than its composition at a moment in time. It thus imposes a dynamic framework, often including a principle of self-regulation, on the phenomenon under study. One can think about the Darwinian model of species change and its subsequent modifications. Linguists often describe languages and anthropologists and sociologists human societies themselves in this diachronic way, which is indicative of how the domain of science has expanded relentlessly far beyond what was imagined at the dawn of the Royal Society.

Whenever the way in which scientific investigation is carried out expands, there are criticisms that what is being done is not science. But in any self-regulating system, it is *competition*—in this case, among definitions of science—that determines what contributes to the goal (knowledge about the world here) and that thus improves the performance of the system. In science, old styles do not replace new ones; they supplement and complement them, in Hegelian style. And at any moment, the methods brought to the problem can be criticized as insufficient. Think, for example, of the frequent criticism of economics or of cultural as opposed to physical anthropology as not being "properly scientific." But to the extent that the criticism sticks, people interested in investigating such problems will develop better methods, and so through nothing more than the workings of the self-regulatory process, their investigations both become more widely seen as scientific and as expanding the realm of questions that science can explore. This conversation continues even now, as physicists struggle with how to accommodate thinking such as string theory, which grew out of

traditionally tested physics, appears so far to be deductively unimpeach-
able, and has widespread support but is not itself currently testable. Some
new thinkers argue that this support can be used, in combination with
Bayesian probability theory, to establish a proposition's scientific accept-
ability. Clearly this conversation about the edges of "science" is ongoing.[28]

In recent years, philosophy has struggled with the question of whether
an objective reality exists. The value and coherence of the scientific process, in other words, has itself come under criticism. In some ways, this
is not new; ancient philosophers in a variety of societies debated whether
that which exists has an unchanging nature that human cognition, beginning with observations attained through the senses, can at least partially
describe. Around the world there are philosophical traditions of supposing
that only the mind exists for certain, and everything else must be subject to
doubt. In their current iteration, such denials that there is comprehensible
reality are often labeled "postmodern," with "modern" in part pointing
to the project, beginning with the Scientific Revolution, to come up with
"laws" about the natural world and human thought and society. In principle, "postmodern" can mean such modernist thinking is like any other,
subject to being refined and even displaced. But actually this view is hostile
to scientific progress. It claims that the scientific method in all its variety is
just another framework for mentally organizing the world and should not
be privileged, because the method is subject to being displaced by other
methods. This is not because these other methods have more "explana-
tory power" in the sense of better conforming to the objective reality; recall here that scientists, after self-regulated competition, have continually
expanded the definition of what "science" is. Rather, it is only better by
being more persuasive to more people—rhetorically more attractive, in
other words. Thus, there is now an extensive critical vocabulary full of
terms such as *perspective*, *socially constructed*, and *contingent*, and of the
dismissal of various empirical claims, particularly in the social sciences and
humanities, as reflecting one "-centrism" or another. The dialectic method
of learning, which implicitly in its ancient Greek uses and explicitly in its
Hegelian formulations was seen as a tactic for getting closer to the Truth,
has ironically now contributed to this belief in the impossibility of that
journey. One claim about reality is always subject to a contending interpretation, and it is impossible to use evidence to arbitrate between them.

Such thinking is all too easily lampooned. There are contests for bad academic writing, often awarded to these kinds of scholars. The physicist Alan Sokal penned an absurd, jargon-filled essay purporting to show that the "discourse" (different, note, from "dialogue" or "discussion," the latter two indicating conversation based on the premise of making progress) of "mainstream Western science" was "contaminated" by "overwhelmingly capitalist, patriarchal and militaristic" language. In fact, the article was intended to test whether the editors of the journal would accept such unbridled nonsense.[29] In recounting this affair, it is not always noted that the entire issue of the journal was devoted to the theme of "Science Wars" and contained over a dozen other nonsatirical articles on the same theme, although without Sokal's deceptive intent. The introduction in particular, by Andrew Ross, placed the word *objectivity* in quotation marks when discussing "scientific 'objectivity.'" Ross did not entirely deny the achievements of science, but he began by arguing that the technological applications of modern science may not be appropriate in a non-"Western" environment (indisputable) and often create relations of dependency on the West for residents of developing countries (debatable), but finally noted (very disputably):

Once it is acknowledged that the West does not have a monopoly on all the good scientific ideas in the world, or that reason, divorced from value, is not everywhere and always a productive human principle, then we should expect to see some self-modification of the universalist claims maintained on behalf of empirical rationality. Only then can we begin to talk about different of ways of doing science, ways that downgrade methodology, experiment, and manufacturing in favor of local environments, cultural values, and principles of social justice. This is the way that leads from relativism to diversity.[30]

"This is" science with a radically reconceived scientific method, in other words.

While such narrations about the importance of competing narrations have potential value like any other (the theme of the next chapter), and perhaps for good reason have proven quite influential in the humanities and to a lesser extent in the social sciences, the natural sciences have proven largely immune to their charm. Instead, groups of people who call themselves scientists (or who approve of the scientific enterprise) define in a way nearly universally accepted in that community (although also subject to change) what is and is not science, and then they do it.

Science as a system is not merely the accumulation of knowledge about the world, a process that extends at least back to the mastery of fire. It is instead a thoroughly self-regulating system, created one step at a time by scientists themselves. Throughout the expansion of science and the scientific method, the objective nature of reality, even if sometimes expressible only probabilistically, has always been maintained. That good science depends on constant criticism, and that this constant criticism when generated from people who accept the scientific method is valuable, is also a key part of the immense progress that science has made in terms of both the intrinsic value of the knowledge itself and its practical value for the human condition. It is self-regulation that ensures that scientific knowledge is continually expanding and that false scientific claims, including fraudulent ones, from menotoxins to Piltdown Man, are purged.[31] In the other two potentially self-regulating processes described in Chapters 4 and 5, the virtues of the self-regulating process will be just as true, even if more disputed.

CHAPTER 4

The Less Unsaid the Better
Self-Regulating Free Speech

Without Freedom of Thought, there can be no such Thing as Wisdom.

THOMAS GORDON (C. 1691–1750)[1]

Ask a citizen of a modern democracy what his most important "right" is, and he is quite likely to offer some variation on "the right to say what I want." Whether it is the most important right (in comparison to, for example the right to try to earn a living, the right to vote, the "right" to health care, or the right to live) is for political philosophers to debate. But the right to write and say what you want, and for that matter to read and listen to what you want, is indeed protected in all of these societies.

There are at least two reasons this right came to be acknowledged. One is an argument from morality: it is not generally ethically justifiable for the state to punish people for what they say or publish (let alone think). The other is an instrumental justification. There is truth out there, not just about the state of the physical world—the province of scientists—but philosophically and morally. The purpose of protecting freedom of communication is to ensure that the competition among competing claims about the nature of such truth is as vigorous as possible. This chapter traces the development of this idea in the context of that of freedom of communication more generally.

PRELIMINARIES

Two facts about the ancient world must be considered in any discussion of this development. The first is that we know little about whatever attitudes existed in preliterate societies. There were smaller-scale societies, often nomadic or pastoral, where leadership took a consultative form. In these societies, people, especially if perceived as wise, were encouraged to advise frankly on decisions about which animals to raise and to buy and sell, whether to move, whether to go to war with neighboring bands or

chiefdoms, and so on. The second is that in societies where writing systems were developed, the fraction of the literate was generally tiny. Monotheistic Judaism, with its need for believers to understand both religious
texts and claims of the burgeoning number of prophets, may have created
a simulacrum of mass literacy. And it has been estimated that between a
third and half of male citizens in Athens during the classical period may
have been literate.[2] However, given the prevalence of slavery and the low
social status of women there, even there the extent of literacy would be
miserable from the modern perspective.

Although the fraction of the population in ancient civilizations that
could employ advanced written communication was very small, intellectual debate was often vigorous. Unlike the modern sense of debate,
it typically played out over decades, if not centuries. Instead of dueling
op-eds appearing within days or even hours of one another, a philosopher or historian might feel obligated to respond to the claims of another
writer long dead but whose ideas nonetheless influenced a large fraction
of current intellectuals. Because of the generally apolitical nature of what
was being discussed, even when ideas had political consequences, there
was no particular risk to the rulers of ancient societies from scholarly,
esoteric squabbles over the nature of reality, what did and did not qual-
ify as ethical conduct, and so on. And so there was vigorous contention
among ideas in almost all literate civilizations: South Asia, China, the
Islamic world, ancient Greece and Rome. It is true that there were occasional burnings, of books and men, by those with political power—
by the Italian monk Girolamo Savonarola (1452–1498) of the former,
by the Chinese emperor Qin Shihuang (259 B.C.–210 B.C.) of both. But
that these cases are so well known is a sign of how infrequent such direct censorship was.

Polemical oratory in particular seems to have been a respected skill in
the classical West. The funeral oration of Pericles (c. 495 B.C.–429 B.C.)
as recounted in Thucydides is remembered in part for its rhetorical excellence, albeit deployed for chauvinistic purposes during a time of war. The
trial oratory of Cicero (106 B.C.–43 B.C.) was renowned even during his
lifetime. Like other legal representatives, he was expected to make out-
landish accusations as part of his trial repertoire. As a writer, he could be
similarly pointed. It is true that after Augustus (63 B.C.–14 A.D.) became

the self-designated First Citizen, he oversaw the burning of numerous prophetic scrolls (not ideological arguments, note) that might have threatened his rule. It is also true that in the empire's remaining life, if Pliny the Younger (61–c. 113) and Tacitus are to be believed, the old Roman tradition of vigorous debate fell victim to some extent to fearful self-censorship.

After Rome fell, such debate, carried out over centuries instead of hours, was far from unknown in the West. The establishment of the first universities beginning in the eleventh century carved out a zone in which such exchanges of ideas could be held generally free of restraint by bishop or king. At this point, all of Europe had been Christianized, and western Europe in particular was in theological matters, and in some lay matters as well, under the domination of the Catholic Church, which appears to have tolerated well enough these internal debates as long as they did not move out of the universities.

The invention of the printing press changed everything. This machine made communicating content of any kind in ways that could escape the scrutiny of secular and religious authorities alike cheaper, something that is always bad news for rulers, even today. Writings of all sorts became far easier to create and distribute. Literacy then understandably rose, which further raised the demand for such writings. Taken as a whole, printing was a major milestone of human progress, not least scientific progress. But from the point of view of rulers of kingdoms who had both ideological reasons (including the belief that they had the divine right to rule) and mercenary reasons to want to stay on the throne, the news brought by the printing press was not good.

INITIAL ATTEMPTS AT CONTROL

In a relatively short period of time, the question of how much expression to tolerate thus went from being essentially a nonissue to a critical issue for the thrones of Europe. The power now came not just from external invasion, usually, as in much of the world, in search of territory sought for God or lucre, or from perceived intolerable internal injustice, a font of resistance that was common elsewhere even before the widespread use of writing. Instead, it came from what people were reading.

Initially, what was printed for them to read was mostly the Bible. (Other dissident movements had earlier spread hand-copied Bibles, but of

course the infectious potential of the ideas they carried was much lower.)
Access to Scripture that more and more individuals could read themselves
meant a diversity of views on what proper Christianity was, which would
generate the Wars of Religion, which finally ended only in 1648 with the
Peace of Westphalia. Meanwhile, the new technology and the ideas it could
make available spread all over Europe and beyond—to Russia by 1563,
the European colonial enclaves of Goa and Macao by 1557 and 1585,
respectively, and Nagasaki by 1590. Printing was here to stay.

The Church then sought in several ways to control the spread of heresy and news of scandal. The Inquisition went after printers, Rome in
1559 drew up the famous banned book list known as the Index Librorum
Prohibitorum (which lasted until 1966),[3] and booksellers were surveilled
by the Church. And state got in on the action too, initially through the
creation of copyright, literally a right to copy. Royal authorities, always
for a fee, granted an exclusive privilege to print a particular text. (This
was the same game played with the first chartered corporations, state-li-
censed trading monopolies that began to be established in the seventeenth
century.)[4] Even in the British colonies in North America, printers were
licensed by colonial governments and, famously, publications of all kinds
were taxed, though briefly, by the Stamp Act of 1765. The first known ap-
pearances of the copyright practice are in prepress fifteenth-century Italy
and then in early sixteenth-century France. Monarchs could decide on a
whim whether to renew an existing copyright or even to impose a new
one on an existing book. To the extent that this worked, it meant that
they had the power of prior restraint. Such censorship that had existed
in the Roman Empire was scattershot, depending on the temperament of
particular emperors and other officials, in the face of a very small number of people who could read, let alone write well, and often took the
form of self-censorship, Here, however, there was an entire apparatus,
leaky though it was, to control what was printed. It was far from perfect;
as always happens when the state tries to prohibit the buying and selling
of things that people want to sell and buy, black markets sprang up for
texts that were banned in this way.

A social system that has always self-regulated, language, was also affected by the new invention. Martin Luther's writing in German served to
significantly align the spoken German of the northern and southern states,

and particular national literatures began to appear because of the wider written use of the vernacular languages in place of Latin.[5] The technology plus the popularity of Luther's translation of the Bible and other works also helped create a huge new variety of information packaging: not just books, but flyers, pamphlets, and, by the seventeenth century, newspapers and journals. Printing was also a condition for the appearance of at least two new literary forms: the essay and, depending on how one defines it, the novel.

The Wars of Religion left a legacy of dread of religious conflict. The West-phalian Peace of 1648 did not generate a consensus among the thrones of Europe that proselytizing and conversion ought to be free. Instead, mon-archs were free to choose the confession within their realm and to impose it on all their subjects (Jews excepted). At roughly the same time these wars were being fought, the Church also was trying to control dissident interpretations of the nature of the universe. From astronomy, the basics of the Copernican heliocentric model advocated by Galileo were not so controversial when used as a navigational tool or even as a source for the calendar, especially given the telescopic evidence Galileo offered in his writ-ings. But his abrasive personality, along with the return to political strength in Rome of the order-and-orthodoxy-obsessed Jesuit order, all contributed to the condemnation in 1633 of his *Dialogue Concerning the Two Chief World Systems*. (Galileo was allowed to live out the rest of his days under house arrest). Natural philosophers who were investigating mathematics and the nature of matter also came under Jesuit scrutiny in the seventeenth century. But this was occurring at a time when individual scientific specu-lation was already growing unstoppably across western Europe, and by the latter part of the century, the struggle to communicate freely was over in the scientific realm.

Restraints on the political communication also enabled by Gutenberg nonetheless continued to be imposed. In England, the court initially estab-lished by Parliament in the Star Chamber Act in 1487 was set up to be distinct from the ordinary courts. It was used in part to enable criminal prosecution of the upper classes, but also to break the political power of the nobility. By the time of Henry VIII (1491–1547, ruled 1509–1547), it was routinely used against political and religious opponents of the monarch. Based on several licensing requirements enacted by the throne over the second half of the sixteenth century, the court was free to punish the publishers of unlicensed books, and in 1632, it banned all newsbooks, short, single-topic publications on contemporary major news stories.

With the freedom to implement the scientific method increasingly in hand, however, and the open scientific inquiry that led to unprecedented scientific progress, theological and confessional explorations also began to be seen as something best left free. This was especially so given the prior century-plus of carnage that had arisen when it had been assumed that these differences could be settled by force. (Indeed, the argument for freedom of scientific inquiry is just a special case of the argument for free communication.)

JUSTIFYING THE RIGHT OF FREE COMMUNICATION

In England, the Star Chamber had assumed the power to punish religious dissidents and ban newsbooks. But in 1640, Parliament, through the Habeas Corpus Act, dissolved the court. Predictably, the amount of publishing soared, including on topics that had previously made the authorities uncomfortable. In 1643, Parliament in response asserted its own censorship rights, independent of King Charles I (1600–1649, ruled 1625–1649), with a passage of the first Licensing Order. The order required that all publications be licensed in advance; that the material submitted to obtain the license include the publication and the name of its author and a single printer; and authorized the confinement on conviction of those who wrote, printed, and published books that would have fallen afoul of the old Star Chamber regulations.

John Milton (1608–1674), known at this point primarily for his signed essays against the hierarchy of the Church of England (*Paradise Lost* would not appear until 1667), in 1644 published the essay *Areopagitica*, a sophisticated defense of the right to publish and addressed specifically against the 1643 act. In it he invoked the value of almost complete freedom of speech (aside from disrespect for the gods, and even that sometimes allowed) in ancient Greece and Rome. Then he presented several arguments against licensing, including the low character of those who sought licensing orders, the likely use of licensing authority by the Catholic Church

he despised, and what would surely be its ineffectiveness. But he also asserted the ignoble nature of prior restraint itself, for example, arguing
that "hee who destroyes a good Booke, kills reason it self; kills the Image
of God, as it were in the eye." Furthermore, a good man cannot possibly
be damaged by reading prurient or heretical material. Those who wish to
be virtuous (in the Christian sense) also could not be expected to do so
without having the opportunity to reject temptation—"for reason is but
choosing." Those who issued the licenses could not be expected to be as
wise as the man who "writes to the world" and thus "summons up all his
reason and deliberation to assist him; he searches, meditates, is industrious, and likely consults and conferres with his judicious friends; after all
which done he takes himself to be inform'd in what he writes, as well as
any that writ before him." Speakers who must answer to a possibly critical audience, in true self-regulating style, would always get closer to truth
then their censors will.[6]

Most of Milton's attention was focused on religious publications, and
there is inspiration in his view of the faithful and those who minister to them
as being more than able to maintain the faith after being exposed to "three
sheets of paper without a licencer." And while he viewed truth as Platonic
rather than something that continuously evolves, he nonetheless argued that
the contention of ideas is necessary to allow us to get nearer to it: "Truth
is compared in Scripture to a streaming fountain; If her waters flow not in
a perpetuall progression, they sick'n into a muddy pool of conformity and
tradition."[7] In the end, he maintained, the licensing of publications and the
embargo of information it would create would be more costly to the people
of England than a physical blockade of all of England's ports. As a whole,
Areopagitica is now seen as a landmark moment in the struggle for free
expression, and it was an act of courage besides. Milton did not apply for a
license yet put his name to the document. While the idea of self-regulation,
that free competition among ideas will lead to the triumph of the best ones,
was not Milton's primary argument, he did raise it.

The Parliament of an England torn apart by civil war and, after the
Restoration, deep religious conflict was unlikely to immediately give up
the power to restrict what people could read. The Bill of Rights of 1689,
passed one year after the Glorious Revolution, made no mention of the
right to expression of opinion. (There was, however, a telling exception:

giving exemption from prosecution to members of Parliament for anything they said during parliamentary proceedings. As is so often the case with political regulation, political regulators exempted themselves from the regulations they enacted.) But as things unfolded during the latter half of the seventeenth century, broader arguments for freedom of expression took stage.

Baruch Spinoza (1632–1677) of Amsterdam in his *Theological-Political Treatise* (1677, published posthumously) opposed attempts by the sovereign to compel certain kinds of thinking, because of the futility of such attempts, and to forbid theological and philosophical speculation. (He did allow that the sovereign should be free to compel the observance of particular religious rites.)

It is true that Spinoza wrote the *Treatise* anonymously, but his name did not remain secret for long, and in any event, the commercially vibrant Netherlands was already developing a reputation as a haven for dissident tracts on politics, theology, and science. (Note the pattern of commerce and freer communication tending to go together.) The 1579 Treaty of Utrecht, one of several historical agreements with that name, united seven northern Dutch provinces during the long war for independence from Spain and included a clause on freedom of conscience (albeit imperfectly enforced, especially in communities with strong Calvinist majorities). As a result of these documents and attitudes, the seven provinces became a haven for persecuted religious minorities and, soon, for people who had provocative things they wished to publish.

Descartes wrote most of his major works, including *Discourse on Method*, during the over twenty years that he spent there. England's John Locke (1632–1704) composed his *Letter Concerning Toleration* (1689) and worked on other essays while in exile there (having fled after suspicion of involvement in a plot to assassinate Charles II and his brother, the future James II (1633–1701, ruled 1685–1688). He returned to England in 1689. In a note circulated to Whig members of Parliament in late 1694 to early 1695 while it was contemplating renewing the newer 1662 Licensing Act, Locke simply said that men should have the liberty to print whatever they would speak and that any crimes that occurred after such publications had appeared should be punished in the names of those crimes. In the *Letter*, he similarly advocated a fundamental liberty of religion.

But Locke's rationale did not much involve any intrinsic social value of a freedom to communicate; he simply expressed it as one of several natural rights, although undoubtedly he was influenced by decades of confessional turmoil in England.

THE GROWTH OF THE SELF-REGULATION ARGUMENT
AND PROTECTIONS FOR FREE EXPRESSION

In Britain (as we may call it after the Union of England with Scotland in 1707), the government, despite refusing to renew its power to license books, did not entirely abandon the power of prior restraint. In 1712 Parliament enacted the Stamp Act, which imposed taxes on each page published in newspapers and other forms of public communication, and it required each periodical to have the owner's name on it. The Licensing Act of 1737 empowered the Lord Chamberlain to deny the opportunity to stage any play; the act persisted in that form until modification in 1843 and was not entirely repealed until the Theatres Act of 1968. The common-law doctrine of seditious libel, in which some criticism of the government (e.g., accusing it of criminal behavior) could be prosecuted as a crime, was commonly used by the authorities during the seventeenth, eighteenth, and early nineteenth centuries. One victim was the writer and activist Daniel Defoe (1616–1731), imprisoned from 1702 to 1704, nominally for having his name on a pamphlet mocking religious leaders. The doctrine also led the House of Commons to order that two books by the deist Matthew Tindal (1657--1733) be burned, a fate also suffered by Defoe's *The Shortest Way with the Dissenters* in 1703. Fearing both religious conflict and heresy, the authorities clearly still held to the belief that they had to limit communication.

So there was still work to be done, ironically because of the growing communication network enabled by rising literacy. Laws had to be passed not because the British sovereign was more censorious than before, but because there was more to potentially censor and more robust networks were being built.

While the Netherlands and Britain were making progress, in the British case with no small amount of struggle, toward freedom of communication, the situation was worse in France and the German states. France, like Germany and the merchant towns of the Dutch coast, had seen an explosion of publications after the invention of movable type. And in 1631, Théophraste Renaudot (1586–1653) founded one of France's first periodic updates on current affairs (i.e., newspapers), the *Gazette de France*. Alas, he did it under the licensing regime prevailing at the time, and the publication gave royal officials, including Louis XIII (1601–1643, ruled 1610–1643) and Cardinal Richelieu (1585–1642), space to report on the doings at court, French military victories, and English military defeats or atrocities, all the while avoiding any reporting on French military crimes. To be fair, Renaudot was able to parlay this propagandistic function into opportunities to bring various proposals for social reform to royal officials. But overall, the control of the press in large states such as France and England was much more effective than in the small states of the North Coast and Germany. Bernstein resolved this paradox by arguing that at a time of very high transportation costs for information (physical texts had to be shipped by land or sea) and when anything subversive would have to come from outside, stopping smuggling of ideas was difficult in a small duchy or city-state. There was a constant flow of commercial traffic into and out of their jurisdiction, but areas with few ports of entry made controlling what came into and went out of the country easier.[8]

Numerous French Enlightenment-era works had to be smuggled out of the country to be published. It is estimated that in the last few decades before the Revolution, perhaps half of all books written in the French language were being published outside France, especially in Holland (notably Amsterdam) and Switzerland, including most of what was written by the *philosophes*.[9] The *philosophes* themselves were divided on the question of freedom of publication, with no less (by modern reputation) a free-speech absolutist than Voltaire coming down on the side of free access to controversial works for the educated, but not for the uneducated masses. Only subsequent writers such as the Marquis de Condorcet (1743–1794) and Diderot took an absolutist position.[10]

All three of these writers looked at freedom of expression through a self-regulation lens, as a tool to pursue the goal of improved knowledge, but the members of the so-called moderate Enlightenment seem to have felt that outside a narrow circle of the elite, self-regulating communication did more harm than good. Jean-Jacques Rousseau (1712–1778) had little to say about freedom of expression, arguing instead that the source of the general will governing the sovereign's conduct was not that generated by reasoned public discussion but by the "voice of duty."[11] The so-called enlightened despot Frederick the Great in 1770 took pen rather than sword in hand, one supposes to his credit, to argue for a limit on the freedom to access the expression of others. It drew a riposte from Diderot in the form of a letter not discovered by scholars until 1937.[12]

The first explicit legislation protecting freedom of written expression, and guaranteeing public access to state records, was created in Sweden in 1766. It lasted until 1772. More substantially for our purposes, in 1770, Johann Friedrich Struensee (1737–1772), the personal physician of the king of Denmark, became chief royal adviser there. A somewhat wild-eyed child of the Enlightenment, he took power as a reformist in the model of Anne Robert Jacques Turgot (1727–1781), whom we will get to know a little better in the next chapter. Struensee dismissed the king's senior advisers and issued a series of radical decrees abolishing traditional feudal labor obligations and state subsidies for wasteful producers, promoting land reform, banning the slave trade in overseas Danish possessions, and establishing complete freedom of the press. The rescript on the last decree, issued on September 4, 1770, read:

We are fully convinced that it is as harmful to the impartial search for truth as it is to the discovery of obsolete errors and prejudices, if upright patriots, zealous for the common good and what is genuinely best for their fellow citizens, because they are frightened by reputation, orders, or preconceived opinions, are hindered from being free to write according to their insight, conscience, and conviction, attacking abuses and uncovering prejudices. And thus in this regard, after ripe consideration, we have decided to permit in our kingdoms and lands in general an unlimited freedom of the press of such a form, that from now on no one shall be required and obliged to submit books and writings that he wants to bring to the press to the previously required censorship and approval, and thus to submit them to the control of those who have undertaken the business until now of inspecting them.[13]

Struensee's proclamation was essentially a self-regulating argument for freedom of communication. While the immediate consequence was ironically a surge in publications hostilely assessing Struensee and his reforms, so that he canceled the decree two years later and lost his job soon after that, the die was cast. The arguments for the truth value of free communication, already well understood in Holland and Britain, began to spread.

The greater ease of smuggling forbidden knowledge in through borders now merged with the generally increasing respect for the idea of enlightenment as a cornerstone of human progress. Combined, the application of the scientific method to human society and a general lack of concern about the consequences of either excessive or excessively threatening speech meant that in Britain, France, and Prussia, while there may still have been nominal prior-restraint obstacles, debate on public affairs, like debate on science, was now largely free. The writer Claude-Adriene Helvetius's (1715–1771) work *De l'esprit* (1758) was a wide-ranging speculation on the human mind and society more broadly, but in the course of it, he specifically used the self-correcting scientific system as a metaphor for how to govern well. In addition he used, as was common then among Enlightenment political theorists, the governance of the Ottoman Empire as the very example of ignorance and corruption. Precisely because the words that rulers there heard were not subject to the refinement of competition, he argued that Ottoman-like censorship bred ignorance:

But even supposing them animated with the desire of doing good, their ignorance prevents their being able to accomplish it; and the attention of the viziers being necessarily engrossed by the intrigues of the seraglio, they have not leisure for rejection.

Besides, to obtain knowledge, they must expose themselves to the fatigue of study and meditation; and what motive can engage them to take this trouble? They are not stimulated to it even by the fear of censure.

If we may be allowed to compare small things with great, let us take a survey of the republic of letters. If the critics were banished from thence, is it not obvious, that authors being freed from the salutary fear of censure, which now compels them to take pains in improving their talents, they would then present the public with only rude and imperfect pieces?[14]

Having to endure the slings and arrows of criticism, in other words, makes for better thought, and therefrom better governance.

Across the Atlantic, in the colony of Virginia in 1776, the Virginia Convention, the successor to the dissolved House of Burgesses, included the freedom of the press in its Virginia Declaration of Rights. This was probably the most proximate source of the First Amendment to the 1787 U.S. Constitution, which enshrined the freedom of speech, religion, and the press and was the first permanent (at least so far) national guarantee of these rights. In 1795 the new Dutch Republic, ratifying what was now standard practice, listed the freedom to reveal one's thoughts to the press or by any other means as one of its guaranteed rights. By the arrival in the French summer of 1789 of the convening of the Estates General and the decision by the Third Estate (the representative of the common people) to declare itself a constitution-making assembly, the time seemed to be propitious there for a firm commitment, on both human rights and human progress grounds, to freedom of communication.

But there was a temporary setback. In France the Declaration of the Rights of Man, enacted by the Assembly on August 26, 1789, asserted in article 4 that "liberty consists in the freedom to do everything which injures no one else." But it went on in article 11 to assert: "The free communication of ideas and opinions is one of the most precious of the rights of man. Every citizen may, accordingly, speak, write, and print with freedom, but shall be responsible for such abuses of this freedom as shall be defined by law." As public anger, often manipulated by Revolutionary politicians, grew faster than the benefits of the liberal 1789 reforms could hope to do, the Revolution collapsed into terror over the next several years. Revolutionary authorities, seeing "abuses" everywhere, both limited antigovernment speech and aggressively prosecuted, in a process often ending at the guillotine, perceived threats to their authority. Governments across Europe became not just fearful of revolution breaking out in their own countries, but paranoid that the secret societies that they blamed for the violent turmoil in France were also active underground in their societies.

Surveillance and attempted infiltration of these organizations, real or imaginary, grew rapidly, as did attempts to control what was published.[15] Having seized power in 1762, the Russian empress Catherine II (1729–1796, ruled 1762–1796) early on revealed herself to be an admirer of free expression, liberalizing private printing in 1783 and authorizing the publication of several major Enlightenment texts. But worried about the events in France and about works published in Russian that she viewed as dangerous, she revoked the right to own printing presses and established committees of prior restraint throughout Russia. The chaos and bloodshed of the Napoleonic Wars only exacerbated the tendency to see secret plots throughout Europe, particularly in the Austro-Hungarian empire under the stewardship of its long-serving foreign minister, Prince Metternich (1773–1859), who seemed to see Enlightenment-driven plots everywhere, with censorship justifications sometimes reaching comical proportions. For example, a proposal to rehabilitate prisoners after their release was turned down for publication by the censorship authorities because "the aforementioned suggestion could be used to blame the government for the fact that no such institutions exist."[16]

On top of this, throughout the two decades after Napoleon's final defeat in 1815, the argument that the enlightened monarch had to cultivate morality by restricting speech was common. The licensing policy of the Habsburg emperors was to aggressively limit publication and the theater, all in the name of encouraging the common people to avoid infection by the revolutionary germ. The Prussian authorities too now resisted for a time any official commitment to freedom of communication outside the scientific realm, where the importance of such freedom was undeniable.

Yet in Britain, where the tradition of freedom of communication was most robust, there was some restraint on the enthusiasm, born of paranoia, to politically regulate the ideas people could access and express. As we have seen, some ability to regulate expression in the courts and in Parliament already existed, and as the Revolution in France turned radical, the British authorities tried to expand these powers. Under William Pitt the Younger (1759–1806, prime minister 1783–1801 and 1804–1806), the government in 1792 banned "wicked and seditious writings," and Thomas Paine (1737–1809), a serial troublemaker in Britain, the American colonies, and France, was brought up on charges for *The Rights of Man* (1791) and duly convicted. Sales of the text nonetheless rose. The clergymen and activist Robert Hall (1764-1831) in 1793 made a self-regulation argument for freedom of communication, saying that "where the right of unlimited enquiry is exerted, the faculties will be upon the advance." As proof, he favorably compared recent British giants of social and political philosophy such as Locke to the ancients.[17]

In 1794, over thirty people, all of them engaged in activities of varying degrees of radicalism to reform Parliament, were arrested on suspicion of treason. Three of them were tried consecutively later that year, but, remarkably, Pitt himself was forced to testify in one of the trials, and the third defendant, John Thelwall (1764–1834), impishly recorded and published the entire proceedings. When all were acquitted, all other charges were dropped. Meanwhile, the recently established newspaper the *Times* solicited correspondence throughout the world, including from military zones. The duke of Wellington noted (disapprovingly) that the British military were "the most indefatigable writers of letters and news that existed in the world."[18] All in all, Britain came through the revolutionary, Napoleonic, and early Industrial Revolution upheavals with its free communication rights, imperfect though they were, essentially undamaged.

Restriction of open discussion of public affairs could not survive steadily building social pressures throughout the rest of Western Europe. Nations on the Continent looked with envy to Britain as the country that had escaped the great poverty trap and had amassed military power and a great empire in the course of doing so. Free communication, along with free markets, was seen as part of what nations had to do to become modern. Expression that was perceived to threaten the Church or the current regime was precisely what most needed to be expressed, precisely the self-regulation argument. In Britain itself, criticism of British imperialism was common, and rebels dangerous in thought or deed from outside the country were increasingly allowed to stir up trouble; examples include Karl Marx (1818–1883) of Germany, Giuseppe Mazzini (1805–1872) of Italy, and Jeanne Deroin (1805–1894) of France. By the time of the revolutionary year of 1848, in many countries, relatively little attempt (and essentially none at all in the United States, Britain, and the British dominions) was made to control what was expressed. In France, the comparatively insipid protections of 1789, further weakened over the years, were strengthened in 1881 by the Law on the Freedom of the Press. A somewhat similar law had been passed under the German Empire in 1874, although the right did not extend to live entertainment. While Italy never had official legal acknowledgment of freedom of speech or the press until after World War II, neither there nor anywhere else in Western Europe was there much restriction on social commentary or social science during this period. The concept of freedom of communication as a condition of modernization spread to China in the late nineteenth century, generating a vibrant intellectual and literary culture that persisted until the onset of war with Japan in 1937. Such freedom in the European colonies was in no way formally guaranteed as it was at home, but numerous anticolonial activists took advantage of press interest to further their cause at home and in the United Kingdom itself from the late nineteenth century on.

DISCUSSION, EXPERIENCE, AND RECTIFYING MISTAKES

That most Western countries had few meaningful constraints on the discussion of ideas by the mid-nineteenth century was a view held by John Stuart Mill (1806–1873), who acknowledged this in his landmark advocacy of the self-regulating society writ large, *On Liberty* (1859). This work essentially depicted human society as in a continuous state of improvement and of social experimentation as the key ingredient in that improvement. According to his own account, he wrote the book in part because the general improvement of human cognition and social organization, along with the elimination of despotism and the arrival of democratic politics, increasingly meant that the popular will was now seen, rightly or wrongly, to be the primary moral consideration in thinking about what the government *should* do. Given that this will could be mistaken, Mill's utilitarian beliefs, and the principle that no one could know much about what social progress looked like without many social experiments both successful and not, he advocated that the government should criminalize only behavior that harms others. Humans become "noble and beautiful" by cultivating as best they can what is distinct about them, which provides more perspectives on how to live.[19] Liberty, in other words, generates information. In turn, it ensures that that information can be productively used in social experiments: experiments as far-flung as the Salvation Army (founded in 1882 and still in existence), Robert Owen's experimental New Lanark community (planned yet not totalitarian, begun in 1813 and today run by a conservation trust), and the Women's Vegetarian Union (1895, no current trace).

With regard to freedom of communication in particular, Mill's logic was the same. No one *knows* what the truth is. Even when certain moral doctrines are accepted as true, if they are not allowed to be challenged, they become stagnant, and adherence to them becomes a matter of rote obedience rather than thorough reflection. In addition, Mill took a dynamic, Hegelian view of truth as something that can progress with new human insights. Extending Milton's primarily religion-specific argument, he rejected simply accepting the growing number of doctrines widely believed to be true, because only freedom to contest one could give an audience the confidence to accept its truth. He repeated Helvetius's argument that only the despot who never hears contrary views can be (unjustifiably) certain that he is right about everything. And he rejected that the container of truths has been filled, both because, given human intellectual progress, new arguments against existing ideas may be discovered and because there remain truths yet undiscovered. "All wise and noble things" were discovered by some individuals somewhere, and it is foolish to think that this work is done.[20]

Mill did view modern society as a stultifying force and seemed to possess a touch of bourgeoisphobia—the belief that the mores of the prosperous masses are a threat to the individual creativity that propels humanity forward. He also suggested that such censorship by the crowd is the norm, and only during rare eras (he listed the Renaissance, the Enlightenment, and the early nineteenth-century German-speaking areas) does humanity meaningfully progress. But he was not a modern libertarian or anarchist. He viewed the state as uniquely capable of defending the country, funding (although not necessarily providing) childhood education, and (provocatively) serving as the storehouse of information about all the social experiments that groups try, and their results. Critically for our purposes, he, like Montesquieu, invoked science as he likened the robustness of ideas tested in the crucible of free expression to the "Newtonian philosophy," in which we can have such confidence only because its claims have been repeatedly tested.[21] (In the twentieth century, even Newton's model would be altered by Einstein and others, something that scientists of course applaud.) In the concluding chapter, Mill also explicitly likened (in principles of operation, if not directly) the self-regulating properties of speech to the analogous properties of markets in making decisions about what to produce and how to produce it. These principles, at the height of liberal political economy, had by this time been demonstrated to his satisfaction by Adam Smith (1723–1790) and David Ricardo (1772–1823). The connecting thread of self-regulating systems thus appears again.

THE MODERN COMMITMENT
TO SELF-REGULATING COMMUNICATION

While Mill, writing in the 1850s, could be confident that all suitably modern nations were committed to the protection of the right of free communication, this protection obviously suffered (along with even more fundamental human rights) grievous setbacks worldwide in the first half of the twentieth century.

The United States, through its Supreme Court, made self-regulation one of the fundamental planks of its increasingly broad protections of freedom of expression in the twentieth century. In 1774, in a document addressed to their fellow (recently conquered) colonists in Quebec, it was noted that Americans had already listed freedom of the press as the fifth of five rights they valued. The founding fathers later drew on this document when drafting and considering the Constitution. The justification of this right appealed in part to its dynamic self-regulating properties:

The last right we shall mention, regards the freedom of the press. The importance of this consists, besides the advancement of truth, science, morality, and arts in general, in its diffusion of liberal sentiments on the administration of government, its ready communication of thoughts between subjects, and its consequential promotion of union among them, whereby oppressive officers are ashamed or intimidated, into more honourable and just modes of conducting affairs.[22]

The second argument in the letter is also striking from a self-regulating point of view because it suggests that given freedom of the press, any governmental excesses will generate a sufficiently effective countervailing force from the citizenry. The founders, in other words, made self-regulating communication a necessary component of Montesquieu's well-balanced republican government.

The Supreme Court did not meaningfully engage issues of the First Amendment freedoms of speech and the press until the World War I era. Under the presidency of John Adams (1735–1826, president 1797–1801), the Sedition Act became law in 1798, but it was not renewed when it expired in 1800. (The requirement that laws periodically be reauthorized requires that legislators periodically evaluate earlier legislation, with a presumption that it will not be reapproved. On self-regulation grounds, this is perhaps an underused legislative tactic.) But the general expansion of government regulation of previously self-regulating activities that occurred beginning in the late nineteenth century (discussed further in Chapter 5) led also to increased controls on speech. U.S. entry into World War I provided the opportunity for controls on what antiwar activists and socialists could say (and thus what their audiences could hear) in particular.

Initially, the Court in 1919 upheld in two opinions both the conviction (in *Debs v. United States*) of Eugene V. Debs (1855–1926) for making speeches opposing the war, and in (*Schenck v. United States*) of Charles Schenck (c. 1877–c.1864) for mailing leaflets to conscription-age men urging them to use all legal means to resist the draft. The Court in both cases relied on the since-repealed Espionage Act of 1917.[23] Debs was imprisoned and was not released until 1921, after Woodrow Wilson (1856–1924, president 1913–1921), who had refused more than once to issue a pardon, had been succeeded in the White House by Warren G. Harding (1865–1923, president 1921–1923). On December 23, 1921, Harding commuted the sentence to time already served, effective on Christmas Day, and he received Debs at the White House on December 26.

Whereas Justice Oliver Wendell Holmes Jr. (1841–1935) wrote the opinion in both these cases, in a later opinion the same year, Holmes, in a dissent joined by Justice Louis Brandeis (1856–1941) and perhaps influenced by criticism of his opinions in *Debs* and *Schenck*, established the famous "marketplace of ideas" self-regulation argument for permitting distribution of pamphlets that opposed U.S. participation in the war. (Again one self-regulation idea reinforces another.) In particular, he wrote, in an opinion that could have been written by John Stuart Mill, had he been American:

Persecution for the expression of opinions seems to me perfectly logical. If you have no doubt of your premises or your power, and want a certain result with all your heart, you naturally express your wishes in law, and sweep away all opposition. To allow opposition by speech seems to indicate that you think the speech impotent, as when a man says that he has squared the circle, or that you do not care wholeheartedly for the result, or that you doubt either your power or your premises. But when men have realized that time has upset many fighting faiths, they may come to believe even more than they believe the very foundations of their own conduct that the ultimate good desired is better reached by free trade in ideas—that the best test of truth is the power of the thought to get itself accepted in the competition of the market, and that truth is the only ground upon which their wishes safely can be carried out. That, at any rate, is the theory of our Constitution. It is an experiment, as all life is an experiment. Every year, if not every day, we have to wager our salvation upon some prophecy based upon imperfect knowledge. While that experiment is part of our system, I think that we should be eternally vigilant against attempts to check the expression of opinions that we loathe and believe to be fraught with death, unless they so imminently threaten immediate interference with the lawful and pressing purposes of the law that an immediate check is required to save the country.[24]

Justice Brandeis, in a concurring opinion in *Whitney v. California*, made an argument even more explicitly grounded in the self-regulating properties of free speech.[25] In it, he urged a very cautious interpretation of what constitutes, as Holmes's opinion in *Schenck* required, a "clear and present danger" of a crime succeeding. The opinion is worth quoting extensively:

Those who won our independence believed that the final end of the State was to make men free to develop their faculties, and that, in its government, the deliberative forces should prevail over the arbitrary. They valued liberty both as an end, and as a means. They believed liberty to be the secret of happiness, and courage to be the secret of liberty. They believed that freedom to think as you will and to speak as you think are means indispensable to the discovery and spread of political truth; that, without free speech and assembly, discussion would be futile; that, with them, discussion affords ordinarily adequate protection against the dissemination of noxious doctrine; that the greatest menace to freedom is an inert people; that public discussion is a political duty, and that this should be a fundamental principle of the American government. They recognized the risks to which all human institutions are subject. But they knew that order cannot be secured merely through fear of punishment for its infraction; that it is hazardous to discourage thought, hope and imagination; that fear breeds repression; that repression breeds hate; that hate menaces stable government; that the path of safety lies in the opportunity to discuss freely supposed grievances and proposed remedies, and that the fitting remedy for evil counsels is good ones. Believing in the power of reason as applied through public discussion, they eschewed silence coerced by law—the argument of force in its worst form. Recognizing the occasional tyrannies of governing majorities, they amended the Constitution so that free speech and assembly should be guaranteed.

Fear of serious injury cannot alone justify suppression of free speech and assembly. Men feared witches and burnt women. It is the function of speech to free men from the bondage of irrational fears. To justify suppression of free speech, there must be reasonable ground to fear that serious evil will result if free speech is practiced. There must be reasonable ground to believe that the danger apprehended is imminent. There must be reasonable ground to believe that the evil to be prevented is a serious one. Every denunciation of existing law tends in some measure to increase the probability that there will be violation of it. Condonation of a breach enhances the probability. Expressions of approval add to the probability. Propagation of the criminal state of mind by teaching syndicalism increases it. Advocacy of law-breaking heightens it still further. But even advocacy of violation, however reprehensible morally, is not a justification for denying free speech where the advocacy falls short of incitement and there is nothing to indicate that the advocacy would be immediately acted on. The wide difference between advocacy and incitement, between preparation and attempt, between assembling and conspiracy, must be borne in mind. In order to support a finding of clear and present danger, it must be shown either that immediate serious violence was to be expected or was advocated, or that the past conduct furnished reason to believe that such advocacy was then contemplated.

Those who won our independence by revolution were not cowards. They did not fear political change. They did not exalt order at the cost of liberty. To courageous, self-reliant men, with confidence in the power of free and fearless reasoning applied through the processes of popular government, no danger flowing from speech can be deemed clear and present unless the incidence of the evil apprehended is so imminent that it may befall before there is opportunity for full discussion. If there be time to expose through discussion the falsehood and fallacies, to avert the evil by the processes of education, the remedy to be applied is more speech, not enforced silence. Only an emergency can justify repression.[26]

Neither this opinion nor that of Justice Holmes in *United States v. Abrams* was binding as to the necessary conditions for controlling self-regulating speech. But these two opinions established a foundational principle in First Amendment jurisprudence: that speech cannot, absent violations of local obscenity standards or advocating violence right now, be regulated on the basis of its content. Justice Brandeis's reasoning was part of the decision in *New York Times Co. v. Sullivan* (1964), which increased the burden of proof in defamation cases for public figures.[27] Self-regulation reasoning has also been used in overturning a New York law that required that accused or convicted criminals hand over to the state any revenues from describing their crimes, to overturn a University of Virginia policy that selectively denied funds to a student organization that promoted a particular religious belief, to uphold the right to burn crosses, and to defend the right to burn the American flag in public.[28]

The United States has the broadest protection of freedom of communication in the world. But most countries observe this basic liberty in name, and many substantially observe it in practice. Some constitutions also explicitly protect, in the manner of the Charter of Fundamental Rights of the European Union, the right to receive information.[29] While the ability to better search for truth through the competitive struggle of ideas is generally not explicitly mentioned, this reason is certainly a major part of the post-Enlightenment understanding of why the freedom to communicate is necessary.

CONCLUSION

The idea that the pursuit of truth, of which scientific truth is an important part but only a part, ought to be free so that self-regulating properties can assert themselves has a long pedigree. It is not clear that the average person attaches as much importance to this justification as to the fundamental nature of the right itself. And it should be noted that even in liberal democracies, people of various political persuasions tend to interpret whatever the authorities set down as justification for restricting speech (e.g., "clear and present danger") as narrowly as possible when out of power and as broadly as possible when wielding it. This gives us cause to reflect whether on, given the instrumental function of the competition of ideas as improvement (broadly defined) for human society, political authority should ever be trusted to set limits on human expression. Under almost any political system, people must ultimately be persuaded that a moral argument is correct—hence the reliance on propaganda in totalitarian societies.

CHAPTER 5

A Better Way Forward

Self-Regulating Socioeconomics

I call great men all those who have excelled in creating what is useful or agreeable.
VOLTAIRE, 1736 letter to Nicolas-Claude Thieriot[1]

The writer James Bessen has noted that the number of typesetting jobs has declined substantially since the early 1980s. At the same time, the number of Web developers, a job that didn't even exist in the early 1990s, has soared. It seems almost certain that the two phenomena are closely related. In 1980, almost no one, let alone any significant political authority, predicted this. It is the result (and surely there are more to come) of a series of innovations small and large, Hegelian in their connectivity, in computing and telecommunications technology.

In the face of new telephone and radio technology, the federal government created a new regulatory agency, the Federal Communications Commission (FCC), to considerably expand on the Federal Radio Commission of 1927 to control how the technology could be structured. Suppose the government had established a similar regulatory apparatus to control and channel the emerging computing technology in, say, the late 1970s. What would we *not* have had? It is impossible to know, but some hints of the cost of such regulation of any emerging technology can be inferred from the long delay between the establishment of such regulatory control (through the FCC voting in 2015 to enforce net neutrality, the first major assertion of ordinary political authority over Internet access) and spectacularly dynamic technological change that happened absent such regulation in the interim. (The vote is currently being reviewed as a I write by an FCC of different composition. The instability of mandates is another problem of political regulation.) This, combined with the trivial (in hindsight) rate of change between the late 1930s and the late 1970s in telecommunication, when the major innovations were the elimination of the call-by-call manual switchboard system and the creation of the touchtone phone, suggests the cost of economic experiments not undertaken. Seen another way, how much better was radio in 1970 than in 1930? How much more useful is telecommunications equipment in 2016 than in 1980? The pace of technological change under political and self-regulation is an anecdote, but surely an instructive one.

That the economy should be left to take care of itself is the most widely known and widely disputed claim made in favor of self-regulating processes. It is thus unsurprising that the paper trail for the arguments for and against socioeconomic self-regulation is the longest. In modern parlance, "the economy" is often used to refer to the trend in gross domestic product, how easy it is to find or lose work, interest rate movements, and so on in some particular geographic area. As we will see, even this meaning assumes that commercial activity, particularly the exchange of individuals' time and talent spent on highly specific tasks for monetary reward, and the use of those rewards to purchase the results of the equally specialized production of others, can be analyzed according to these discrete geographical units. People thus like to speak of such activity there as a unified whole: the Japanese economy, the Silicon Valley economy, and so on. But the origins of the word *economy* reveal another meaning. According to the *Oxford English Dictionary*, the ancient Greek *oikonomia* combines smaller words meaning "house" and "manage," and later was also used to mean "thrift." In Hellenistic Greek, it also referred to "administration," "principles of government," "arrangement of a literary work," "stewardship," and "plan." The original word had a connotation of top-down system management. Thomas Leonard argues that the term also included management of household slaves.[2] Only in the early modern era did a different sense of political economy emerge. How was the socioeconomy regulated in the interim?

THE HISTORICAL BACKDROP OF THE DEBATE

For as long as humans have existed, there has been tension between the desire to gain by cooperating with others and by taking what others have. Throughout most of recorded history, settled agricultural societies, as opposed to pastoral societies or societies based on hunting and gathering (the latter two generally nomadic and easier to exit), were generally dominated by hereditary ruling elites. Those in the former societies who actually cultivated the sustenance of life were often relegated through equally heredity-based rules to living life in the assigned misery, the only potential reward coming after death. Rulers' control over the construction of irrigation projects strengthened their control over social order generally, a tendency reinforced by their close ties to, and to some extent control over, traders who brought goods in from outside a particular empire or its capital city. Overall, while history testifies to many examples of rebellion in ancient peasant societies, the combination of a lack of any ability to conceive of better alternatives, very slow technological improvement, strict religious reinforcement of the existing hierarchy, and military support of the ruling class's right to rule combined to produce a general acceptance at all levels in peasant societies that having to take orders was just the way things were.

This is not to say that there was no role for economically essential activities outside of planting and harvesting, especially in societies where there were numerous urban centers. Kautilya in the *Arthashastra* noted that the wise ruler—an archetype found, with different specifications, in Plato, China's Mencius (c. 389 B.C.–272 B.C.), and elsewhere—must make sure first that the people are prosperous before concerning himself with charity and human wants, "inasmuch as charity and desire depend on wealth for their realization" (1.7).[3] Trade and lending were both mentioned as the proper task of the *vaishya*, the fourth social group in the evolving Hindu social order, who initially did agricultural work and later included merchants and financial middleman. Recall the contrast between this respect given to merchants and lenders, who have at least an implicitly indispensable social function to perform, and commentary in other places, where commerce falls considerably short of learning as an admirable trade.[4]

Similar skepticism of commerce and property is found in Plato's *Republic*, where labor was necessary but done at the expense of the pursuit of wisdom; the accumulation of wealth was a fundamentally corrupting force. (In fairness, Plato did invoke the value of the division of labor, but only from the perspective of designing the ideal city and assigning the proper proportion of people to the various unchanging tasks.) This tone of disdain continued in Aristotle's *Politics*, where in book I, he contrasted the habits of tilling, hunting, and (strangely) brigandry, which are honorable activities, to wealth acquisition via exchange, which are "justly censored;

for it is unnatural, and a mode by which men gain from one another."[5]
While he noted in *The Nicomachean Ethics* that both parties agreeing to
an exchange must be made better by it, he also postulated that two goods
exchanged for each other must be deductively equal in terms of the work
needed to create the goods. Indeed, the primary benefit of money is the
ability to define prices that can adjust not to equalize quantity supplied
and demanded, but to render two goods completely different by nature
or function equal, in the same way a scale can tell us whether two objects
of different compositions or dimensions nonetheless weigh the same. The
apparent need to impose order on trade—here, order as a universal logical
rule that must mathematically characterize all of it—is another feature of
his thinking on economic matters. The idea of microexperiments continually changing the macro-order would not emerge for centuries.

From ancient Greek philosophy, we get the contrast of the actual state of
affairs in production and exchange to an ideal state that the philosopher's
guidance can point us toward, an example of the ideal social structures
that were noted in Chapter 2. We also get a contrast between lamentably
necessary commerce and the higher things that are separate from it. There
is thus an implied disappointment in the way Greek scholars in particular
contemplated the actual state of human affairs versus what could be (if
philosophers ran things, notably). In such thinking, there is no scarcity,
only imperfection.[6] Economics as a description of the competition for resources to further different human ends rather than a way to formulaically
satisfy fixed human needs is a relatively recent conception.[7]

Again the Indian subcontinent stands out. The idea that rulers can
merely improve the commercial environment, but the welfare of the people
ultimately is achieved by merchants and farmers on their own, without any
particular guidance from those rulers, was found in ancient thought there.
There was as yet no explicit advocacy of the idea that merchants must
be left alone for the system to take care of itself through self-regulating
processes. Nevertheless, at least there was in Indian philosophy the willingness to see them as part of a well-functioning social order and neither
compare that order to an ideal nor seek to actively manage it. Given that
merchants, because they could accumulate significant wealth and often
traveled, had some measure of independence from any particular ruler, this
policy of taking commerce as it was rather than specifying how we wish

it were was preferable to one of diagnosing its ethical shortfalls. To many relatively globalized Indian thinkers, they were unrepairable in any case.

In the medieval West, the perfectionist, impurity-cleansing approach to politically regulating society continued for centuries, not just because of the classical philosophical heritage but owing to the dim view that the dominant form of Christianity also took of wealth accumulation. Aquinas in the *Summa* speculated about ideal goals rather than actual principles of market operation. He was not so much investigating what the price of the thing is under different conditions of buying and selling (let alone whether what it is in any self-regulating system has any virtuous qualities) but about what it *ought* to be. He thought prices were set by sellers rather than the result of bargaining, and thus the primary question was whether the price charged was sinful, as both lending with interest and attempting to monopolize a market were argued to be. To be fair, he indicated that when a merchant arrives in a place where a shortage of what he is selling prevails and he is aware that other merchants offering the same goods will soon be arriving, it is not a mortal sin for the first merchant to charge whatever (high) price is prevailing there. In addition, consistent with his analysis of the rest of creation, he believed that buying and selling were governed by laws that could be detected through human reason. He and the subsequent Scholastic writers believed that, along with everything else, the task at hand in economics was to search for the "universal, transcendent ideas that govern everyone," that "apply equally to all people in all places."[8] But like prior writers, he focused on the act of buying and selling among particular individuals. The analysis of what we now call a market, let alone the interaction among all markets—in other words, the socioeconomy as a system—would have to wait.

FIRST STEPS TOWARD A NEW WORLD: SALAMANCA, MONTCHRÉTIEN, AND THE BIRTH OF POLITICAL ECONOMY

The late Renaissance and the early modern period brought dramatic political and economic changes. These followed a historically unprecedented flow of new ideas (and recovery of old ones from the classical era), vastly increased availability of information once mass printing replaced copying manuscripts by hand, new financial innovation and growth in England and the Dutch Provinces, and contact during European conquest of overseas territories with civilizations seemingly vastly less complex. These collectively created a growing desire to understand differences in technological and economic achievement and, from that, the idea of social progress. This strengthened the Thomistic confidence that with the application of reasoning about what one saw, the world, now in the European mind a much broader entity than it had been, could be understood.

In the early stages, this new thinking in the economic sphere, which involved not just how to be prosperous but how the state could be powerful, could hardly help but default to central control. Proto-mercantilists in 1500s England such as Thomas Starkey (1495–1538) and John Hales (1516–1572) argued for avoiding the trap of exporting raw materials and importing the manufactures of others because otherwise the value added inherent in manufacturing would be reaped elsewhere. Barthélemy de Laffemas (1545–c. 1611), comptroller general under France's Henry IV (1553–1610, ruled 1589–1610), anticipated by almost three centuries Friedrich List's (1789–1846) argument in his 1841 text, *The National System of Political Economy*, for avoiding dependence on foreigners for critical products. Antonio Serra (precise birth and death dates unknown, but who lived in the late sixteenth and early seventeenth centuries) wrote perhaps the first definitive tract on political economy, *A Short Treatise on the Wealth and Poverty of Nations* (1613), which argued for specialization in manufactures rather than agriculture, because the former was subject to economies of scale, the latter to diseconomies. And in *De Cive* (1642), Hobbes addressed the broader issue of how to secure order, not just to allow the people to secure their right to life but to tend to their affairs effectively by enabling them to enter into enforceable contracts in particular. He justified his argument for the powers of the sovereign, made almost a decade before the publication of *Leviathan* (1651), on the idea of individual will, the exercise of which is a basic right alongside the right to life. The ability of individuals to manage their own affairs subject only to the sovereign's monopoly of violence had not yet coalesced, but the ideas of each person's particular aims in life and of individual right had by now. Human nature of course had long been discussed by many people in many places. But the growing consciousness of the importance of individual agents with their different purposes is what is new here.

The individual was gradually coming to be seen as the motive force in the creation of broader social outcomes and someone whose unique self-assessed welfare had to be considered in thinking about the functioning of society as a whole. For a self-regulating system to be analyzed, it must first be seen as a system with purposeful agents. Paradoxically, to investigate the operation of the economy and society as a whole, a new kind of what we would now call microeconomics, a departure from Scholastic musings on a just price or Aristotle's concept of a good's use value, was needed. Individuals, and their motives and the resulting outcomes, had to be thought about as a question of science as much as of ethics. While it had long been understood that, for example, droughts might cause grain prices to rise, this systematic, predictive, and prescriptive socioeconomic thinking was new.

While later English-speaking writers get the most attention from English-speaking readers, in fact the initial breakthroughs were made first in Spain. It has been speculated that the rising tide of commerce in parts of Europe and contact with distant peoples through early-stage imperialism sparked curiosity about the nature of the entire commercial system.[9] In any event, the commercial portion of the divinely inspired order began to draw attention from moral theologians at the University of Salamanca.

The seed of this intellectual tree was planted by Francisco de Vitoria (1492–1546), who is most famous for, in response to a request for his views from the Holy Roman Emperor and Spanish king Charles V (1500–1558, ruled in various places 1516–1556), defending the rights of the aboriginal peoples of the New World against Spanish predations. On economic questions, he accepted the prevailing Catholic theology in its entirety, including beliefs about the existence of and concomitant obligation to charge a "just price" for particular goods. However, he interpreted this to mean any price that was the result of voluntary interaction (under implied conditions of free competition) between buyers and sellers. When bad things happened to merchants, it was because they were mistaken in what they thought they knew or unlucky. In either case, the observed market price was, given sufficient competition (important!), the fair one.[10] Remarkably, there is little previous evidence of any belief that the "just price" could be anything but one negotiated among the guilds and royal courts, then enforced by the monarch.[11] Vitoria instead depicted such a price as emerging through self-regulating interaction between market participants on both sides. The idea that it was precisely a critical function of the market price to convey information about changed conditions had yet to be developed. However, that it would adjust in response to such changes and that it was better to simply accept that price than try to fix it by royal *diktat* was the first implicit claim that the market was statically self-regulating.

Soon the most important work in advancing the idea of the self-regulating economy moved to France. The writer Antoine de Montchrétien (c. 1575–1621) in his 1615 *Treatise on Political Economy* (*Traicté de l'économie politique*), a work credited with introducing the term *political economy*, produced two innovations. First, he saw the economy as a system that tied together individuals, whose behavior had to be part of any analysis of the workings of the whole. Second, he argued that while individuals were self-centered, this vice could nonetheless be turned into a public virtue. However, he asserted, unsurprisingly for a Frenchman writing in the early seventeenth century, that it took the strong hand of a beneficent monarch to properly harmonize the constituent parts of this economy so that it would work for the interests of society as a whole. For example, agricultural workers, disinclined to work, must be incented to do so by limiting the burden of royal taxation. His primary policy recommendations were order, good governance, job training, the favoring of domestic production, and the elimination of quality standards for French goods, which had been imposed by Louis XIV's finance minister, Jean-Baptiste Colbert (1619–1683), but had raised domestic production costs.

Thus, the key task for politics now was to arrange laws so that they were in harmony with the emerging principles of political economy, so that overall social welfare could be enhanced by prompting individuals to do what ought to be done. Richard Cantillon (c. 1685–1734) wrote in the posthumously published *Essai sur la nature du commerce* (1755) that "wealth is nothing more than the sustenance, the conveniences and the comforts of life."[12] What it was not, conspicuously, was the stock of precious metal within a country's borders, something many contemporaneous mercantilist authors were contending. Instead it was something produced by a collection of sectors that could all be connected (save for landowners and princes, who, he thought, had independent sources of income) by mutual self-interest. Friedrich Hayek (1899–1992) argued that the *Essai* contained a thorough description of the movement of prices toward equilibrium, a critical component of any theory of the operation, if not necessarily the value, of a self-regulating market, this even though Cantillon's discussion was carried out at a macroeconomic level.[13] François Quesnay (1694–1774) in his Tableau économique (1758) also depicted the interdependent nature of different parts of the economy.[14] Its functioning began to be seen as analogous to that of a machine with many parts or, perhaps more telling, Newton's clockwork universe.

How to achieve harmony and order given intrinsic conflict among sectors or individuals with differing interests was identified as the key social problem. These writers and others had their preferred policy prescriptions that ought to be carried out before the economic machine could function properly, which involved prioritizing the agricultural sector, mercantilist trade laws, or other forms of state intervention.[15] And so the virtues of the self-regulating market as the best response given self-interest as motivating behavior, a logical extension of Cantillon, nevertheless remained to be laid out.

To so describe it required thinking systematically about what motivated individuals in the market, and this required thinking more deeply about them as agents. Such individualist social/political analysis was already apparent in Hobbes's derivation (in *De Cive*, as well as the better-known *Leviathan*). He saw the legitimacy of sovereign power as emanating from the need to protect the safety of individuals and their ability to make their way in the world without fear of chaotic social disintegration (even though this required obeying whatever it was that the sovereign commanded). For Hobbes, the attainment of life goals, in other words, was clearly a goal of a political system.

Locke amended Hobbes's argument in his 1690 essay, *Second Treatise of Government*, which posited that the function of the sovereign is to impartially enforce the natural law, which includes enforcement of the right to property. This right is in turn acquired by mixing one's labor with unclaimed land. The function of property rights is to enable man to improve the land "originally given as it was to the children of men in common" (5.37) through work and thrift. The earth is given to man to use, not to waste through letting land go unused. (Locke also argued that the monetization of society, by enabling trade, is a necessary condition for such investments in improvement to be rational—thus advocating the creation of money prices as a standard to help people trade.) He therefore embraced the idea of a future in which there would be, given only the proper incentives, more to go around—a future, in other words, of growth, the dynamic goal of a self-regulating socioeconomy. And growth is a function of human effort. Referring to the development of idle land, he argued in the same chapter in the *Second Treatise*:

I think it will be but a very modest computation to say, that of the products of the earth useful to the life of man nine tenths are the effects of labour: nay, if we will rightly estimate things as they come to our use, and cast up the several expences about them, what in them is purely owing to nature, and what to labour, we shall find, that in most of them ninety-nine hundredths are wholly to be put on the account of labour. (5.40)

To the extent that enforcement of property rights is similar to benevolent state neglect of the economy, this is a justification for limited government in pursuit of self-directed and self-regulated social improvement.[16]

Locke's insight is important for our purposes because it looks to human nature to deduce that humans, when left alone, will seek out unexploited land and the resources on or under it to improve their lives, and therefore to improve the state of human society generally. Liberty was not just a basic right, although that was perhaps Locke's primary point. It was also a way to give humans incentives to do what was best for the species. Here we can perhaps speculate that this way of thinking was in the air during this time. In *An Essay on Human Understanding* (1689), Locke indicated that there can be no complete comprehension of the world. Humanity can have a better understanding of some phenomena than others, but the process by which this understanding is generated is inherently limited. Human cognition, in other words, is scarce. At birth we possess no innate knowledge that will emerge as we age. Instead, the mind is an empty vessel (the famous "blank slate" metaphor) that is fueled by the perceptions of the senses. From these perceptions, we craft simple ideas, which can be shaped into more complex ones.[17] We must, however, use language to carry out this craftsmanship, and words do not map exactly onto natural phenomena. At any time, they can be recombined (as new hypotheses or "ideas") to further our ability to make sense of the world, and each repackaging can be replaced at any time when new information (e.g., experimental results or better hypothesizing) emerges. Note again the common ground shaping this view of human knowledge generally, as in Newton's contemporaneous account in the *Principia* of all scientific knowledge as subject to amendment and Hegel's subsequent imaginings about social and intellectual progress generally.

This description of scientific understanding provides an idea of promotion of a goal, better understanding of how the natural world works, which gives us a yardstick by which to measure the efficacy of any scientific system. Gradually the scientific community discovered practical mechanisms that amounted to a dynamically self-regulating system: lesser hypothesizing is naturally displaced by better hypothesizing once these institutions are in place. Locke, along with Newton, was one of the founding members of the Royal Society, and in the *Essay*, published a mere two years after the *Principia* (which Locke read while in exile in the Netherlands), he specifically praised the "incomparable Mr. Newton."[18] It is not too much to suppose that this idea of knowledge generated according to the scientific method as, under appropriate conditions, tending toward gradual improvement also influenced the way Locke viewed human flourishing more generally. In the *Second Treatise*, he made the same argument about a society's material improvement as he did about the improvement of human understanding in the *Essay*—that it takes effort, but given the appropriate environment it can happen.

"GREED IS GOOD," SAID SOMEONE
WHO WASN'T ADAM SMITH

Locke's argument did not describe the inner workings of the system that yields the improvement he sought to promote; he more or less took for granted that given the opportunity, people will improve themselves and thus society. The first significant argument that explicitly connected human motivations to the need for and the ability of both producers and consumers to manage their own affairs was actually seen at the time as a vulgar one, written by the Dutch author Bernard Mandeville (1670–1733). Not much is known about his early life, which is surprising in light of his notoriety. We do know that he was born into a prosperous Dutch family and acquired degrees in both philosophy and medicine. At the beginning of the eighteenth century, after having moved to England, he began writing in English. In light of his social criticism, some of his sexually explicit writing (by the standards of the time), and ultimately of the popularity of his most famous work amid establishment rejection, it is perhaps not surprising that he is less often included in any list of philosophical or Enlightenment luminaries. But he is a major figure in the spread of the idea that like communication, the economy, if not the entire socioeconomy, is best left to regulate itself.

This most famous work was published in 1705 as *The Grumbling Hive, or Knaves Turn'd Honest*. This poem told the story of a prosperous hive of bees whose society is run not along the lines of "Tyranny" or "wild Democracy" but by kings whose "power was circumscrib'd by Laws." The result? Avaricious insects desirous of the instruments of luxury on the one hand, yet many of whom worked energetically to supply them on the other. Physicians care about wealth and not health, lawyers care about fees and not justice, and yet, as an expanded 1723 version had it,

> The root of evil, avarice,
> That damned ill-natured baneful vice,
> Was slave to prodigality,
> That noble sin; whilst luxury
> Employed a million of the poor,
> And odious pride a million more:
> Envy itself, and vanity,
> Were ministers of industry.[19]

In the end, some of the bees hypocritically bemoan the lack of virtue amid their plenty, and the gods in response banish greed and envy. As a result, the unmotivated bees will work no more, and so the hive's prosperity collapses.

While many took Mandeville's tract as an obvious attack on Christian charity, he followed it up with several versions of a book, *The Fable of the Bees: Or, Private Vices, Publick Benefits*, all of which contained the poem and his commentary on its reception. By the time the last version appeared in 1732, it contained a wide variety of strikingly prescient reflections on the division of labor, the subjectivity of goods' valuation, and the difficulty of an outsider's appreciating the unseen advantages of the commercial networks that people have constructed on their own, without guidance by guilds, princes, or other external regulation. But in claiming that individuals driven by purely materialistic and selfish concerns would thus choose in a way that redounded to the greater benefit of society (which the antihero Gordo Gekko rendered as "greed is good" in the 1987 movie *Wall Street*), he was making an argument that Adam Smith, whose thinking on both moral questions and economics was more complex, was later caricatured as believing. Yet it was also the argument that the self-regulating socioeconomy needed—even though motivated by something other than some overall "social" interest, individual agency could nonetheless produce outcomes that furthered that interest.

TURGOT AND SMITH

Not much later and just a few years apart, two writers on opposite sides of the English Channel essentially completed the task of building the first comprehensive vision of the self-regulating economy. To Anglophone readers, by far the less well known is the Frenchman Anne-Robert-Jacques Turgot (1727-1781), the very representative of Enlightenment faith in continual progress. He was not just a disciple but an apostle of the scientific method, by now well ensconced. He wrote in his paean to comprehensive progress, *A Philosophical Review of the Successive Advances of the Human Mind* (1750), that unlike mathematics, with its deductive nature, science is a process in which initially absurd (in hindsight) speculations give way to less absurd ones thus, again anticipating Hegel, proceeding toward the understanding of truth.

While a younger man, Turgot had also fallen under the influence of a French doctrine that almost immediately came to be known as physiocracy, a neologism coined from the Greek roots meaning "nature" and "rule." Earlier physiocrats had extended the idea that buyers and sellers left alone will find the price that best harmonizes the amount desired with the amount offered for any particular good, and that the way to achieve this is to avoid mercantilist protectionism (done in the mistaken belief that this is the way to maximize a country's gold stocks and, hence, wealth). In writing in 1762 against Rousseau's earlier invocation of an inchoate "general will," Pierre Paul Lemercier de la Rivière (1720–1793) had argued that only liberty of commerce could ensure the attainment of the best attainable outcome:

Do you wish a society to reach its greatest possible degree of wealth, population and power? Entrust its interests to liberty; and let this be universal; by means of this liberty, which is the true element of industry, the desire to enjoy, stimulated by competition and enlightened by experience and example, you are guaranteed that each will always act for his greatest advantage, and consequently will contribute with all his might to the greatest possible growth of the sum of these particular interests, which together form what can be called the general interest of society, which is composed of the common interests of the head and each of its members is composed.[20]

This was the temper of the times, in France anyway. (France did not yet have Britain's long-standing devotion to the idea of natural rights.) And if Lemercier was a man of theory, Turgot was a man of action. Given the latter's view of the value of the scientific method in discovering the nature of nature, it is perhaps not surprising that his economic views, published in 1766 in *Reflections on the Formation and Distribution of Wealth*, were written while he could gather data during his work as a local tax collector. He was appointed minister of finance in 1774, and during this time, he tried to sweep away long-standing competitive restrictions imposed by medieval guilds, along with the *corvée*, the forced labor imposed by French landowners on peasants, often to build or maintain nominally public works. But despite (or perhaps because of) advocating an end to the oppressive tax burdens also inherited from previous centuries and proposing significant reforms to French governance, like Struensee he generated and lost a bureaucratic power struggle and left office within two years.

Reflections, a short work, made two arguments. The first was that rates of return on investment tend to equalize as people move investment funds from lower- to higher-return activities, thus presenting the idea of a *competitive* homeostatic equilibrium. Second, in crude form by modern standards, was the idea that free competition was the only way to maximize what consumers and producers could get together out of participating in a market (what economist today call consumer and producer surplus). Critically, Turgot later raised the self-regulating property when he noted that when a "duped consumer" (*un consommateur dupé*) is the victim of a "cheating merchant" (*un marchand fripon*), the market's immune system gets to work: "The cheated consumer will learn by experience and will cease to frequent the cheating merchant, who will fall into discredit and thus will be punished for his fraudulence; and this will never happen very often, because generally men will be enlightened upon their evident self-interest."[21] He compared this process favorably to government policing of such behavior, which he saw as preposterously unworkable.

The phrase *self-interest* is most often associated with Adam Smith, although he never used it in the 1776 work that brought him global renown, *An Inquiry into the Nature and Causes of the Wealth of Nations* (TWN). He did use it several times in his 1759 work, *The Theory of Moral Sentiments* (TMS). Smith is justifiably thought of, along with David Hume (1711–1776), as one of the two stars of the Scottish Enlightenment. But the reputation he has among some in the general public is misplaced, because of the absurdist reduction of those views, by some of his admirers and most of his detractors, to the idea that everyone's selfish individual action is sufficient to ensure prosperity for all.

In fact, Smith was first a moral philosopher, and his innovations in political economy in TWN are, if anything, less powerful than the thoughts on the human condition found in TMS, published while he was chair of moral philosophy at the University of Glasgow. Before and while holding this position, his lectures concerned rhetoric, logic, and human nature. Although he hinted at the eventual publication of TWN in the last paragraph of TMS, he had already become famous for the latter by the time the former was published in 1776.

TWN largely completed the idea of the static self-regulating economy. Many of the ideas in it that were celebrated for their revolutionary nature contemporaneously and by subsequent generations were probably not original to Smith. In addition to Turgot's anticipating the idea of different prices for the same good and different rates of return across economic activities both tending toward equality, versions of the division of labor are found in Turgot, Mandeville, Ibn Khaldun, Xenophon (c. 430 B.C.–354 B.C.), Plato, and Aristotle. The last two seem to have thought of it as the inevitable motivator of social formation rather than, as Turgot and Smith thought, the key ingredient of prosperity. As we saw, the idea that suppliers and demanders are best at finding the natural price can be traced back at least to the Salamanca school. Even the idea contained in Smith's most famous phrase, the "invisible hand," has been argued to have been anticipated over half a millennium prior by a Chinese historian, Sima Qian (c. 145 or 135–86 B.C.). It is, however, far from clear that the Chinese text on this point has the sophistication that Smith's analysis does, and in any case Sima's ideas left no trace in subsequent Chinese writing.[22]

Smith's great achievement (in addition to the remarkable moral insights found in TMS) is to depict the entire economic system as generally capable of correcting its mistakes provided only the absence of political interference, which is almost always damaging. The division of labor is not mandated by heaven but is grounded in human nature, in "the propensity to truck, barter, and exchange one thing for another" (I.2).[23] This natural propensity is in turn driven by the ability to rely on the "self-love" of a potential trading partner to give someone what he desires.[24] In TMS and TWN taken as a whole, the primary paradox of modern society is that each of us is most sympathetic with those closest to us, yet we depend for our prosperity on the induced cooperation of multitudes of people we never meet, who nonetheless work to provide us with the things we desire. The division of labor achieves this, and it develops naturally (I.2) from the human desire to trade. Moreover, this division that naturally develops as we all seek to improve our condition is thoroughly self-regulating (I.2, III.1). The desires generated by the nascent commercial society lead to the creation of money (I.3). A society will have a natural rate of wages, profits to capital investment, and land rent, from which it may depart for a short period of time but to which it will always return (I.7). Given excess supply, competition forces the price of a good or productive factor back down (I.7). When wages or profits are higher in one activity, they will usually be equalized when labor or capital flows out of the lower-return activity and into this higher-return one (I.9; this is also a Turgot argument). The only exceptions are wage differences owing to (in the case of returns to capital) a different willingness to take risks or (in the case of wages to labor) differences in skill or the unpleasantness of the work (e.g., for an innkeeper, the disutility of being "exposed to the brutality of every drunkard," I.10).[25]

Smith argued equally fervently from the opposite starting point not for free trade but against political interference, noting numerous cases in which state restriction of individual choice frustrates self-regulatory mechanisms. State-chartered corporate monopolies are charged numerous times (I.7, I.10, V.1) with charging high prices. This most famously comes in his accusation (often erroneously cited by people who criticize unfettered markets as promoting social domination by business) that "people of the same trade seldom meet together, even for merriment and diversion, but the conversation ends in a conspiracy against the public, or in some contrivance to raise prices" (I.10.82).[26] But he was equally disparaging of labor cartels, in the form of guilds and the apprenticeship laws that supported them, as damaging to customers (I.VII, I.X). Revisionist historians who cite his anticorporate arguments in particular as evidence of his allegedly anticommercial sympathies fail to note that the corporations he was talking about were artificial anomalies, given exclusive access to a market domestically or abroad in exchange for kicking back a percentage of their revenues to the crown; the British East India Company was a notorious example. He was, in other words, criticizing not business but the absence of competition.

Contrary to the long-held belief that buyers and sellers of labor are in intrinsic conflict, Smith criticized the corporate and guild apprenticeship statutes, which required would-be entrants in certain careers to be trained while working for free for a fixed period. Both, he argued, foolishly limited the competition that incents cooperation. It was not only the obviously "economic" patterns that were affected by state limits on competition. Smith was equally critical of laws limiting the ability of the poor, whom local parishes were responsible for caring for under English law, to move freely about the country—not least because it interfered with their right to try to earn a living, a right they possessed, he argued, in equal measure to other subjects (I.10). He opposed as well the prohibition of transport of grain for sale within and outside England (I.10) and laws that prevented "the free cultivation of the Vine" in France, enacted supposedly because vineyards were too common and corn and pastureland were scarce, yet unnecessary, because profits would naturally fall in wine and land would then be converted to other uses (I.XI).[27] He criticized as well the requirement that landed estates be subject to primogeniture, handed down in total to the eldest son if he existed (III.2).

While TWN covers a wide and indeed eccentric range of topics, certain themes run throughout. One is that men (Smith seldom spoke of women in either of his texts) have a natural tendency to pursue a higher profit or wage, whatever their individual purposes might be; if we let them do that, good things will usually happen. In addition, the market self-organizes; this is why we have the discovered and perfected division of labor and the opening of new markets, for example. The idea of "natural" wages and rates of profit also frequently appears and reflects the idea of static self-regulation: in the face of changed market circumstances, owners of labor and capital react to bring things back to equilibrium. But there are two qualifying remarks here. The first is that free competition is *required* to bring about these good results, while limits on competition correspondingly frustrate their achievement. The second is that "natural liberty" or "perfect liberty" (phrases Smith used about two dozen times combined in TWN) is a necessary and sufficient condition for such competition to exist.

Smith's insights were enormously influential, even in a France that had its own record (at least among intellectuals) of preferring an economy that could adjust on its own to one that was politically regulated. The specific idea that the entire socioeconomy could self-regulate featured prominently in the writings of Thomas Paine, who spent several years in France during the Revolutionary turmoil there. They even extended to William Godwin's (1756–1836) advocacy of anarchism precisely because social harmony was better achieved than under the state.[28] And while Smith did not live to see anything beyond the initial stages of the Industrial Revolution, this event was perhaps the greatest testimony in history to the power of not just Smithian static but dynamic self-regulation. Individuals driven by the desire to make money, do great things, help humanity, and become famous (proportions naturally vary from one entrepreneur to another) use the signals given to them by social feedback, including market prices. Sometimes their powers to persuade the holders of capital that their ideas have merit can remake the human condition a little or a lot.

One could look to almost any industry as an example, but railroads will do nicely. These were made possible as a completely unpredictable by-product (and how important these unexpected by-products are in human progress!) of the harnessing of steam power and the building of rails for hauling goods by horse-drawn wagon, ideas laid down many decades prior. The first invention and trial of a steam-powered locomotive is credited to John Blenkinsop (1783–1831), and the first intercity route opened in 1830.

It involved not London but the two great commercial cities of Manchester and Liverpool. Naturally, the first version of this transportation system was not ideal, and the same kind of dynamic self-regulation led to the enclosure of many of the tracks to protect them from damage, signaling to enable single tracks to carry more trains, and the creation of the caboose (or its English equivalent, the brake van) to house idle crew (and the later elimination of the caboose when these crew became too costly relative to the gains they brought). In addition, for passenger train service, ticketing and standardized time to enable scheduling were created, and train stations, a new experiment in architectural creativity, were erected. (Even now, train stations are often an architectural highlight in both big cities and small towns worldwide.) The railroads also generated the first very large, purely private companies, as opposed to the even larger, in terms of scope, chartered monopolies that Smith so objected to.

Most of this evolution of not just the locomotive machine but the whole system of rail transport was trial and error, with consumer valuation and the opportunity cost of resources needed for providing new forms of service provision the key ingredients in determining success and failure. From a long-term point of view, the main effect of the railroad was to enable the mass movement of people, raw materials, and products. These products included oil and meat, now available at much lower costs to serve new human purposes. They also included the standardized wares that displaced local handcrafted ones, to the obvious dissatisfaction of the makers of the latter, who could, at a time when belief in socioeconomic self-regulation was ascending, do nothing about it but try harder to sell good wares at good prices. The shipping of such products by rail, including the refrigeration of railcars, also facilitated static self-regulation by standardizing prices around the world.[29]

The precise extent to which the creation of the liberal revolution in purely economic thinking can be parceled out among Smith, the Salamanca school, and the French liberals of the seventeenth and eighteenth centuries is a matter for specialists to sort out. But without question, Smith was the most influential, not just in his own country but in others as well. His work over the next century was judged, often by the criterion of having facilitated the power of the British Empire, as sufficiently important to be translated not just into French, German, and Danish, but Japanese,

Chinese, and Russian as well.[30] It is, and was seen at the time as, a revolutionary work, and for our purpose of tracing the path of the idea of the self-regulating economy, that is sufficient.

To Adam Smith and in fact to most other Enlightenment writers, buying and selling, today known as "the economy," were together merely one stage where the drama of the much larger human project was staged.[31] The idea that humans could be trusted to take cues from their environment and quickly do what ought to be done spread beyond commerce. In one arena after the other, it began to be believed that people left unmolested would in combination form both a homeostatic and a progressive society, so that agents in pursuit of their own goals caused society as a whole to function with remarkable harmony.

The most direct extension of the self-regulating idea to emerge from the new writing on commerce was the *doux commerce* hypothesis. This line of reasoning is best known for tying transnational commercial ties to peace between countries, an argument with extensive empirical support.[32] But in fact collectively, the hypothesis as originally posited is a much broader claim about deepening commercial ties generating a refinement of the human spirit through evolutionary promotion of the most mutually beneficial activities. In this view, the commercially unregulated society causes us to live together peacefully far better than the world of mercantilist, statist rivalry, and it also brings moral improvement by promoting virtues such as trust that enhance trade. Intergovernmental tensions generate offsetting reactions from those with the most to lose from such conflict—static self-regulation. The view made its first well-known appearance in *Spirit of the Laws*, in which Montesquieu argued that commerce promotes wealth and wealth promotes civilization (see especially XX.2). If humanity wishes to dynamically move toward a society of greater harmony, free commerce promotes this. He granted that the merchant's life can take the refined individual's attention away from pure virtue. Nevertheless, he wrote, it is "a cure for the most destructive prejudices" (XX.1), all in addition to providing a superior, "more refined" alternative to military conquest for acquiring that which one desires (XXI.21).[33]

After Montesquieu, the commercial-peace hypothesis became something of an Enlightenment zeitgeist. Voltaire in two of his twenty-four *Letters Regarding the English Nation* (written first in English and about the English and their ways, and with several English titles) noted (letter 6) a virtuous, self-reinforcing cycle between commerce and liberty in England. He identified as part of a broader metaphor about the commercial peace the peculiarly pacifying effect of stock trading on religious quarrels (letter 10).[34]

The view reached its apex with the work of Immanuel Kant (1724–1804), who was also a believer in long-term dynamic self-regulation, in the form of moral progress. In the first supplement to his third proposal for perpetual peace (a peace that he said ought to be everyone's "cosmopolitan right," i.e., the right not to be treated as an enemy when abroad) he argued, "Perpetual peace is insured (guaranteed) by nothing less than that greater artist *nature (natura daedala rerum)*, whose mechanical process makes her purposiveness visibly manifest, permitting harmony to emerge among men through their discord, even against their wills."[35] The road is long and painful, but elements in human nature nonetheless facilitate their cooperating for mutual gain (a Smith argument too). Commerce is one route to building ties through which "by virtue of their mutual interest does nature unite peoples against violence and war."[36] More recently, Deirdre McCloskey has argued that commerce serves as a key component of self-regulation by giving people an alternative route to individual glory besides conquest and thus channeling their impulses away from violence.[37] In sum, people can do evil, as writers have long conceded, but in a vibrant commercial sector, these impulses are rechanneled in productive directions. Commerce thus builds broader human cooperation.

PUTTING THE SOCIO IN SOCIOECONOMY: OF ART AND ETHICS

The other great human endeavors of arts and ethics are also subject to dynamic self-regulation. What is more, extending the analysis to these areas allows us to more clearly see how progress in some areas of such endeavor often generates further progress in others. The logic of self-regulation extends far beyond buying and selling of goods, as important as that has been for human progress— hence, the importance of the term *socioeconomy*.

Art

Images, sounds, and words are different tools for expressing the same thing: ideas. Sometimes the ideas partly involve less purely intellectual phenomena such as beauty—a well-crafted poem, a provocative piece of music, the *Mona Lisa*. Intellectual concepts and beauty can mix in equal measure; think of a compellingly written novel that also has valuable things to say about the human predicament. As we have already seen in the cases of science and expression, ideas can be born, struggle against one another, recombine, and vanish.

But art, whether it involves words or not, is not like science. Science has a goal of accurately describing the universe, and while many artists also believe that they are pursuing the Truth, the self-regulatory process is different. Scientific ideas persist only as long as they are not falsified. If they are, new hypotheses that better fit the new results are developed. Discarded ideas from the past are not included in the training of young scientists and are mainly of interest to historians of science. But as new techniques and media are developed in art, it may be that old techniques and media are less often practiced; nevertheless, older art itself does not lose all value to the present generation, as the unending stream of visitors to the cave paintings in Lascaux testifies.

The primary benefit of artistic innovation comes in the form of more variety, not replacement of the obsolete. Some can enjoy Hindi music done in a cappella style (for a current example of this unusual hybrid, see the group Penn Masala) or silkscreen painting, and others can enjoy Elizabethan-era music or Byzantine religious icons. The people may even overlap. In this, art much resembles communication; indeed it *is* a form of communication. In art, new ideas are always additive, not substitutive. New art unquestionably builds on existing art, sometimes in a specifically oppositional way, as with atonal music in the early twentieth century. But more is always better, so progress is measured in increasing variety. Artists take inspiration from other artists, the stock of artistic information is always increasing, and these make art dynamically self-regulating.

Ethics

Ethics, in contrast to art, can clearly be defended, like science, as something that improves through networked, self-regulating improvement. A moral code can be seen as a Platonic absolute, based on religious or secular reasoning. But it can also be seen as something that is continually refined without ever reaching any end point. The latter argument for the nature of morality appears in, for example, Hume's *A Treatise on Human Nature* (published in excerpts from 1738 to 1739) and is implied in Hegel. Hume explicitly argued that morality evolved to serve general human interests, which would provide the goal analogous to those in the other self-regulating systems investigated here. Seen this way, morality is also a dynamic, progressive self-regulating process, but even (allegedly) unchanging moral codes can compete in the human imagination. "All" that is required for ethics to be dynamically self-regulating is that moral thinkers take the work of other moral thinkers as a starting point and view their own work as a way to improve morality. The remaining question is whether morality has improved.

To be sure, the claim that we are more moral than we used to be, while obvious to many, is not universally accepted. It is common for people of a conservative disposition to believe that things used to be better. Indeed, that is the very definition of conservatism, although many conservatives oppose sudden, substantial, politically imposed change rather than change itself. (Edmund Burke, 1729–1797, is the classic example.) Still, almost anyone—including many a conservative—taken back in time several centuries would see common, even morally compulsory, conduct that would appall him. It is equally likely that anyone transported to the present from several centuries in the future would feel the same way. It is difficult to see this as anything other than moral progress. The only ways not to see it that way are to believe that what constitutes moral conduct is either timeless or arbitrary.

And morals *are* dynamically self-regulating, in the direction of progress. For example, there would be no belief in human rights without the willingness to believe that humans in a moral sense are at least presumptively equal. As Steven Pinker argues, the ability to think abstractly about people you do not know and liken them to yourself is a condition for the development of this idea of moral equality; that cannot happen until the idea that some are naturally born to rule is questioned.[38] The progress of the concept of human rights is clear: from not existing, to existing only within a certain society and only for men of a certain intellectual or moral sophistication, to all men of a certain ethnicity or religion, to men generally, to men and women, to all people without regard to the accident of where they were born.

It is true that some current schools of thought contend that human rights, like all other ideas, are just a rhetorically effective moral claim without broader content and that individual rights cut against the "rights" of collectives, especially those organized around religions or artificially defined ethnicities. (For an ancient indictment of the idea that morality is simply successfully persuasive rhetoric, see Socrates in Plato's *Gorgias*. For a more modern advocacy of the idea that morality is empty of anything beyond being good at winning an argument, see, for example, the work of Richard Rorty.[39]) But unless these moral claims are institutionalized by politics, they will have to compete, like all others, to prove their worth.

It is one thing to argue that the economy is homeostatic when politicians leave it alone or even that self-interest drives continuous improvements in the standard of living. But it is another thing to claim that people will become morally superior—less cruel, more beneficent, more decent—by the same route. And yet by the mid-eighteenth century, this is precisely the argument that was being made.

Such a claim is associated with two people whose ideas will long be yoked in the mind of many intellectuals, the Englishman Herbert Spencer (1820–1903) and the American William Graham Sumner (1840–1910). Both were advocates of laissez-faire in economic policy and anti-imperialist, the latter a view that put them in the minority in their respective countries at the time of the Boer and Spanish-American wars. Both were subsequently criticized as social Darwinists. While this term has seldom been rigorously defined by those who use it, it is invariably considered a pejorative in the English language as a way of disqualifying the ideas in question from reasoned discussion. In stereotype, it is thought to mean that people get what they deserve in (and only in) a laissez-faire society, which thus operates to the benefit of the species; therefore, both public and private efforts to ameliorate material distress are mistakes.

While relegating the thought of Sumner and Spencer to this category of intellectually irredeemable ideas is common even now, it was not always so. The obituaries of the two men in the *New York Times* did not even mention these aspects of their thinking. An editorial on December 9, 1903, marking the death of Spencer described his theorizing across many

fields as having "survived nearly a half a century of examination and attack, until it has come now to such wide acceptance that of habit and
almost unconsciously it guides the thinking of a great part of intelligent
mankind."[40] His achievements were accurately noted as sweeping: he was
a theorist in ethics, psychology, sociology, and evolutionary biology itself.
(It was Spencer, not Darwin, who coined the phrase "survival of the fittest" in *Principles of Biology* in 1864, which appeared after Spencer read
the first edition of *On the Origin of Species*. Darwin added the phrase to
later editions.[41]) Spencer in fact was a Lamarckian: he believed that traits
acquired before one became a parent, such as strong muscles acquired in
the course of a career as a miner, were then transmitted to children. Gregor
Mendel's (1822–1884) experimental findings from cross-breeding of plants,
in true self-regulating style, caused the Lamarckian view to be rejected.

And, critically, in Spencer's thinking, human ethics was thought to
have progressed through this kind of evolution. In particular, Spencer believed that as humans learned to cooperate, they developed traits that were
passed down through the generations. The expected result of this process,
according to the *Times* account, was "the law of progress, a continual advancement toward a better state and higher things."[42] Spencer did argue
that it was evolutionary competition with one another that made humans
better. But precisely because he was a Lamarckian, "human evolutionary
competition" meant that the species proceeded from violent barbarism to
cooperation, so that there was an "evolutionary ethics." Spencer described
self-regulating moral evolution this way:

The theory then was, as the theory still is, that those mental products of sympathy constituting what is called the "moral sense," arise as fast as men are
disciplined into social life; and that along with them arise intellectual perceptions of right human relations, as become clear as the form of social life becomes
better. Further, it was inferred at that time as at this, that there is being affected
a conciliation of individual natures with social requirements; so that there will
eventually be achieved the greatest individuation along with the greatest mutual
dependence—an equilibrium of such kind of that each, in fulfilling the wants of
his own life, will spontaneously aid in fulfilling the wants of all other lives.[43]

In other words, he believed in self-regulating moral progress, hardly
advocacy of the proposition that the poor deserve whatever happens to

them. On at least one occasion in 1882, Spencer expressed in a lecture the belief that "the American passion for 'business' and 'money getting' was soul destroying. This was the true lesson of evolution."[44]

Sumner's case is more complicated. His sympathies were consistently with the common man, as seen in this excerpt from his best-known work, *The Forgotten Man*, who is the man who pays higher taxes and higher prices for goods and services because the government, often for distinctly noncharitable purposes while subject to the "jobbing" of powerful business interests, provides alleged "charity":

When you see a drunkard in the gutter, you are disgusted, but you pity him. When a policeman comes and picks him up you are satisfied. You say that "society" has interfered to save the drunkard from perishing. Society is a fine word, and it saves us the trouble of thinking to say that society acts. The truth is that the policeman is paid by somebody, and when we talk about society we forget who it is that pays. It is the Forgotten Man again. It is the industrious workman going home from a hard day's work, whom you pass without noticing, who is mulcted of a percentage of his day's earnings to hire a policeman to save the drunkard from himself. All the public expenditure to prevent vice has the same effect. Vice is its own curse. If we let nature alone, she cures vice by the most frightful penalties. It may shock you to hear me say it, but when you get over the shock, it will do you good to think of it: a drunkard in the gutter is just where he ought to be. Nature is working away at him to get him out of the way, just as she sets up her processes of dissolution to remove whatever is a failure in its line. Gambling and less mentionable vices all cure themselves by the ruin and dissolution of their victims. Nine-tenths of our measures for preventing vice are really protective towards it, because they ward off the penalty. "Ward off," I say, and that is the usual way of looking at it; but is the penalty really annihilated? By no means. It is turned into police and court expenses and spread over those who have resisted vice. It is the Forgotten Man again who has been subjected to the penalty while our minds were full of the drunkards, spendthrifts, gamblers, and other victims of dissipation. Who is, then, the Forgotten Man? He is the clean, quiet, virtuous, domestic citizen, who pays his debts and his taxes and is never heard of out of his little circle. Yet who is there in the society of a civilized state who deserves to be remembered and considered by the legislator and statesman before this man?[45]

Self-regulation as social Darwinism? Perhaps. But Sumner was a consistent opponent of anyone using political regulation to get what he couldn't get through cooperation with others. Elsewhere in the essay, he did indicate that people who wish to help the poor, the drunk, or "loafers" should be completely free to do so. However, they should be mindful that in so doing, they are taking scarce resources from productive companies that are creating products that make people's lives better. He was no admirer of the rich or of colonialism. He was instead a long-standing opponent of plutocracy. He consistently opposed tariffs and other special favors for big business, the Spanish-American War, and any postwar attempt to colonize and "civilize" the residents of the Philippines. He was no advocate of simply letting Darwinian processes cull the herd in human society but believed that competition could improve humanity.[46] As in Spencer's case, the *New York Times* in its obituary did not raise this latter idea because it was not then seen as the way he saw the world. Instead, it saw fit to describe him as the teacher of a beloved course at Yale, Science and Society, and "an ardent advocate of free trade and the gold standard," before listing his books, about which it spoke no more.[47] (Charles Darwin's much longer obituary, in contrast, began immediately with a discussion of what was seen as his major legacy, *On the Origin of Species*.[48])

How then did both Spencer and Sumner come to be known as proponents of such a cruel doctrine? Indeed how did the term *social Darwinism* even come to be used to indicate that people should be left to struggle or fail on their own in the jungle of laissez-faire? Much of the credit, if that is the term, belongs to Richard Hofstadter (1916–1970), a public intellectual of great renown from the 1940s to the 1960s. He was a critic of what he saw as the cruelty of the unregulated market (and even, when he was younger, of the market itself, to the extent of joining the Communist Party briefly in the late 1930s), and of the intellectual atavism of the people who supported reliance on market forces (meaning substantial property rights and competition unhindered by political regulation). In this regard, his most influential work was *Social Darwinism in American Thought, 1860–1915* (1944). The term *social Darwinism* was almost unknown in the English language literature prior to this book, and began to rise much more rapidly afterward, as Figure 5.1 indicates. The figure is a plot using Google's nGram Viewer (http://books.google.com/ngrams) of all of the

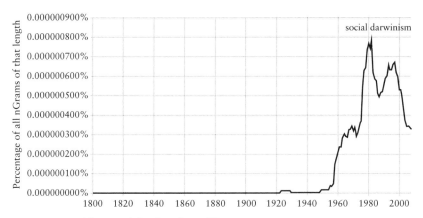

FIGURE 5.1. *The rise of the idea of social Darwinism.*
Source: books.google.com/ngrams (Search term: "social darwinism").

(case-indifferent) uses of the phrase "social Darwinism" in all English-language books available each year from 1860, the year after the publication of the first edition of *On the Origin of Species*, to 2008. As the figure makes clear, the term explodes in use only after the publication year.[49]

Thomas C. Leonard has argued, along with other recent scholars, that for Hofstadter, "social Darwinism" described anyone who believed in the laissez-faire that he despised, because the latter in his view connoted a belief that people deserved whatever rewards or punishments the battle for survival of the fittest meted out.[50] Such a rhetorical sleight-of-hand is inappropriate in the case of Spencer and only marginally appropriate, if that, in the case of Sumner. Yet after 1944, this was how the two men were most frequently known to the educated public, Spencer's published record as a polymath notwithstanding. In fact, the truth is nearly the opposite: commercial culture induces moral progress by promoting "a culture of cooperation, fairness and respect for the individual."[51]

THE SELF-REGULATING SOCIOECONOMY AND SELF-RESTRAINING POLITICIANS

The idea that people, left politically unmolested, could achieve whatever it was possible to achieve reached its height during the liberal era of the mid-nineteenth-century. This was particularly clear in the United Kingdom, where at the behest of its Parliaments (whose strengthening during the seventeenth century had been significantly due to the perceived need to restrain the sovereign's arbitrary taxation powers), the overall legislative trend was one of encouraging decentralized individual decision making, to take advantage of society's self-regulating powers.

This trend reached its height under the work of William Gladstone (1809–1898), a four-time prime minister between 1868 and 1894 and twice chancellor of the exchequer before that. As a young politician, Gladstone took some illiberal stands that he later outgrew; for example, he supported a cap on railroad prices and the maintenance of the long-standing bans on Jews in Parliament and on non-Anglicans as teachers at Oxford and Cambridge, not to mention opposing Whig proposals to expand the franchise. But by the time he became a member of Tory and then later Liberal Parliaments (he helped formally found the Liberal Party in 1859), he usually opposed foreign wars and what he called the "colonial lobby," from the first Opium War in 1839 through wars in southern Africa and Afghanistan in 1879. His second government, having taken office in 1880, ended the first Boer War in 1881 by being willing to cut British losses.

Driven substantially by the growing Irish famine, he was one of the main parliamentary advocates in 1846, joined from outside Westminster by the Anti–Corn Law League, for a repeal of the anti-self-regulation Corn Laws. Between 1815 and that year, those laws had imposed tariffs of varying degrees to keep corn prices high so as to raise the compensation of farmworkers and aristocratic landowners at the expense of grain consumers. He was a thorough believer, both before becoming prime minister for the first time and in his three nonconsecutive terms ending in 1894, in market negotiation as the best determinant of the prices of things, hence making the standard of living of consumers (especially poor ones) as high as it could be. In general, he thought that wars, if they were to occur at all, should be paid for out of present income and not by borrowing, because this would serve as an incentive not to get into them. Many years after his death, his one-time private secretary, John Arthur Godley (1847–1932), the first baron Kilbracken, remembered him this way:

It will be borne in mind that the Liberal doctrines of that time, with their violent anti-socialist spirit and their strong insistence on the gospel of thrift, self-help, settlement of wages by the higgling of the market, and non-interference by the State, were not very different from those generally held by the Conservatives of the present day. I think that Mr. Gladstone was the strongest anti-socialist that I

have ever known among persons who gave any serious thought to social and political questions. It is quite true, as has been often said, that "we are all socialists
up to a certain point"; but Mr. Gladstone fixed that point lower, and was more
vehement against those who went above it, than any other politician or official
of my acquaintance. I remember his speaking indignantly to me of the budget of
1874 as "That socialistic budget of Northcote's," merely because of the special
relief which it gave to the poorer class of income-tax payers. His strong belief
in Free Trade was only one of the results of his deep-rooted conviction that the
Government's interference with the free action of the individual, whether by taxation or otherwise, should be kept at an irreducible minimum.[52]

   If this testimony is to be believed, one of Gladstone's fundamental principles was that there should be full equality before the law. Under those
circumstances, people would find their way to the best solution achievable
because of their ability to prosper and because of the signals they would
get from the rest of society.

   That Gladstone believed that these signals were not limited to market
contexts can be gleaned from his long-standing practice, as a devout Christian, of personally ministering to prostitutes in London—even, remarkably,
while prime minister. This activity exposed him to the potential of politically fatal public backlash and would be unthinkable now both because
of fear of this backlash and the general lack of this kind of faith among
the political classes in the power of individuals organizing themselves to
correct social problems. But he was undeterred. Once in 1853 during one
of his "nocturnal rambles," he was observed in one of his rescue attempts
by a man who then demanded a job, threatening to go to the newspapers
if he did not get one. Unfazed, Gladstone immediately reported the event
to a policeman, pressed charges of blackmail against the man, and appeared in court himself. The man was convicted, and there is no evidence
that the incident hurt Gladstone politically or that he was ever unfaithful
to his wife of fifty-nine years.[53] Overall, "Gladstonian liberalism" is still
with us as a term for low taxes, minimalist government, and a general
belief that the free society is the best achievable society.[54]

   In the rest of Western Europe, the transition was a little rockier. But
the leaders and peoples of other nations saw Britain's stunning transformation and decided that self-regulating liberalism was a major part of it.

In 1806, Prussia's defeat at the hands of Napoleon brought pressure from that country's monarch with the middle-class mores, Frederick William III (1770–1840, ruled 1797–1840), to modernize. In particular, he led the drive for the use of modern scientific methods at the new universities explicitly set up for that purpose, the elimination of feudal labor obligations and land rights, an end to guild cartels, and the social liberation of Jews, much of this in the face of significant opposition from the country's nobles. One of his goals for this socioeconomic liberalization, significantly influenced by Adam Smith's revolution in thought, was the belief, according to Christopher Clark, that "every individual should be free to achieve 'as much prosperity as his abilities allow.'"[55]

Admittedly, much of the spread of the idea of self-regulation was due to military pressure. Napoleon's armies brought the self-regulating economy as part of a larger package of modernization wherever they went. The growing extent of belief in the market's self-harmonizing properties in Japan grew in the face of rising Western military and economic pressure there, culminating in the arrival of American battleships in Tokyo Bay in 1853, and in China with its military defeats to the British in the first Opium War in 1842 and the Japanese in the first Sino-Japanese War in 1895. Russia too was driven by defeat in the Crimean War to partially liberate its serfs in 1861. For a brief historical moment, the state was discredited and self-regulation almost universally accepted, the culmination of a political process that had begun with Turgot. And the chaos that the market clearly generated was something to be facilitated rather than controlled. British industrial success also provided targets for entrepreneurs in other countries to aim at, thus also increasing dynamic self-regulating tendencies.

FAITH IN DYNAMIC SELF-REGULATION
AMONG THE PUBLIC AT LARGE

It was not just British prime ministers who had faith in self-regulation and applied that faith to social improvement. It is important to appreciate how radical these increasingly influential ideas were, seen against the entire backdrop of recorded human history. The ideas that there could be social progress and that people could affirmatively act to make it happen without political instruction were almost unknown across time and space. While social improvement in principle can be imposed by order of the state, in practice almost all of it has been generated independently, most of it when the sufficient conditions for it are implemented politically. And while much contemporaneously desired large-scale social change (e.g., a change in a society's prevailing religion) has been accomplished through horrendous violence, beginning in the second half of the eighteenth century people began to sense that it was the "little man" who drove much of history, not least in Britain. It was there, according to the economic historian Joel Mokyr, that most people for the first time could buy and sell labor in markets and invest their savings and could benefit from the widespread trust among strangers. Objective measures of merit and individual effort also began to replace personal connections (especially to political power) as a determinant of whether individuals could achieve their objectives.[56] In the United States, the best-selling economics textbooks strongly emphasized the ability of market processes to motivate agents to make society materially and morally better. In the first half of the century, the Rev. Francis Wayland's (1796–1865) *Elements of Political Economy* argued that such processes rewarded the industrious and penalized the indolent. In the second half, Latham Perry's (1830–1905) later work of the same title claimed that unhindered competition did much the same and also emphasized the destructive effects of government-created special privileges on both prosperity and moral health.[57]

Increasingly people organized and worked together not just to produce more pins per hour but to create genuine moral progress. The most vivid and perhaps most important example was the antislavery movement. Human enslavement was not, contrary to what one sometimes hears, present in all eras and all places. If by "slavery" we mean to be born (or converted under the threat of death) into a condition of being forced to labor for others, we may say to a first approximation that it was found more in societies characterized by settled agriculture and less so in nomadic societies or societies where emigration was easy. Certainly it was common, with varying degrees of severity, in ancient Greece, Rome, Egypt, China, and parts of the pre-Columbian Western Hemisphere. But the moral imperative to end it was distinctly a product of Enlightenment thinking.

By the 1780s, the view that slavery—the mass commercialization of which had ironically been perfected by Britain, France, Spain, and Portugal since the 1500s—was intrinsically evil and had to go was a significant social phenomenon in the former two countries. Despite the presence of powerful monied interests with a stake in its continuance, the Society for the Abolition of the Slave Trade in 1787 in Britain and the Société des amis des Noirs in 1788 in France were established, each learning from the other how to promote abolition. Over the next forty years, in true self-regulating style, first the transatlantic slave trade and then Western Hemisphere slavery itself throughout the British Caribbean territories were done away with by the mother country. In the French colony of Haiti, it was accomplished violently, and there were numerous violent although small-scale revolts in the British Caribbean colonies prior to the ban in 1833. Nevertheless, the elimination of the scourge was by historical standards (outside the United States) done with remarkably little bloodshed, and was the product of attempts by citizens independently pursuing a first contentious, ultimately widely accepted moral goal. The power of free communication in the service of moral progress has seldom been more powerfully illustrated.[58]

A similar public campaign led to the repeal of the Corn Laws. This was followed by repeal in 1849 of the Navigation Acts, which had been passed in the seventeenth century to protect British shipping. Then tariffs were vastly lowered across the board, bringing Smith's self-regulating system of international trade largely (by historical standards) to fruition. Global prices for standardized goods such as grains and mass manufactures begin to be roughly the same all over the world, a clear sign of static self-regulation (what economists call arbitrage) in action. By the mid-1860s, Europe was essentially "a free-trade area, from the Pyrenees to the Russian border."[59] Most of this was liberalization with the active support of the poor, who wanted the lower prices that competition would deliver. The belief was widespread that things should be made wherever market prices indicated they should. By the end of the century, dynamic self-regulation had created a global financial industry first centered in London and later developing a second pole in New York.

This pattern of self-regulating responses to all manner of social problems spread with the social upheaval caused by industrialization. Some of it—for example, destruction of production machinery and buildings by workers in the first part of the nineteenth century, part of what is known as the Luddite movement—has little to recommend it.[60] Soon some of it turned toward political restrictions on commercial freedom, a topic taken up in the next chapter. But the nineteenth century also witnessed a blossoming of private activism to achieve social improvement. Reacting to the perceived injustices—the gaps between the immense wealth generated for many and the crowded, filthy living conditions for the urban poor in both Britain and the United States—Christians, including clergymen, increasingly preached that the devout had to go out and not simply save souls but improve the lives of the poor.

While the movement also had its political side, it was dominated by people who thought that the first task was to work directly to improve the lot of the urban impoverished. Settlement houses such as Toynbee House in London and Hull-House in Chicago were initially built with the idea that the social and material separation between rich and poor was lamentable, even disgraceful, but that it was up to the reformers themselves to heal this breach—in part by encouraging the wealthier to mingle socially with the poor. This would serve the dual purpose of familiarizing the wealthier with the poor and their problems and socializing the poor to proper behavior. Some modern readers will find this characterization of the difference between rich and poor lives objectionable, but what was clearly rejected was any idea that the poor deserved their fate.

Note the contrast with the modern view that the obligation for the wealthier to help the poor must be, and often is completely, discharged by paying taxes to the state. One could argue that leaving this problem to politics to solve has coincided with, if not led to, the wealthier and the poor becoming increasingly segregated, residentially, educationally, and socially.[61]

In sum, the approach was to diagnose a problem and then act promptly oneself to solve it. The result would be that society would become less imperfect over time, the essence of the self-regulating idea. And while we now increasingly defer to the state to provide social services, from colonial times people in the United States continuously and spontaneously formed (often ethnically based, sometimes owing to segregation) fraternal societies that with remarkable effectiveness provided life insurance, retirement benefits, medical care, funerals, and numerous other social welfare services. Unlike the modern welfare state, which often exercises little regulatory function over citizens' behavior (there are no codes of moral conduct governing eligibility for Medicaid, for example), these fraternal societies had numerous rules about private conduct, which they saw as serving to discipline their members and facilitate better life choices. For such nongovernmental charities, there were no entry barriers, few start-up costs, and none of the other obstacles that modern economists sometimes assert prevent effective matching of resources to social ends. No socioeconomic arena was too difficult; after the antislavery campaign, the era of self-regulation consensus saw the formation of groups like the Red Cross, temperance groups, and even the Communist International. (Two of these movements turned to political regulation amid the rising tide of impatience with self-regulation that followed in a few decades.)

Given that all of these groups rose spontaneously in response to perceived social needs, and did so with the aim of addressing these needs and thus improving society, they were the very example of dynamic self-regulation in action. Their flexibility and, in the case of the United States, their ability to flourish among black Americans in particular despite their legal restraints on participation in society, speaks to their strengths. The impact of such spontaneously organized problem addressing should not be underestimated.

THE TEMPORARY GLOBAL TRIUMPH
OF THE SELF-REGULATING SOCIOECONOMY

The economic transformation of the late seventeenth and eighteenth centuries launched what was the greatest recombination in history of resources, including human talent and drive, land, the buildings on it, and the more traditional resources extracted from the ground. In addition to the creation of new machines and commercial and financial networks, there was a massive movement of people, including a tidal wave who escaped southern and central Europe, as well as China and Japan, where old customs were still powerful.

There was a movement, powered initially admittedly by conquest, of Westerners (mostly British and French) into their colonies, bringing what the French called *la mission civilisatrice* with them, and in the opposite direction by the subjects of these new empires to the heart of the new self-regulating societies. To less prosperous regions of Europe, and to a significant extent in the lands Europeans made their way to in the nineteenth century, the arrival at least in theory of norms where contractual relations based on mutual interest displaced circumstances of birth as the prime determinant of how far one could go was a thoroughly liberating force. People could flow freely among tasks, so that each of these tasks would be done better, enabling these people to have at least the promise of a better life.

For the first time, many people around the world were introduced to the idea of upward (and its inverse downward) mobility. Indeed, this two-way mobility was itself part of the increasingly widely accepted "bourgeois bargain": I have the opportunity to go as far as my talents will take me, but on condition that I grant you the same opportunity.[62] Requiring that success be earned through the competitively sought approval of others led to broader and faster social improvement, with such improvement itself sometimes a radical idea. To the extent that people in countries that have modernized since World War II have preserved this ethos of success even as they have mixed in features of their own cultures in the course of successfully modernizing (think of successful members of the middle class in Korea or India), and especially to the extent that they come from groups that suffered poorly in the old regimes of status, so much the self-regulating better. Faced with the challenge of modernizing, they retain those norms that mix well with it and abandon those that do not. Even self-regulating moral progress was on display when, for example, people and societies exposed to the "modern" socioeconomy began to engage in the kind of organized philanthropy (e.g., merchant-funded disaster relief in China, the Middle East, and India) that was historically the domain in these places, if it existed at all, of the state.[63]

These are the things out of which revolutions in human affairs are made. For a time, self-regulation had broad, if never universal, public approval in the West. It had widespread, if lesser, admiration in other parts of the world as well. If we must pick a date, we can say that in roughly 1874, the end of Gladstone's first term as prime minister, the idea of the self-regulating socioeconomy was at its height.

Alas, this socioeconomy, especially in a democratic society, carries the seeds of its own destruction in that the more complex it is, the more voices (typically of those people who see themselves as losers right now) there are for limiting its spontaneous evolution, and rechanneling that evolution politically in a direction that favors them. The development of this backlash is described in Chapters 6 and 7.

CHAPTER 6

Realignment

Fine Tuning in Light of Self-Regulation's Deficiencies

Laws excessively good are the source of excessive evil.
MONTESQUIEU, The Spirit of the Laws[1]

The late nineteenth century was the apex of the belief in self-regulating social processes in the Western world. With regard to "the economy" particularly (although the term itself would not come into widespread use until after World War II), there was a widespread and rising confidence that free, self-regulating commerce powered by people pursuing individual goals and given the legal space to improve their circumstances had brought about the miracle of industrialization-powered socioeconomic transformation. Spectacular progress in Britain and then France and the German lands after the elimination of the old traditions of control and obligation in the name of stability, inherited from feudalism, were taken as evidence that it was the control and obligation themselves that were the problem. Thinkers, politicians, and, most important, many ordinary people saw that such people could do good work given the opportunity, so it was better to give them the chance than to tie them down with the chains of tradition or law. Especially in the West, a rising tide of thought indicated that left to their own devices in a world of uncertain outcomes but powerful incentives, humanity would improve both materially and morally.

Confidence in such processes requires belief that the pursuit of individual goals in such an environment conduces to the overall social good. But no sooner had the self-regulating vision been ensconced than it began to be systematically and seriously challenged. The criticisms fell into two categories. The first, that the liberation of self-regulating forces was essential to progress but that political regulation was necessary to remedy its flaws, is the subject of this chapter. The other, that the basic premises on which self-regulation is based were false, is explored in Chapter 7.

Most of the first genus of skepticism initially fell on purely economic self-regulation. In science, the only people even potentially damaged in a self-regulating environment are scientists whose hypotheses are rendered obsolete by new results. But the scientists whose hypotheses were displaced amid burgeoning scientific research in the nineteenth century were themselves by profession loyal to the scientific method, and so there was no rage against self-regulating science, whose progress they, along with society as a whole, were benefiting copiously from. And despite attempts here and there to control communication that allegedly threatened public safety or order, free exchange of information was now seen as a key element of modernity.

Confidence in economic self-regulation was considerably more fragile, because from a sufficiently short-term point of view, it became increasingly believed that when some people were making more money, others had to be making less. As noted earlier, rebellion over unequal distribution of wealth has a long history; what was new here was the belief that the recent radical reorientation of the socioeconomy itself was fundamentally unfair.

There is without question some irony in pointing to the rise of intellectual skepticism about self-regulation as a force in its decline. Such skepticism is itself likely to be generated through self-regulating communication— not just reaction to the seeming excesses of the industrial age but from the incentives public intellectuals have to say something counterintuitive. But once the belief that external political control was (only sometimes, initially) superior to benign neglect captured much of the political imagination during this period, it made self-regulation more difficult, with sometimes catastrophic effects.

THE SHORTCOMINGS OF
THE SELF-REGULATING ECONOMIC ORDER

The building of the mass production economy meant truly dramatic improvement in the standard of living for ordinary people, including desperately poor immigrants to North America and the rising bourgeoisie in the cities of Europe. But it also begat previously unseen levels of population density and the resulting disparities of wealth in such teeming cities as London, Manchester, New York, and Chicago. The first reaction was the spontaneously generated and self-directed social reform: the choice by individuals facing appalling sights to directly help the people affected and encourage them to take the reins of their own future. But soon pressure began to rise for politics to constrain the seemingly out-of-control industrial beast. Some of this was driven by the simple visibility of poverty. Prior to the rise of the modern city, poverty was ubiquitous, but it was mostly confined to the countryside and ameliorated somewhat by the traditional feudal and religious obligations of landlords to their desperately poor tenant farmers. In addition, it had unfolded before the creation of modern journalism—meaning daily newspapers with professional correspondents, specifically looking for news of general interest—in the mid-eighteenth century and the invention of photography in the first half of the nineteenth.

Combined with society's rising ethical sophistication, the new information generated pressure to do something right now rather than wait for problems to spontaneously call forth many competitive, nonpolitical responses. This anxiety was heightened by the rising tide of macroeconomic instability. Although episodes of such instability have been traced back centuries, this instability accelerated substantially with the intrinsic uncertainty about what opportunities and losses would be generated next by the unprecedented rapid economic transformation.[2] The industrializing world was more and more characterized by periodic sharp spikes in unemployment as economic experiments were continually tried and tentatively duplicated, sometimes to be weeded out ruthlessly later. This, combined with easy-to-see and therefore cognitively salient and, from a sufficiently short-term point of view, seemingly intractable urban poverty meant that even as self-regulating socioeconomic liberalism and its industrial fruits were revolutionizing society, distrust of it began to grow.

As suggested earlier, there is a love of order that occupies part of the human soul and an eagerness to attribute material poverty and poverty of the spirit alike to a decline of such order. Disorder—the word suggests that regimented order is the goal—and chaos are often seen as self-evidently bad. But the word *disorder* can mean "lack of stability." And some stability—legal stability and a preservation of the tendency of members of society to trust one another and not behave in a predatory manner—is critical to the self-regulating socioeconomic order. But sometimes—given social immobility, technological stagnation, or long-standing special privileges attached to being members of a particular social group—stability and self-regulation are at cross purposes. The Industrial Revolution and the legal changes that accelerated its spread beyond Britain shattered the old class structure, the geographic distribution of people, and the whole notion of the behaviors and social relations associated with a life well lived. We should not be surprised that there was resistance to this actually most fruitful form of instability. Much of the resistance was initially religiously motivated, and some of it involved a distaste for the seeming obsession with money that the growing prosperity seemed to be generating. Most important, some of it was a direct response to the perceived excessive individualism of the new liberal thinking.

And so a new doctrine was born: socialism—the idea that there exists a "society" specifically thought of as larger than the recently lionized individual. According to Google nGrams, the word *socialisme* made its first appearance in the French written corpus in 1787. In the 1840s, it began to grow rapidly there, and *socialism* first appeared in English. In the early years, socialism was simply another part of the stream of dynamic self-regulation. Self-organized communities arising in Western Europe and North America engaged in Mill-style experiments in building societies on the principles of common access to resources and cooperative/democratic decision making rather than by vesting owners of private property with complete control over how that property could be used. These societies were seen as ways of avoiding material inequality, even in the face of an unprecedented increase in overall wealth and the competitive cruelty that seemingly characterized mass industrialization. Such inequality was seen as inherent in a socioeconomy run for increasingly vilified profit. Even experimental family structures and sexual practices were implemented in some of these communities. The process was one in which some became convinced that industrial society, with its alienation, poverty, and destruction of what was best in human nature, had to be replaced. Evidence for this proposition was gathered through lifestyle experiments designed to prove that socialism was better. These attempts were subject to self-regulating forces rather than political command, and usefully so.

While such experiments have continued since—examples are kibbutzim in Israel, communes in the 1960s in the United States, or recent back-to-the-future Maoist farms being operated in China[3]—most of them have had modest impact on or left little trace in society. Such societies were and are often criticized for their "unrealistic" view of human nature (a telling criticism in a self-regulating society, albeit one that deserves to be tested), and yet done this way, socialist or any other sort of social experiments can be carried out as long as they do not threaten social institutions that support self-regulation.

Other thinkers went further and said free commerce and the resultant cutthroat competition over money were changing human nature for the worse and turning allegedly long-standing harmonious cooperation into a life-or-death struggle between the allegedly small minority who "controlled" money and power and the vast majority who correspondingly suffered. The self-regulating spontaneous order, in other words, was being shown to have failed and had to be replaced by a new, more "cooperative," less competitive society, imposed from on high if necessary.

Some of these thinkers shared with the prophets of self-regulating liberty a belief, a fruit of the Enlightenment, that the trajectory of humanity was ever upward. But for them, industrialization based on private property and the unequal distribution of power between workers and owners was a mere phase. What it should be replaced with varied from thinker to thinker. For France's Henri de Saint-Simon (1760–1825), the new science and industrial technology were certainly progress, but should be managed for the general good not by self-regulated industrialists but by a meritocratically selected class of managers. For Charles Fourier (1772–1837), the building was the thing; his ideal structure, known as the *phalanstère,* was designed to house a community where work, play, and the cultivation of children and adults were all combined. Well before his time, he was also an advocate of women possessing the right to perform any job, and he rejected the stigma of homosexuality and other minority sexual orientations. This kind of proposed social (re)design—the one way that is better for everyone—has a long history in Western thought, including Plato's Republic and various examples of utopian fiction.[4] While they were not terribly influential during Fourier's lifetime, numerous groups of people, notably in the United States, established communities on his principles.

FROM SOCIAL EXPERIMENTATION
TO SOCIAL CONTROL

As long as these communities were merely hypothetical or freely established, they could only but add to the vitality of Millsian self-regulation.

But before long, European thinkers and activists began to advocate, in the manner of the French Revolution, the use of politics to boldly transform society. This was, to be sure, part of a much larger reform project, including the previously mentioned self-organized campaigns to politically end slavery. Similar campaigns were waged in Britain to expand the franchise and lessen the population disparities in parliamentary districts.

As the Industrial Revolution proceeded, the self-regulating market was increasingly seen as part of what had to be reformed. Gradually the view that people must turn to politics if they wished society to progress further took hold. While the rising size and wealth of the middle class were already obvious in Britain and France (not to mention in the United States and Canada, where opportunity for personal advancement was already seen as merely requiring, for the white male population, the freedom to try), it was noticeable elsewhere as well. As dissent against industrial transformation was, paradoxically, rising in tandem with this growth, other revolutionary impulses equally hostile to self-regulating forces—a desire to overthrow not just the existing political authorities but the very structure of the societies they presided over—also began to stoke the fires. The most important of these noneconomic yet ultimately crucial impulses, because it enabled much of the political regulation that followed, was nationalism.

Creating the Nation

In Europe on the eve of the historically decisive year 1789, the British and the citizens of the Dutch territories had, by the standards of the time, a long history of relatively free movement and a significant right to work free of royal or feudal restraint. Elsewhere, the new replacement of long-standing feudal customs now led not just to socioeconomic but political upheaval. The revolutionary years in France from 1789 to 1795 were hugely influential in persuading people all over Europe that a national government invested with powers to regiment and reorganize was needed to sweep away the old order and regulate what followed.

Many began to sense the power of this new tool to organize mere societies as comprehensive nations to keep up with the British in "international competition." By the end of Napoleon's rampage across Europe, a new national model was on the scene. Previously the relevant sovereign facts—a large number of kingdoms and principalities based substantially on opportunistic marriages and the aftermath of wars—often carved up peoples who spoke the same languages (think of Germany and Italy) or united many who did not (the Hapsburg Empire). The overthrow of Louis XVI gave the Revolutionary authorities an opportunity to create an alternative to the king's realm, namely, a *nation*: a set of people who share a geographic space and are ruled not by a family dynasty but by a new class of rulers selected through some process (sometimes violent, sometimes not) other than heredity. (Recall from Chapter 2 that I distinguish between the nation, an entity more complex and hence more capable of more comprehensively regulating society, and Elman Rogers Service's mere state.)

The idea of the nation was a technological improvement of sorts, an increase in the ability to politically regulate. To call a politician in modern Europe a "nationalist" is, mainly because of the Nazi experience, to describe him as potentially dangerous. But in mid-nineteenth-century Europe, the nation was the wave of the future. Initially, what increasingly cohesive nations often wanted to do was improve the space for self-regulation to work its magic, free of long-standing and senseless restrictions.

From the point of view of self-regulating societies, however, the rise of national power was also in many ways a pity because the nation is in fact a requirement for extensive political regulation of modern, complex self-regulating processes. Monarchs often corruptly rewarded friends and punished enemies, and under a Louis XIV or Frederick the Great, they could occasionally try to extend state ordering of society into areas where it had not reached before. But it takes *national* leaders to ask (and to claim to know how to answer) questions such as, "How should French schools be run?" or, "How should the German economy be managed?" Chancellors and parliaments ask those questions; kings and queens seldom did. Perhaps lamentably, the leaders of nations more urgently wished their people to think of themselves not as members of a particular religion or subethnicity, but to be loyal to a new sort of tribe, the national one.

Like all other tribalism, nationalism emphasized commonality and therefore worked against individual-level experimentation and the social improvement that inevitably followed. The fate of the "Italian nation" or "German nation" became critical the way the fate of the French Republic had been in 1792, the year French people thinking of themselves as *citoyens* rallied to the defense of *La République* against counterrevolutionary invaders at the battle of Valmy. In lieu of self-regulating liberalism, the nationalist philosophy emphasized a common destiny. As some societies grew more complex, almost entirely through self-regulating processes, the belief took hold, paradoxically, that the nation (more accurately, the national government) needed new tools to control the problems that self-regulating processes generated and to point the nation in a different direction than such processes would otherwise take it in.

The exploration for new knowledge, sometimes scientifically carried out and sometimes done so merely with a scientific patina on fundamentally unscientific methods, turned in new directions in service of the national ideal. Diachronic linguistics sought to demonstrate the distinctive characteristics and history of particular languages, culminating in the Sapir-Whorf hypothesis, which in the 1930s argued that a language's grammar determines and is determined by the culture of its speakers. (This is now largely rejected by linguists, if not by the broader public.) Myths of national founding, while around since ancient times (think of the Roman Republic's Romulus and Remus), grew in importance in places as far-flung as Germany, Japan, and the newer United States. There was a growing market for anything that promoted the idea of "the people of this nation are different, in ways that reflect well on us." Lamentably, most of the aspects of "national culture" that were seen as distinct were ironically themselves substantially the results of dynamic self-regulation: language, arts, food, and social mores, for example.

Subordination to the Nation

The creation of the nation, in which the government became the defender of the unique "national identity," was destructive in many ways, and to self-regulating processes in particular, because of the combination of a desire to prevent national contamination and the ability of national governments to enforce national "hygiene." Mobilizing the nation required stressing its common features and destiny, and convincing its people to oppose any infections from outside the national body that self-regulation might introduce. It is to the credit of global science (driven in part, surely, by its obvious payoffs) that it was able to resist this pressure as much as it did. Science continued to be a transnational system, although national governments emphasized the importance of having "our" scientists outperform "theirs," a pattern that may be even stronger now in the age of large-scale government funding of science and the attention paid every October to how many Nobel Prize winners have come from various nations.

National leaders took it upon themselves to reinforce, and often create, this identity, which they used to push out other elements of individuals' identity portfolios. This required action against religious authorities, as seen in campaigns against the Catholic Church in Italy and the German Southeast during and after the unification process in those nations. It led to often opportunistic campaigns against linguistic minorities in the Hapsburg territories and, despite the general pattern of full legal emancipation, against the Jews in some countries. In addition, more prevalent democratic governance became a way for the "will of the nation" to make itself manifest, a will that necessarily overrode the desires of individuals, who became internal enemies of the nation.

At the top of the new nation-based enemies list was the "cosmopolitan" personality type, who had a sinister loyalty to people of his transnational group and was therefore unpatriotic. This was a charge that was first leveled against aristocrats in the late eighteenth and early nineteenth centuries; then at various times, it was also used against industrialists and especially financiers, and finally used to disinter old suspicions against Jews, Catholics, and other ethnoreligious minorities. The rising power of the nation, plus the growing complexity of "international" economic relations (a term suggesting that commerce transcending a national border is somehow peculiar), began to reinforce each other in lamentable ways. International commerce provided more targets for opportunistic nationalist politicians to aim at, for example.

Questions of classical liberal or conservative, religious or traditional, of class loyalty and conflict now had to contend with and were often subsumed by issues about what was best for the nation, a sometimes historically arbitrary geographical collective. That many socialists enthusiastically supported their nations' participation in World War I, for example, is well known. In short, the nation, a creation of the nineteenth century, stood above more traditional tribalisms by the beginning of the twentieth. In the twentieth century, even politicians of the Soviet Union, in principle a postnational government by a working class in solidarity with its cohorts in other nations, resorted to nationalism, especially during World War II.

By the time Germany unified by rallying most of the German-speaking peoples to mobilize resources to militarily defeat the first modern nation, France, in 1871, the outcome was to create a unified German nation, now called an empire. That society not only could be but *ought* to be left to order itself now became a proposition with fewer and fewer takers. It was not firms or individuals but nations that competed for colonies, competed industrially, and competed in the revived Olympic Games, laden as they were with national flags and anthems. It would take only approximately half a century between the time Italy was unified, on admittedly defensible grounds that a people sharing a common language should not be ruled by speakers of other languages, to devolve into the first fascist society. The entire point of governance in Italy became to overcome the fissiparous tendencies—conflicts between workers and management, between rich and poor, between the religious and irreligious, the common factor in each case being conflict—that were now seen as the inevitable result of self-regulation. Competition in the factories, among businesses, and among political parties was less and less a benefit but a cost to the abstract collective known as the nation. It thus had to be managed by national authority.

At the same time, the new nations were building up their record keeping and surveillance capacities, a legacy in part of the Revolutionary authorities in France. Historical records from the eighteenth century are full of accounts of disasters on the water where the death toll could only be estimates. Such events still happen in developing countries today. But in modern countries, when there is a deadly incident of any scale, the survivors and fatalities are quickly documented; this is a measure of how thoroughly government identification has permeated such societies. Such documentation is useful in a great deal of commerce, but it also enables (and was originally motivated by) the need of the new nation to keep track of its people. The establishment of national documents of all sorts and the increased reliance on passports, not just as government authorization for movements across national borders but within them, grew between the French Revolution and World War I. Data collected by and organized around the nation led national authorities to think further in terms of using "their" government to solve national problems. The creation of statistical theory enabled this trend by allowing analysis of "national" data.[5] John Cowperthwaite, a colonial official given significant credit for the postwar

British policy of abstaining from politically regulating the economy of Hong Kong, once was asked which of his accomplishments he was most proud of. He answered, "I abolished the collection of statistics."[6]

These tools remain useful to some governments amid the widespread fear of immigration in now prosperous democracies, many of whose "nationals" fear large-scale immigration of low-skill people from troubled or failing societies. The greatest threat such immigrants carry with them is to "national" cohesion, whether to the social schemes of the twentieth century or to the sense of national identity carefully sculpted by government schools since the nineteenth.

It seems almost impossible now to imagine that prior to the immigration control legislation first implemented against the Chinese in 1882 and extended to people from all nations in 1924, millions of immigrants entered the United States with nothing in the way of formal documentation, and once they got here, they faced only a cursory inspection at the port of arrival. To be in favor of any interaction across national borders, for example, through free trade with people from other nations, also began to be seen suspiciously. If anything, this nation-based form of conflict has been worse than previous forms of the group conflict to which we are prone. The argument is not that before the nation, there were few tribal conflicts. But the potency of national identity and the unprecedented power of the nation to influence the thinking of its members significantly increased both the opportunity for and the perceived importance of control of self-regulating processes by the national political apparatus in particular, and the belief that broad cultural and commercial exchange across national borders was itself a failure of self-regulation.

The inability of even democratic national governments to satisfactorily control socioeconomic evolution also interacted toxically with the new national consciousness. While some of the new nations lacked thorough democracy, in nations that did become progressively more democratic, election results became synonymous with a "national will." In such an environment, the expression of individual agency that cut against electoral outcomes, including international free trade, expressions of solidarity with fellow members of subnational tribal groups, or transnational social movements involving, for example, the "working class," could now be seen as dangerous to the nation. This impulse, part of the broader sacralization of "national" identity, explained why economics-based opposition to the self-regulating order often came to be seen as unpatriotic. (Think of the frequency with which people even now impugn those who seem to advocate policies that threaten "American jobs," as if a particular job at a particular time were not the result of bargaining based on those particular circumstances but could "belong" to some nation.)

DISSATISFACTION FROM BELOW

Running in parallel with the nationalist-driven construction of the means to control the self-regulating economic order was the increasing anger at its visible results. The experimental small-scale socialist and other planned communities eventually became, despite their frequently short life spans, a movement for political regulation of this seemingly failing order. The visible, wrenching urban poverty that new media increasingly reported came in part to be seen as a national problem that the national government had to solve. In England, the movement to substitute political for self-regulation of socioeconomic exchange began with the Factory Act of 1831, which mainly addressed child labor, seen already as a damning indictment of "unregulated" exchange. An influential factor, especially in Britain, in the growing belief that the market could not be trusted to self-regulate because the poor suffered the most was the Irish famine of the late 1840s, one of the last disasters of this kind on the European continent.[7] While the British government that then ruled Ireland employed many destitute Irish to allow them to earn some income, and despite the fact that the Corn Laws were in effect until 1849 (so that cheaper grain from other countries was largely unavailable during the famine), the fact that grain was frequently exported from Irish ports even as people in the interior starved caused liberal economic doctrine to take much of the blame for the catastrophe.

In such a climate, and with the disappointments of the mostly failed revolutions of 1848, working-class consciousness could not but grow. The Frankfurt Assembly, democratically elected to write a constitution for all the German-speaking lands, met in 1848 and 1849. It was dominated by liberals, but the document it produced was not accepted, and German politics turned more radical. Even in France, with a somewhat stronger liberal tradition, 1847 and 1848 were partly marked by students largely from the middle class but of a radical bent plotting revolution. This contributed to the overthrow of the bourgeois king Louis Philippe (1773–1850, ruled 1830–1848) in February 1848, followed at the end of that year by the ersatz emperor Napoleon III (1808–1873, ruled 1848–1870).

Meanwhile, the belief that the modern economy was inevitably zero sum grew: the amount of economic fruit to be bestowed was fixed, and the only question was how it should be distributed. Wherever revolution was contemplated or attempted from 1848 on, both inside and outside Europe, it was to be carried out in the name of "the people." The implication was a singularity of purpose obviously hostile to a society governed by rules enabling different social experiments to be carried out to try to address competing human problems. That socialist and other nominally transnational revolutions were carried out one nation at a time, so that even nonnationalist revolution was harnessed to the national apparatus, is informative. The first meeting of the International Working Men's Association (First International) was held in Geneva in 1866. Trade union leaders became more active in the increasingly democratic politics of France, Germany, Britain, and elsewhere, despite varying degrees of hostility from the political authorities. What in Germany is now called the Social Democratic Party was founded in 1863, the postunification Italian Socialist party in 1892, and the British Independent Labour Party (which had previously run candidates through the Liberal Party and was the forerunner of today's Labour Party) in 1893.

OBJECTIONS FROM ECONOMIC THEORY

People who studied what by the year 1900 had become "economics" and even "economic science" contributed heavily to the decline of confidence in the self-regulating order. The first version of the monumental *Principles of Economics* by England's Alfred Marshall (1842–1924), released in 1890, made unprecedentedly extensive use of mathematics to model economic ideas and powerfully illustrated the virtues of competition in moving resources from where they were less to where they were more valuable at the margin. Marshall also emphasized the role of competition and freedom in giving all a fair chance to escape poverty and "excessive mechanical toil." He noted as well the civilizing effect commerce had on the treatment of people outside one's own extended family and of women generally, an extension of the commercial-peace argument for a self-regulated socioeconomy. He invoked what he called the law of substitution, whereby less costly options are substituted for more costly ones when the means to do so are discovered, as a reason why competitive markets with self-regulating properties promote the social good.

Clearly having read his Mill, Marshall applauded the value of increasing social variety that competition brings about as valuable. Like others before and after him, he invoked scientific analogies. For example, money served as "a *mean sun*" does for navigators, a reference point for people who wish to transact in the market, and price differences that drive resource reallocation are like the movement of fluids between chambers of unequal pressure. Moreover, all markets must be considered together rather than separately, which he likened to the necessity, when a system of balls is subjected to a force, to consider the effects of each ball on every other in determining the final outcome.[8]

Still, while applauding the role of the market in promoting prosperity and the role of prosperity in promoting Aristotelian happiness, he also raised the concept of market failure, though in an imprecise way. As he saw it, the national government's purpose in the generally self-regulating era was "to increase the good and diminish the evil influences of economic freedom." He was not certain about what that entailed, but among these tasks might be enabling those of lesser means to enjoy the higher things in life, the promotion of at least some scientific research, rectifying the "evils arising from the unequal distribution of wealth," and the need to break poverty arising when the poor lacked the resources to provide their children with a better future.[9] As is so often the case, it was an essentially free-market Marshall who saw the potential of the poor and not their victimhood, and he saw the solution to poverty as giving them the capacity to improve themselves. In his case, this was especially compelling because of the rising tide at that time of racial and IQ-based determinism as the explanation for multigenerational poverty. (Chapter 7 discusses this in the context of political regulation.)

With the exception of industries with increasing returns, which Marshall clearly indicated deserved public subsidy, he did not develop concrete principles for using the state to supplement self-regulating competition. But repeatedly he invoked the idea that the state must do the small number of things that such competition will not.

On that basis, subsequent economists developed three categories of market failure, meaning that the static market equilibrium fails to produce the best achievable results, given what consumers want and the current ability to combine resources in different ways to bring it to them. The first category is externalities, which occur when the participants in a transaction generate positive or negative effects for people who are not contractually part of the transaction. This concept was characterized mathematically by A. C. Pigou, although there is preliminary discussion of it in John Stuart Mill's economics textbook.[10] In Pigou's characterization, if the externality is positive, these external parties have insufficient incentive to contribute resources to encourage expanded production; if the externality is negative, they are similarly unable to make their displeasure known by placing a higher bid for the resources that contribute to the activity that generates it, meaning that the good is overproduced. They are, for example, unable to convey to automobile producers the damage they suffer from pollution when car buyers drive cars. (And, hence, car producers ignore that damage when deciding whether to produce these cars and, if so, how to price them and how much pollution control to install in them.) Pigou looked at this as a problem of incorrect prices, even under competition, that the state can correct by imposing taxes or subsidies.

A second problem involves nonexcludability, which economists have a habit of dividing into two separate problems. When people who do not pay the price asked cannot be excluded from consuming a good, even though that means others, now or in the future, cannot use it, this is known as the tragedy of the commons. (This term is attributed to the biologist Garrett Hardin, although Hardin credited the economist William Forster Lloyd.[11]) An example is overfishing in unowned ocean water. Since fishermen will not be able to harvest any fish spawned later by fish they choose not to take today, they do not have any reason to take account of the effect of their fishing on these future fish, that is, to manage the fish population properly—a problem owners of privately owned fish farms (just like owners of fenced-off cattle ranches) do not face. Bacterial resistance from overprescribing antibiotics is another example, as is obtaining government subsidy of particular activities, with costs imposed on taxpayers generally, which results in "overgrazing" of the fiscal commons. When people cannot be excluded from consuming the good itself and the good is nonrivalrous (consumption by one does not lessen the amount available for others), this combination of nonrivalry and nonexcludability generates what is known as a public good, which is not the same thing as "a good that members of the public can use." Henry Sidgwick in 1883 proposed as an example that lighthouses would not be built by firms in pursuit of profit because any passing ship would enjoy the benefits without the light-house builders being able to impose a fee on them.[12] Paul Samuelson gave a precise mathematical specification in 1954.[13]

The final posited "market failure" was the one most readily grasped by the general public: imperfect competition. Many economists claim there is "perfect competition" if and only if the price for which a good sells, a measure of its marginal value to consumers, is equal to the marginal cost of producing it.[14] By maximizing profits, each identical firm in some indus-try then uses the exact amount of resources that maximize the net of the value to consumers of its product over its social cost—that cost being the value that could be created for consumers if this industry did not exist and the resources claimed by it were instead used for other purposes. (Any modern microeconomics textbook will discuss this perfect-competition model.) In this model, the price is identical across the identical companies, and unless it has been driven down by competition to the average cost of production, profits exist, elicit entry by new firms, and thereby eliminate those profits. In this model, competition is nothing more than mere static self-regulation. It generates consumer satisfaction in excess of the oppor-tunity cost to society of using those resources for some other purpose. The benefits to society are maximized when there are no profits because they have all been competed away, reaped instead by consumers. That the ben-efits of competition come from reducing profits through price cutting rather than increasing them through innovation is a striking feature of the model and the microeconomic thinking, friendly to political regulation, that fol-lowed it.[15] Ordinarily, this "zero-profit" equilibrium requires large numbers of producers, so that each producer is so small that its entire production has no effect on overall market conditions. When such competition fails to obtain because the number of existing firms is too small and the cost of opening new ones too high, the market has "failed."

Generations of economics graduate students have learned these "fail-ures," often simultaneously imbibing the idea that the state could and hence should use its powers to address them in four ways: (1) taxing, subsidizing, forbidding, or requiring activities that generate negative or positive externalities; (2) producing public goods itself; (3) policing excessive use of goods from which nonpayers cannot be excluded; or (4) breaking up or nationalizing companies that are too big to be competed against effectively. Competition continued to be seen as potentially beneficial, but substantially on grounds of lowering prices. The idea that it could also benefit society by introducing entirely new ways to satisfy human purposes became very secondary. If price, and not innovation, were the primary margin of competition, the social costs of "imperfect" competition were easier to establish. It became an uphill struggle to persuade economists and politicians that exercising property rights could overcome externalities without state intervention, as when restaurants solve the problem of secondhand cigarette smoke by establishing separate smoking and nonsmoking sections. (The idea that externalities can be seen from either side is owed to Coase.[16]) Thinking about competition merely as charging lower prices for an identical product also neglects the robustness of the human urge, which a self-regulating socioeconomy capitalizes on, to cooperate to solve problems even against an observer's narrow conception of her own immediate self-interest. Examples are the norms that are continuously developing to govern open source software and copying in fashion and other forms of art.[17] The scientific method is another such gradually evolved norm.

The textbook model of competition ignores the general disposition to invent new forms of social and business organization to address unmet needs. If one accepts the ubiquity of such reactions, generalizing any blackboard exposition of a specific evanescent "market failure" into a broad, permanent pattern requiring constant political oversight and interference is very risky, since it makes such solutions generated through market self-regulation much harder. Dynamic self-regulation generates many responses. Political regulation generates one at best.

THE POLITICAL REWARDS
TO POLITICAL REGULATION

Economists did their part to depict self-regulating economic forces as periodically failing, but increasingly the public also believed that the failure of the self-regulating socioeconomic order was its injustice. This played out as an increasing willingness to vote for parties of "the left."

In modern use. "the left" is a broad label. It encompasses views on market exchange, particular components of it such as health care and retirement income, human interaction with the natural world, the role of ethnicity in society, and opposition to traditional mores. But many of these political controversies are fairly recent; "left" parties were for many decades mostly united by dissatisfaction with socioeconomic self-regulation. Some said socialists should control the national government, others that workers should replace it with some postpolitical way of regulating production and consumption. Some favored parliamentary means to achieve their agenda, others violence. By the 1880s, we may speak of moderates and radicals with respect to the desired pace and extent of political control of socioeconomic change and how much violence was acceptable in bringing that change about.

European Democracy

Stefano Bartolini has conducted a study of the pattern of voting for parties of this broad left in various Western European countries between 1880 and 1989. He finds that the level of electoral support rose continuously from 1896 to 1939, and after World War II, it stabilized at roughly a third of the popular vote. In most countries, the share of the vote going to Communists and other hardline anti-self-regulation parties in particular peaked (Italy, with its active postwar communist party, aside) during the early 1930s. This radical extension was driven first by what was seen as the foolish enthusiasm of socialist parties for World War I and then by economic chaos in the 1920s and 1930s.[18] The source of hostility to self-regulation differed from country to country. In Britain, it was the large and increasingly radical trade unions that led the charge for laws "protecting" current workers in their current jobs, for example, or more heavily taxing the wealthy, while the Fabian socialists viewed socialism as the perfection of democracy itself, the apex of social progress. In Germany, all socialist parties were banned between 1878 and 1890 (breaching the freedom to communicate), and during this time, the German left was substantially captured by people heavily influenced by Marx (about whom more next chapter), resulting in a more radical left. German chancellor Otto von Bismarck (1815–1898, governed united Germany 1871–1890) introduced the welfare state in the 1880s to siphon off support for this left. In autumn 1918, in the last days of a war that was now clearly about to be lost, several radical uprisings by workers and former soldiers succeeded for a short time in a number of cities there, before being suppressed in 1919.

The catastrophe of the war, which had severely tarnished liberals and socialists alike, was followed by dramatic attempts by ambitious men of varying degrees of commitments to democratic means to use the state to defeat the fatal conflicts to which a socioeconomy left to regulate itself was seen as inevitably prone. Increasingly the presumption was in favor of sweeping political control. The first of such believers to take power was Benito Mussolini (1883–1945). A man thoroughly familiar with the intricacies of socialism, for which he had written vivid propaganda, he had lived for various stretches in Switzerland, Austria, and Italy prior to World War I, including in one of the Italy's prison cells for five months. After fighting in the war, he became a rising leader on the socialist left before his acolytes in his National Fascist Party broke a general strike in July and August 1922 by manning public services and then, in response to public acclaim, seizing power.

The word *fascist* comes from the Latin *fascis* (modern Italian *fasces*), a collection of wooden rods tied together. In Roman times, this collection was used as a symbol of authority. That Mussolini chose this name for his party is informative.[19] By 1922, the cornerstone of his political philosophy, which was receiving growing support throughout the Western world, was that liberal democracy had failed, a victim of endless squabbling among social groups and the parties that claimed to represent them. It was the job of a fascist party to monopolize power to overcome these differences, which in the absence of violence are actually fundamental to a self-regulating socioeconomic order, not by annihilating these groups but by arbitrating among them. (Note the difference of Mussolini's fascism from the path to progress in Lenin's Soviet Union, Mao's China, and other communist regimes in other places, where annihilation was often the preferred tactic.) Mussolini, while no wallflower when it came to cracking heads in the name of the revolution, lacked Hitler's genocidal beliefs. Nonetheless, with regard to social order, Hitler too believed that the function of the state was to impose order on an inherently and destructively disorderly bourgeois world. In both countries, disagreements between, for example, labor and management, business and consumers, and farm and city were failures that the right kind of governance could overcome. And what was that right kind of governance? Corporatism, which means that all interest groups should come together, state their goals and concerns, and have the state play mediator or arbitrator. (The word *corporate* comes from the Latin word for "body," *corpus*, and like *corporation* denotes distinct agents being treated as a collective.)

American Progressivism

As Italy's economy seemed to boom in the 1920s and Germany's in the early 1930s, the idea of the state in its wisdom organizing these squabbling groups into a whole greater than the sum of the parts had growing appeal in United States as well. Faith in the self-regulating order had already taken a number of blows. In the 1870s and 1880s, as in Europe, the belief that business looked out for a collective "itself" at the expense of the rest of society was far from rare. In the United States, the breathtaking scale of many of the new corporations turned the argument first in the direction of concern about fairness rather than about intrinsic flaws in the market itself. The suddenly ascended president Theodore Roosevelt (1858–1919, president 1901–1909) in his first message to Congress in December 1901 accepted as uncontroversial that the fortunes of many of the new industrial magnates were due to the "condition of conferring immense incidental benefits upon others. Successful enterprise, of the type which benefits all mankind, can only exist if the conditions are such as to offer great prizes as the rewards of success." Antitrust action was to be reserved only for truly excessive concentrations of production. He used the 1890 Sherman Antitrust Act to break up "powerful" firms such as John D. Rockefeller's (1839–1937) Standard Oil and J. P. Morgan's Northern Securities Company, a northwestern railroad trust.[20] But it took Woodrow Wilson (1856–1924, president 1913–1921), the only president to have possessed a Ph.D., and in the increasingly social engineering–oriented discipline of political science at that, to act on the belief that the state should not just cut extremely large companies down to size but should generally substitute its own judgment for that of the market's damaging self-regulation.

Wilson viewed the president as the only available incarnation of the national will. In his writings before entering politics, he criticized the fragmentation of power intrinsic to the American constitutional system. He preferred a parliamentary system, and, given the constraints of American checks and balances, he wanted the president, as the only public official representing the entire nation, "to be as big a man as he can."[21] It was the abstract state, not concrete individuals undirected, that should evolve by taking on more authority to meet the changing needs of the nation. He was the very representative of the Progressive movement, an American term for diagnosing problems as being of a national magnitude and of using the state to address them. (He, like many contemporary progressives, supported American colonization of lands like the Philippines that were inhabited by "children" so as to drag them in the direction of progress.[22]) Upon becoming president, he inaugurated a sort of cult of experts—people with advanced degrees who could diagnose and act on whatever national-scale problems they discovered. To this day, presidential administrations and indeed congressional legislation are, respectively, substantially run and written on this principle of politics solving problems (and often actually looking for problems to solve) rather than the principle of adherence to principle itself. This is why people running for president are often asked what their "plan" for resolving this or that contemporary problem is.

To regulate the economy more aggressively, Wilson signed legislation creating the Federal Trade Commission and the National Farm Loan Association and authorizing more aggressive antitrust enforcement—the Clayton Antitrust Act, the 1914 successor to the insufficiently powerful Sherman act.[23] The Federal Reserve Board was established in 1913 to control both the financial system and macroeconomic instability. A constitutional amendment authorizing the income tax, which had had a brief existence in the 1860s, only to be declared unconstitutional, was adopted by the states in 1913, and the first 1040 form followed shortly after.

To Wilson's credit, he managed to avoid entry into World War I for a time even after the sinking of the *Lusitania* in 1915, but in his second term, the United States did enter the war, and the extent of political regulation of the socioeconomic order increased significantly. The Food and Fuel Control Act of 1917, its very name reflecting the ideological shift, gave the executive branch the power to control pricing and distribution for any activities judged to affect the public interest. It was designed to expire after the war ended, but in 1919, Wilson got it extended before its most onerous provisions were either repealed after he left office or were declared unconstitutional by the Supreme Court.

The federal government during this time even encroached on self-regulating speech through the implementation of the Espionage Act as amended in 1918, which declared that certain forms of communication were a threat to the war effort, and the Committee on Public Information, which published propaganda to correct what the administration saw as the more objectionable results of unfettered public conversation. Overall, analysis of discourse in presidential State of the Union speeches suggests that 1917 was a decisive moment for the legitimization of substantial political regulation, at least at the presidential level.[24]

Much of the Progressive agenda was similar to the planning and harmonization that was the core of Mussolini's economics. But unlike on the Continent, after the war, the fever broke under Presidents Harding and Coolidge and the United States stepped back from this planned paradise. Despite the fears of the economic disruption that would emerge when hundreds of thousands of soldiers returned from Europe with no work and a sharp depression in part necessitated by the need to adjust to the end of Wilsonian controls, the 1920s was a decade not of senseless speculative boom but of the thorough, if uncertain, integration of usefully disruptive technologies such as electric power, the private automobile, and radio. But the decade famously ended with the economic crash of October 1929, followed by what quickly became the worst economic contraction in modern world history. In the eyes of the American people, doing nothing would not do.

Politically Regulating the Depression Away

The U.S. stock market collapse of late 1929 was perhaps symptom as much as cause of economic imbalances, but either way, it was followed by an epidemic of bank failures and a soaring rate of business failure and unemployment, exacerbated by the Smoot-Hawley tariff increase of 1930. This kind of macroeconomic event, which is perhaps best thought of not as a result of neglected political regulation but as necessary housecleaning after an unexpected innovation-driven economic boom, has a long historical record.[25] But the frequency and severity of such crashes in particular seemed to accelerate with the general social upheaval of industrialization in the later nineteenth century. (The same kind of instability has been generated by the last four decades of telecommunications-technology improvement.) The 1873 depression was unusually severe in both North America and Europe, and the crash immediately after World War I was the last such episode for which the president of the United States (Warren G. Harding, 1865–1923, president 1921–1923) was able to resist what was by now massive public pressure to "do something" about the "business cycle." This misnamed term, which implies a nonexistent regularity to economic change, tellingly makes its first continuous appearance as an nGram in the English-language corpus in 1897.[26] Between the Civil War and 1929, the belief took hold among many intellectuals, including many economists, in the United States that "the economy" was not a self-regulating system but a complicated machine that could break down at any time; it thus required continual supervision and repair, in the manner of a car engine. The antitrust laws and the establishment of the Federal Reserve were symptoms of this belief, as were Wilson's wartime serial interventions, which he saw as the precursor to permanent features of American life. Within only a few years after the 1929 crash, the American public, seeing the economic collapse around them, shared this view.

Contrary to conventional understanding, Herbert Hoover (1874–1964, president 1929–1933)had not adopted a hands-off response to the Depression that was rejected by the electorate in 1932 in favor of an activist Franklin Roosevelt (1881–1945, president 1933–1945). In fact, Hoover (trained as an engineer, i.e., someone whose job was to rearrange matter in specific ways to solve problems) was active in trying to use the power he had as president. He successfully persuaded business executives he personally knew to maintain wages and prices and spending in spite of self-regulating feedback to lower them, asked labor leaders not to ask for increased wages, agreed to legislation substantially expanding (admittedly from a small base) federal public works spending, and signed the 1930 tariff.[27]

And yet the situation worsened. When Franklin Roosevelt was inaugurated in 1933, his "brain trust" (suggestive wording in that it indicates that what was needed were smart people to direct the resolution of the crisis) included people who were influenced by both Wilson's experiments and the Soviet experience since 1917, the latter described in Chapter 7. The number of government regulatory commissions, which had already grown under Theodore Roosevelt and Woodrow Wilson, mushroomed, as did the scope of their authority.

The most dramatic of these initiatives was the National Recovery Agency, which was created in 1933 and gave the government sweeping authority to regulate pricing and output (despite the economic impossibility of specifying both at once) in a wide variety of industries through negotiation between labor and management. Some research indicates that it actually worsened the Depression, until it was declared unconstitutional in 1935.[28] By being granted exemption from antitrust laws, organized labor was vested with rights to collude previously denied it. In a manner reminiscent of Mussolini's economics, federal machinery was then set up to mediate disputes between these unions and management.

This legal structure was trimmed back between 1936 and 1950, but the most important legacy of the political regulation apparatus remains: the administrative state. Cabinet departments have long been authorized to issue rules interpreting federal legislation, but it was the creation of the Interstate Commerce Commission in 1887 that launched the independent *regulatory* agency, designed to correct the malfunctions (later seen as the rule and not the exception) of the self-regulating socioeconomy. Staffed by members of the "civil service," a term enabling contrast with government workers subject to being replaced after the next election, whose independence from the political authorities was gradually strengthened starting in the late nineteenth century, agencies such as the Securities and Exchange Commission and Environmental Protection Agency live forever unless explicitly repealed (which very occasionally happens). These "servants" have authority that is better characterized as only limited ad hoc and post hoc rather than affirmatively and explicitly authorized by congressional legislation.

Over time, these agencies have become the main source of socioeconomic political regulation. The number of individual, self-regulating activities that have come under their purview, whether because they have seized that authority or because Congress has given it to them, has grown dramatically. The growth of arguably more corrupt (because of the direct interest politicians have in reelection) direct legislative control has also been substantial, with the length of tax law itself now standing at perhaps 2,600 pages.[29] These two indexes in particular proxy for the growing extent of political regulation of otherwise self-regulating activity. Similar patterns occurred in European countries and Canada, and this structure of political regulation is now growing rapidly at the transnational level in the form of the European Union.

Roosevelt, like the fascists and communists who ruled contemporaneously with him, was quite skilled at using the new mass media to try to persuade the public to see things his way. Roosevelt himself was neither fascist, communist, nor totalitarian. But his view of politics as a correction to failed self-regulation was that of the times.

Radio was a new, distinct kind of communications technology that could easily facilitate one-way government-to-citizen expression as a replacement of two-way, self-regulating communication. The new so-called mass media enabled the instructively named broadcast of a single message to many simultaneously. In principle, it is possible to have many radio or television stations, but it is easy for a national government to dominate this technology. Even in a liberal democracy such as the United States, skilled leaders can dominate it if they play their cards right, as Roosevelt certainly did with his fireside chats and as Ronald Reagan did later with his first-term televised addresses to ask voters to call Congress and demand support of his 1981 tax cuts.

Radio and television are unlike their predecessor, the telegraph, and their much more powerful successor, the Internet. These technologies allow people to communicate both one-to-one and in both directions, which facilitates the generation of the new ideas that are key to self-regulating expression. Thus, it is not surprising that broadcast media were state monopolies in the planned societies of both the communist and fascist stripes. Even now, totalitarian societies exercise vigorous control over the much more dangerous Internet.

Postwar Control of the Excess of Self-Regulation

In 1945 the election manifesto of the Labour Party of Britain, with Clement Attlee at its head, included the following:

But if the slumps in uncontrolled private industry are too severe to be balanced by public action—as they will certainly prove to be—our opponents are not ready to draw the conclusion that the sphere of public action must be extended.

They say, "Full employment. Yes! If we can get it without interfering too much with private industry." We say, "Full employment in any case, and if we need to keep a firm public hand on industry in order to get jobs for all, very well. No more dole queues, in order to let the Czars of Big Business remain kings in their own castles. The price of so-called "economic freedom" for the few is too high if it is bought at the cost of idleness and misery for millions."

What will the Labour Party do?

First, the whole of the national resources, in land, material and labour must be fully employed. Production must be raised to the highest level and related to purchasing power. Over-production is not the cause of depression and unemployment; it is under-consumption that is responsible. It is doubtful whether we have ever, except in war, used the whole of our productive capacity. This must be corrected because, upon our ability to produce and organise a fair and generous distribution of the product, the standard of living of our people depends.

Secondly, a high and constant purchasing power can be maintained through good wages, social services and insurance, and taxation which bears less heavily on the lower income groups. But everybody knows that money and savings lose their value if prices rise so rents and the prices of the necessities of life will be controlled.

Thirdly, planned investment in essential industries and on houses, schools, hospitals and civic centres will occupy a large field of capital expenditure. A National Investment Board will determine social priorities and promote better timing in private investment. In suitable cases we would transfer the use of efficient Government factories from war production to meet the needs of peace. The location of new factories will be suitably controlled and where necessary the Government will itself build factories. There must be no depressed areas in the New Britain.

Fourthly, the Bank of England with its financial powers must be brought under public ownership, and the operations of the other banks harmonised with industrial needs.

By these and other means full employment can be achieved.

Britain needs an industry organised to enable it to yield the best that human knowledge and skill can provide. Only so can our people reap the full benefits of this age of discovery and Britain keep her place as a Great Power.

The Labour Party intends to link the skill of British craftsmen and designers to the skill of British scientists in the service of our fellow men. The genius of British scientists and technicians who have produced radio-location, jet propulsion, penicillin, and the Mulberry Harbours [temporary harbor equipment developed by the British for D-Day] in wartime, must be given full rein in peacetime too.

Each industry must have applied to it the test of national service. If it serves the nation, well and good; if it is inefficient and falls down on its job, the nation must see that things are put right.

. . .

The Labour Party is a Socialist Party, and proud of it. Its ultimate purpose at home is the establishment of the Socialist Commonwealth of Great Britain—free, democratic, efficient, progressive, public-spirited, its material resources organised in the service of the British people.

But Socialism cannot come overnight, as the product of a week-end revolution. The members of the Labour Party, like the British people, are practical-minded men and women.

There are basic industries ripe and over-ripe for public ownership and management in the direct service of the nation. There are many smaller businesses rendering good service which can be left to go on with their useful work.

There are big industries not yet ripe for public ownership which must nevertheless be required by constructive supervision to further the nation's needs and not to prejudice national interests by restrictive anti-social monopoly or cartel agreements—caring for their own capital structures and profits at the cost of a lower standard of living for all.

In the light of these considerations, the Labour Party submits to the nation the following industrial programme:

1   Public ownership of the fuel and power industries. For a quarter of a century the coal industry, producing Britain's most precious national raw material, has been floundering chaotically under the ownership of many hundreds of independent companies. Amalgamation under public ownership will bring great economies in operation and make it possible to modernise production methods and to raise safety standards in every colliery in the country. Public ownership of gas and electricity undertakings will lower charges, prevent competitive waste, open the way for co-ordinated research and development, and lead to the reforming of uneconomic areas of distribution. Other industries will benefit.

2   Public ownership of inland transport. Co-ordination of transport services by rail, road, air and canal cannot be achieved without unification. And unification without public ownership means a steady struggle with sectional inter-

ests or the enthronement of a private monopoly, which would be a menace to the rest of industry.

3   Public ownership of iron and steel. Private monopoly has maintained high prices and kept inefficient high-cost plants in existence. Only if public ownership replaces private monopoly can the industry become efficient.

4   These socialised industries, taken over on a basis of fair compensation, to be conducted efficiently in the interests of consumers, coupled with proper status and conditions for the workers employed in them.

5   Public supervision of monopolies and cartels with the aim of advancing industrial efficiency in the service of the nation. Anti-social restrictive practices will be prohibited.

6   A firm and clear-cut programme for the export trade. We would give State help in any necessary form to get our export trade on its feet and enable it to pay for the food and raw materials without which Britain must decay and die. But State help on conditions—conditions that industry is efficient and go-ahead. Laggards and obstructionists must be led or directed into better ways. Here we dare not fail.

7   The shaping of suitable economic and price controls to secure that first things shall come first in the transition from war to peace and that every citizen (including the demobilised Service men and women) shall get fair play. There must be priorities in the use of raw materials, food prices must be held, homes for the people for all before luxuries for the few. We do not want a short boom followed by collapse as after the last war; we do not want a wild rise in prices and inflation, followed by a smash and widespread unemployment. It is either sound economic controls—or smash.

In the interests of agriculture, housing and town and country planning alike, we declare for a radical solution for the crippling problems of land acquisition and use in the service of the national plan.

. . .

And the effective choice of the people in this Election will be between the Conservative Party, standing for the protection of the rights of private economic interest, and the Labour Party, allied with the great Trade Union and co-operative movements, standing for the wise organisation and use of the economic assets of the nation for the public good. Those are the two main parties; and here is the fundamental issue which has to be settled.

Similar efforts occurred in Europe and its newly independent former colonies. The overturning of the presumption of socioeconomic self-regulation was complete. Planning by national governments using data, laws, and regulations nourished by them and shrewd political appeals was essential to the genuine achievement of the "national" interest. In Britain as in the rest of the West to varying degrees, state regimentation of social order increased. While it never reached the extent of Fascist Italy or the level achieved by communist parties that obtained political power, parties of the democratic left *wanted* to plan. So persuasive were the combined moral and theoretical objections to a self-regulating socioeconomy that by the early twentieth century, it already heavily influenced anticolonial resistance in China, India, and elsewhere. That many of these advocates had learned these arguments after studying in a West grown modern on self-regulation yet more and more hostile to it was a special irony. Many colonial resistance groups saw the wisdom of self-regulating communication and used it without irony or regret to debate in print and in person how, and how much, to eliminate broader self-regulating forces in their societies. (Upon taking power after independence in former colonies, many of these independence advocates would largely eliminate rights to free communication.)

In Britain this lasted until 1979, when public dissatisfaction with growing social chaos led to a Conservative government, which, among other reforms, significantly privatized state industry and diminished the power organized labor had under legal privileges previously given to them to stifle production. Countries such as Sweden that had been most willing to substitute state planning for self-regulating order subsequently engaged in the most dramatic reforms.

Currently the countries of northwest Europe, while characterized by high marginal rates of taxation on the highest incomes and substantially government-directed provision of services such as health care and retirement benefits, now have very lightly regulated markets for labor and business creation. Meanwhile, the communist example, having failed so spectacularly amid the unparalleled, industrialized human suffering it generated, now inspires few. Nonetheless, the extent of public confidence in the principle that individuals under competition generally choose best from the point of view of the entire society is not held nearly as widely in the countries that made the most of it by achieving the great escape from poverty that occurred in the nineteenth and twentieth centuries. While the "immorality" of competition drove much of the opposition prior to and immediately after the war, doubts about the very foundations of self-regulating order are sometimes at least as responsible for such skepticism now. We next turn to these beliefs.

CHAPTER 7

Rebuilding

Systemic Changes to Counter Self-Regulation's Flaws

> God works through the State in carrying out His purposes more
> universally than through any other institution.[1]
>
> RICHARD T. ELY (1854–1943)

By the late nineteenth century, after a period of confidence in the discovered principle of socioeconomic self-regulation, its strength was increasingly doubted. Initially this doubt took the form of using politics to adjust the socioeconomy in a more favorable direction. But by the dawn of the twentieth century, the society sculpted by self-regulating forces had come to be doubted in a more fundamental way, which required rebuilding it.

The objections had the common feature that people, as the experimenters and evaluators at the heart of all self-regulating processes, were inadequate to these tasks. Throughout the rise of self-regulating thinking, many had thought that as long as the state truly reflected the general view or even the majority interest (neither of which it should be assumed to do), then it could, as needed, justifiably supersede the individual plans made by various socioeconomic agents. But the argument that people should not always be allowed to act on behalf of their individual interest now became that they *cannot* do so. This can happen, thinkers of the last century and a half have assured us, because they are helpless driftwood cast about by the social tides, mere atoms subject to the scientific laws governing not individuals themselves but the society composed of them. Alternatively, their cognitive capacities are simply not up to the task. Under either of these conditions, a Kantian moral agent capable of acting on his interests is a myth, and building a society around such a myth is a mistake, if not a crime.

DETERMINISM: HOW HISTORY IS NOT MADE

Lamentably if predictably, people—especially people of the first school, who saw history as the sweep of grand social forces and not the results of individual decisions—now argued that the state, if placed in the hands of the right people, could overcome these intrinsic weaknesses and forcibly rebuild society for the better. One of the earliest, most influential, and certainly most notorious examples of this kind of thinking was published in 1867 under the innocuous-sounding title (translated into English) of *Capital: Critique of Political Economy*.

Marxist Determinism

Karl Marx and Friedrich Engels (1820–1895) were both born in post-Napoleonic Prussia at a time when belief in self-regulating economic liberalism was ascending throughout Europe. In their youth, they witnessed the spread and growth of industrial society, and the rise of the associated social instability, including the tumultuous events of 1848. As young men in the late 1830s, they became enamored of Hegel, Marx at the University of Berlin and Engels while working joylessly as an unpaid clerk at a Manchester cotton mill owned by his father. Marx and Engels did not meet until 1844 in Paris, although while working at a radical newspaper in Paris, Marx first came to admire Engels's writings on the working conditions in Manchester factories.

The two nineteenth-century men would go on to lay the intellectual foundation for changing the history of the twentieth century. While *Kapital* (published by Marx alone in 1868) is the more intellectually heavyweight work, the *Manifesto of the Communist Party* (written by the pair, published in 1848 and translated into English in 1852) is where the communist "inevitablist" conception of history was introduced. World history, Marx and Engels said, is a sequence of struggles among social classes. Now, with breakneck industrialization monetizing all previous tradition-bound social relationships, the final class struggle between workers and the bourgeoisie or capitalists was at hand. (In German, they used both *bourgeoisie*, borrowed from the French, and *Kapitalisten*.) The class struggle between those two groups had largely made national borders and distinct social roles for men and women obsolete. And modern social norms concerning justice, property, and family were not moral progress but merely the product of the needs of modern industrial production. History is not the outcome of heroism, any struggle between good and evil, or critical decisions made and not made. Rather, according to the manifesto's opening:

The history of all hitherto existing society is the history of class struggles.

Freeman and slave, patrician and plebeian, lord and serf, guild-master and journeyman, in a word, oppressor and oppressed, stood in constant opposition to one another, carried on an uninterrupted, now hidden, now open fight, a fight that each time ended, either in a revolutionary reconstitution of society at large, or in the common ruin of the contending classes.[2]

A more dramatic exposition of individual irrelevance is found in Marx's very brief preface to *Contribution to the Critique of Political Economy*:

In the social production of their life which men carry on they enter into definite relations that are indispensable and *independent of their will*; these relations of production correspond to a definite stage of development of their material powers of production. The sum total of these relations of production constitutes the economic structure of society—the real foundation, on which rise legal and political superstructures and to which correspond definite forms of social consciousness. The mode of production in material life determines the general character of the social, political and spiritual processes of life. It is not the consciousness of man that determines their being, but, on the contrary, their social being that determines their consciousness.[3]

Human society thus moves along a track propelled by the changing terms of class struggle, which will culminate in the last stage: the replacement of highly complex but antagonistic collective production with cooperative worker direction of same. In *Kapital* Marx stipulated that "capitalists" are mechanistically driven to accumulate "capital" not so much to spend on themselves as for its own mindless sake, and in the course of this relentless and endless accumulation, they take advantage of competition among endless numbers of perfectly substitutable workers to keep wages at the subsistence level. Only near the end (which, in Marx's and Engels', view, was imminent) would tensions reach the critical level, so that antagonistic class struggles could be forever banished by communism—an end of history reminiscent of Hegel's Absolute.

This was history as putative science—as predictable as the orbits of the planets. But unlike actual scientists guided by the scientific method, there was neither a desire nor the ability among the partisans of the new historical "science" to conduct any controlled experiments. And contrary to Marx and Engels's analysis, communist revolutions did not take place in the most industrially advanced countries, although revolution was attempted in post–World War I Germany. When they happened, it was in largely agricultural societies such as Russia, China, Cuba, and Vietnam. (In modestly industrialized postwar Central Europe, communism was imposed by the force of Soviet arms.) And in communist societies in practice, there was not, as Engels predicted, a withering away of the state but an almost immediate need to establish totalitarian control over all social processes.

The deterministic argument may have been inspired by the ideas of biological evolution, which were in the air even before the publication of *On the Origin of Species* in 1859. But biological speciation is a process that is both unguided and devoid of ethical content; biological evolution simply happens. Human society, of course, is, in the Marx/Engels conception, as in the twentieth-century progressive one, also subject in the broadest sense to an evolutionary track. The Marx/Engels vision was an even more deterministic one: individuals do not choose; they merely play their part in the scripted historical drama.

It would be excessive to say that Marx and Engels absolutely rejected the idea of individual agency. Marx granted that some individuals are bolder than others—Napoleon Bonaparte versus Louis Napoleon, to take his most devastatingly satirical example.[4] But the most any individual can hope to be is the lever that brings about a particular historical transformation at the appropriate time, when the tension in the old production relations has reached full flower, rather than someone who can change history himself. The individual plays no historical role outside these relations, and even then, he is specified entirely by his place in the class structure. That he could better himself or possessed much control over his life was at best an irrelevant claim and at worst a false distraction from what had to be done. Indeed, contra the beliefs that motivated earlier individual efforts to help the individual poor, individuals in the new materialist history could not actually perfect themselves; it was only at the level of society that such improvement was meaningful.

Communism in Action

Soon enough, the 1917 Bolshevik Revolution was fought in the name of this "science." The new leadership, having seized power from a collapsing primitive democracy, now wanted to structure society to the last detail. Vladimir Lenin (1870–1924) had been an excellent student in school, and later he was an intellectual and polemicist, as had been Leon Trotsky (1879–1940). (Joseph Stalin, 1878–1953, was neither.) With the financial backing of the kaiser's wartime Germany, Lenin took a train from Switzerland to St. Petersburg after the overthrow of Nicholas II (1868–1918) in February 1917.

In November of that year, Lenin and his close underlings took advantage of the chaos caused by the ongoing collapse of the Russian army, radicalization of the urban workforce, and growing food shortages. They seized power on October 24–25. (Lenin actually took a routine municipal train to the revolution, in particular to the decisive meeting of workers' councils where the coup took place.) On his second day of what soon became absolute power, Lenin ordered the closing of the free, self-regulating (or as the communist revolutionaries were now wont to call it, "bourgeois") press. Several years of civil war followed, which, along with the new Soviet agricultural planning and Lenin's terror, caused a famine that killed over 1 million people. In desperation, Lenin retreated and allowed peasants and the still extant small business owners some freedom to sell in the market during the New Economic Policy of the early 1920s. But even before he suffered a debilitating stroke in March 1923, it was clear he thought of this as a temporary expedient.

Following Lenin's death, Stalin constructed the first essentially completely politically regulated socioeconomy in modern history—the first totalitarian society. In 1928 the Soviet bureaucracy created its first Five-Year Plan, which specified what would be made and where, even if new cities had to be built to accommodate it and the cities' residents forcibly brought in. Housing too became entirely a planned enterprise, as it was until the end of the Soviet Union. Due to the usual foibles of economic planning without the knowledge that businesses and customers possess about "the particular circumstances of time and place,"[5] what was planned and what happened were dramatically different. It was in the nature of both Lenin and Stalin to see in the failure of their plans nothing but sabotage driven by classes that were being swept away by history. They were indifferent to, if not gleeful about, the imposed terror and starvation that accompanied their democidal facilitation of historical inevitability, the slaughter itself a response by those who think they know everything and are first surprised by and then contemptuous of others who know differently. Nonetheless, by the late 1930s, Stalin had overseen the complete collectivization of agriculture and massive construction of heavy-industry facilities.

After the desperate struggle against Hitler and especially after Stalin's death, the brutality declined (although the worst of it was yet to come in China, Cambodia, and elsewhere), but the political planning of the socio-economy remained. The power, always forcibly seized—no nation has ever voluntarily elected a government of the completely controlling communist sort—was always deployed in the belief that a self-regulating society was fundamentally exploitive and inimical to human progress. Only state (i.e., Communist Party) planning could move the abstract entity of society forward. Planning even extended to individuals, who, under the guidance of the party, had to be directed away from the bestial instincts that capitalism had bequeathed them—a reconstruction to be achieved not through self-regulating competition among ideas but by party directive. From the Soviet Union to China to Cuba, Communist regimes sought to use, as needed, propaganda, the school curriculum, and labor camps to teach the citizens to love the working class and its representatives in the party and to emulate model citizens who worked beyond the call of duty and produced the ideal children needed to build the future.[6] People were being trained, in other words, to abandon the agency that powered the self-regulating socioeconomy.

The Residue of Marxist Determinism

Marx's economics and class struggle conception of history are now largely spent forces, but his materialist explanation of social structure and claim that individual ideology is simply a product of class structure remains. His legacy among intellectuals is ironically now found almost entirely outside economics. For example, Marxist literary criticism would have us accept the novel—in reality, an artistic breakthrough with regard to the ability of readers to identify with the other (in the form of the novel's characters) as people with the same dreams, problems, and rights as themselves—as merely an unconscious manifestation of class conflict or economic determinism. Stories about heroes and villains or tragedies and triumphs are the product not of individual creative genius but of socioeconomic forces. In this way of thinking, the Renaissance conception of genius as the essential ingredient of artistic progress was undone.

Sociology in turn developed concepts such as "world systems analysis," in which human civilization in its entirety is the result of the interplay of global-scale productive forces, with struggle instead of cooperation, among groups and not individuals.[7] Here, language and culture too are now deterministic in a negative limiting sense. Michel Foucault (1926–1984) diagnosed "discourse" as supraconscious—collectively and therefore mysteriously imposed by the abstract ruling classes rather than consciously chosen by individual agents. It was a way to fence off discussion of what is not permitted by the current power structure and therefore to limit individual choice by erasing from individuals' minds some of what they might choose.[8]

The vast postcolonial literature launched by Edward Said (1935–2003) described the imposition of entire mental frameworks not by individual propagandists but by the abstraction of power, in particular by dominant Western cultures on weak colonized ones.[9] This strain of work has collectively had an astonishing influence on intellectuals worldwide, with its potential to delegitimize any beliefs held by non-Westerners if the beliefs are Western in origin. In postcolonial thinking, to be, say, a Millsian liberal in Egypt or a Burkean conservative in India is no longer to have weighed the evidence and reached a conclusion, but to have been assimilated by an alien mode of thought and, perforce, to be disloyal to the only legitimate way of understanding one's nation (recently formed though it sometimes was) and history, the anticolonial one. Even the cultural works—essays, film, education curricula—of the dominant Western culture are produced by a Newtonian culture machine, whose operating principle is not individual creativity but supporting the current arrangement of rulers and ruled. To be sure, arguments that technological progress relentlessly drives social organization and laws are common. But where do the machines with these powers come from? Are they creations that magically appear from time to time, or is a self-regulating process required to generate them and to weed out the less useful ones? Of this, in postcolonial theorizing usually nothing is said.

By rendering individual choice impotent, such grand determinism makes individual liberty illusory and agency an idea with no particular dignity or importance. Instead, society is prone to crises of various sorts, driven by contradictions in the system or the machinations of "power." The solution is to rely on wiser experts to diagnose the illness and then prescribe the cure, often by reframing and then permitting only imposed "discourse" so as to remake people's thinking along better, designed lines, an idea incompatible with individual assessment of self or the world more generally.

Antonio Gramsci (1891–1937), an Italian Marxist who believed in the efficacy of individual activism, was a somewhat more restrained advocate of the idea of capturing the future by capturing the language; Lenin was a considerably more sinister one. Between the constraining of acceptable ways of thinking asserted by postmodern and postcolonial thinkers and the irrelevance of agency in "systems"-based analysis in determining an individual's life outcomes, determinism reduced society to a structure of collectives of rulers and ruled, and for believers gutted the idea that society even could, let alone should, self-organize. There was no invention, no creativity—only power, and which classes had it and which didn't.

The displacement of purpose-driven individuals with broad collectives and social forces as the movers of history was made manifest in ways that led to things difficult to conceive of in a self-regulating society. It led first in communist societies to reasoning that still resonates today: (1) people's will and consciousness are shaped by the environment; (2) the society that results is flawed; (3) it is thus necessary to remake its members in a new mold, creating an alternative type of human more in tune with a brighter future. Ironically, this tactic, so common in totalitarian regimes in the twentieth century, was a mutation of the thinking of several great Enlightenment liberals. In *An Essay Concerning Human Understanding*, Locke made his blank-slate analogy, arguing that the human mind is a product of its experiences. It thus followed that it could be shaped to a higher purpose rather than be a captive of a baser conception of self-interest, something advocated by Rousseau in *Emile: Or on Education* (1762) and Helvétius (1715–1771), who argued in his posthumously published) *A Treatise on Man: His Intellectual Faculties and His Education* (1772) that "the different interests of man render them good or bad, [and] the only way to form virtuous citizens, is to unite the interest of the individual with that of the public."[10] This Enlightenment conception of trainable man found its way into Jacobin ideology in Revolutionary France and into such pre-1917 Russian Revolutionary literature as Nikolai Gavrilovich Chernyshevsky's (1828–1889) *What Is to Be Done? The Story about the New Man* and Maxim Gorky's (1868–1936) *Mother: The Great Revolutionary Novel*. Both told of heroic revolutionaries who serve as examples of the new, better postbourgeois man; both works were said to have significantly influenced Lenin's building of the Soviet educational system.[11]

POLITICAL REGULATION MEETS THE SOCIAL ORGANISM

More ominous, according to Nikolas Rose, determinism led to the equating of whole societies—or, rather, of their closest available approximation, nations—with complex organisms subject to survival-of-the-fittest competition. Just like an individual body subject to contamination and deterioration, a society had to monitor its health and remove the influences that caused it to fall "ill."[12] While the scientifically built model of the human body had proved extremely useful—groups of cells forming tissues, tissues forming organs, and organs connected via flows of blood, other fluids, and oxygen—it was now very unfortunately extended to society itself. Society was a living thing, and like animals and plants, it functioned poorly if stricken by toxins. (Recall that this view of internal enemies had already increased with the development of the modern nation.)

At some level, this is a useful approach. Clean air and water and public health are all legitimate concerns, and perhaps it does not do much harm to view their maintenance as akin to controlling a microbial infection. But once society became an organism, the use of politics to improve the literal body politic, all too often by purging its toxins, became too attractive to resist. One such toxin was weaker breeds of humans.

The word *eugenics* was coined by Francis Galton (1822–1911), a true Renaissance man whose contributions span what are now the fields of statistics, detective work (he studied the classification of fingerprints), exploration (going to what is now Namibia after joining the National Geographic Society), and many other fields. He was also fascinated by the extent to which human traits were inheritable; it was he who coined the phrase "nature versus nurture." In 1883 he defined *eugenics* (literally "good birth") as

the science of improving stock, which is by no means confined to judicious mating, but which, especially in the case of man, takes cognisance of all influences that tend in however remote the degree to give the more suitable races or streams of blood a better chance of prevailing speedily over the less suitable than they otherwise would have had.[13]

And whereas the idea was derived from similar practices that farmers had long practiced on animals and plants, "improving stock" immediately took on the connotations of improving the overall character of society when it was applied to humans.

Certain people thus became undesirable not just because they had the wrong religion or because their cultural beliefs were so odd and so firmly held that they simply could not be assimilated (although both of these beliefs were far from unknown), but because they were intrinsically "lower quality" in the sense of a spindly pig. Many political attempts to improve the quality of the race, which could mean the nation as well as having its modern quasi-anthropological meaning, took the form of sticks rather than carrots. Approaches including mandatory sterilization, forced or strongly urged abortion, and segregation and immigration control were employed in countries all over the world from the early twentieth century through the 1970s, including the United States, Switzerland, the Scandinavian and Baltic countries, Germany, Turkey, and prerevolutionary Cuba.[14] Intellectuals in a wide variety of fields not directly linked to genetics or anthropology supported the movement. Note the contrast with William Graham Sumner, the opponent of political regulation of social processes. He too believed that individuals (*not* races) were divided by intelligence and discipline, but he thought that the way to achieve social improvement was to rely on competition to allow great men to rise and lesser men to sink. No social sterilizer he; the dangers of displacing self-regulation with political regulation have seldom been more vividly demonstrated.

In fact, to the extent that people were concerned about dysgenesis accruing from excessive indulgence of the less fit, it was largely believers in politically directed progress who saw not just individuals but lower nationalities and "races" (the initial attempt to rank such races was in vogue then) as bringing degenerative forces with them. At a time of unprecedentedly high immigration, this was for them a major public policy concern. The problem that political regulation was supposed to address more effectively was the declining genetic profile of the population, which self-regulation had generated. Among the self-termed socialists and progressives who advocated government *control*—sometimes coercively, sometimes merely through aggressive encouragement of contraception—of a nation's genetic capital were, in the United Kingdom, the Fabian socialist Sidney Webb (1859–1947), John Maynard Keynes (1883–1946), and George Bernard Shaw, who went so far as to advocate that the genetic elite meet to breed and then part forever rather than gamble society's future on random procreation through marriage. Shaw concluded, "There is now no reasonable excuse for refusing to face the fact that nothing but a eugenic religion can save our civilization from the fate that has overtaken all previous civilizations."[15]

Among the many public figures in the United States who included eugenic reasons for having the state control fertility were Woodrow Wilson (who had criticized Reconstruction in part because it eliminated the supervision of an inferior race by a superior one), Herbert Croly (1869–1930, founder of the progressive journal *The New Republic*), and Margaret Sanger (1879–1966, founder of Planned Parenthood).

In addition to the ordinary racism of much of the general public, eugenicists drew their support from the work of intellectuals. Here is Richard Ely, a socialist and one of the founders of the American Economic Association, and a man after whom a prestigious annual lecture at the association's meetings is still named, on this theme:

Let us next take up the degenerate classes, and ask whether any effort is being made to prevent their reproduction. Little has as yet been done, but in civilized society the subject has never before attracted so much attention, and never before probably has there as much been done as now to prevent their reproduction, while there is reason to believe that a great deal more is going to be done in the future.[16]

Ely's argument often took on a racist cast, as did those of other eugenicists:

Moreover, there are classes in every modern community composed of those who are virtually children, and who require paternal and fostering care, the aim of which should be the highest development of which they are capable. We may instance the negroes, who are for the most part grown-up children, and should be treated as such.[17]

Beyond Ely, other contemporaneously well-known intellectuals who supported eugenics included the economists John R. Commons (1862–1945), Henry Rogers Seager (1870–1930), and the sociologist Edward A. Ross (1866–1951).[18]

Commons feared free competition between superior races on the one hand and blacks and undesirable immigrants on the other, and he supported a minimum wage in part to price the latter groups out of the labor market. Seager was simultaneously an advocate of state-provided social insurance and politically regulating labor market competition. He filled out his vision of political regulation by averring that "if we are to maintain a race that is to be made up of capable, efficient and independent individuals and family groups we must courageously cut off lines of heredity that have proven to be undesirable by isolation or sterilization of the congenitally defective."[19]

Ross bemoaned "race suicide," a process through which lower races would come to the United States and outbreed higher ones, threatening their standard of living. While on the faculty at Stanford, he gave a speech in 1900 arguing vehemently against continued immigration from China and Japan, proposing that violence might be necessary to keep such undesirables out of the country. Shortly after, he lost his job; Leland Stanford's widow (her husband's bequest had founded the university) found these remarks intolerable after she had long criticized Ross's "socialist" inclinations and partisanship at the university generally. The incident proved important in the founding of the American Association of University Professors, which sought to defend freedom of communication on campus.[20] While the firing of Ross is often attributed to his broader views on the need for government to regulate society, it is seldom noted that the speech that got him fired involved a standard argument at the time of those who admired political regulation: politically improving society required filtering out the weak—in his case, the racially weak in particular.

No less a progressive luminary than Justice Oliver Wendell Holmes Jr., a fancier of social spontaneity when it came to expression but of democratic despotism otherwise, wrote the opinion in *Buck v. Bell* (1927), a case in which the Court upheld the sterilization mandated by the state of Virginia of a woman on grounds of society-threatening mental incompetence. The most notorious lines of the opinion are:

We have seen more than once that the public welfare may call upon the best citizens for their lives. It would be strange if it could not call upon those who already sap the strength of the State for these lesser sacrifices, often not felt to be such by those concerned, in order to prevent our being swamped with incompetence. It is better for all the world if, instead of waiting to execute degenerate offspring for crime or to let them starve for their imbecility, society can prevent those who are manifestly unfit from continuing their kind. The principle that sustains compulsory vaccination is broad enough to cover cutting the Fallopian tubes. Three generations of imbeciles are enough.[21]

The Court opinion, and the eugenics movement generally, were the product of beliefs that science could guide political regulation to improve society, thus replacing the results of the self-regulating order. It was based, in other words, on the idea that when it came to the fitness of the human race, society could not take care of itself through self-regulation. Some of the enthusiasm for state eugenic planning was based on explicitly racial considerations. Some of it manifested as the need to keep women at home raising children for the good of the workforce. On those grounds, eugenics was a big part of the attempts to politically regulate the labor market through women-only minimum-wage and maximum-hours laws, which priced them out of work that was considered properly men's. Such sex-specific efforts ended when the Supreme Court overturned one such law in *Adkins v. Children's Hospital* (1923), which held that it violated women's right to contract freely.[22]

In its entirety, eugenics was based on substituting the will of government experts and scientific results (for eugenics was, properly speaking, science) for the results of decisions taken by individuals. Genetic planning was like any other sort of social planning, reflecting a deep skepticism that society could tend to its own affairs. It was a new moral claim, a response to new scientific discoveries. But it was a bad idea, and fortunately the self-regulating tendencies of science and morality were sufficient (after over 20,000 mandatory sterilizations of the unfit in the United States in the 1930s[23]) to snuff it and its political manifestations out.

When it came to politically regulating the composition of the population, sometimes the concerns were ethnic, but sometimes they were class based. The more politically regulated society was, the more energetically and violently the population itself was managed. The Leninist Soviet Union and, later, Mao's China, Pol Pot's Khmer Rouge, and Castro's Cuba were all controlled by those who believed in the ability to create the new man through socialist education. Many also believed in the impossibility of retraining at least some of the hopelessly tainted bourgeoisie from l'ancien régime and had the firing squads to prove it. And this is not to mention National Socialist Germany's efforts against peoples who threatened because of their dysgenesis to lower the quality of the German nation, including its conquered territories.[24]

World War II ended most enthusiasm for state-directed eugenics in Western countries, although Swedish doctors persisted in sterilizing women, some on grounds of being sexually promiscuous or otherwise antisocial, until the 1970s. The need to limit the offspring of such people was explicitly emphasized as a reason for such actions.[25] Private efforts to improve the life prospects of one's own offspring through selective mating have long existed, and such cognitive assortative mating is, if anything, now more common in the United States, and presumably other advanced countries, due to the increasing tendency of the social elite to go to the same highly competitive schools and otherwise participate in the same social networks.[26] But such individually driven tendencies to fall in love with people from similar social tiers are obviously considerably less alarming than attempts by the state to issue edicts to improve society by exorcising its weaker elements.

State-directed eugenics is a trend that for now is in abeyance. Nevertheless, it is strikingly illustrative of the dangers that can occur when society, even in the pursuit of what might be seen to be the laudable goal of improving the mental and physical health of individuals, is politically regulated. In some circles, the goal has now moved beyond saving the human species from its constituent viruses and to view humanity itself as the virus that threatens its "host," the natural environment. Environmentalists often see human activity as damaging the earth and its ecosystems, which are themselves sometimes argued to be a single homeostatic system, analogous to a life form, but which human self-organization threatens to destroy. An example is the advocacy of avoiding all human activities that are not, in the vague language, "sustainable." (One might well ask, as a proper scientist would, how we would know sustainable and unsustainable processes when we saw them.[27]) When analysis of social phenomena is carried out in language that suggests society itself is a plastic organism, and in particular when specific, identifiable groups are seen as the enemy of the broader society, or of nature, nothing good can come of it. In this regard, perhaps recent attempts to treat violence as a public health problem should be viewed with alarm.[28]

FROM VERY BIG TO VERY SMALL

The self-regulating society was also vulnerable from the opposite perspective. While the above criticism talked of the individual as meaningless against the omnipotence of such grand forces as technological change, class conflict, and racial characteristics, another school of thought arose in the late nineteenth century. This one suggested that the fault lay not in the social cosmos, but within the mind itself. It held that society could not regulate itself because individuals could not make truly self-interested choices. To use "rational self-interest" as a basis for constructing a society where mistakes were corrected through feedback given proper social institutions, so that happiness and achievement were maximized, was a mistake because "rational" choice was frequently an illusion.

At least in terms of subsequent impact, the erosion of the link between the purposeful individual and the well-ordered society starts in a corpus that does not often find its way into discussions of political liberalism: that of Sigmund Freud (1856–1939). Freud's revolutionary ideas were ironically built on a bourgeois rationalist background. He was born the son of a wool merchant in what is now the Czech Republic. He initially studied under Theodor Meynert (1833–1892), a neuroscientist who advocated a materialist theory of cognition—in particular, that abnormal brain function caused psychiatric problems. It was later, in France, that Freud began to develop his quite different ideas about memory repression, psychological projection, and the role of the unconscious in decision making, which he presented most influentially in 1899 in *The Interpretation of Dreams*.[29] His details of how cognition comes to be formed (the mind's division into id, ego, and superego), like much Freudian theory, have been largely abandoned by the psychotherapeutic community. Nevertheless, the broad idea that motivations unknown to choosers determine their choices could not be less Kantian, yet largely remains. (Notice the similarity to Marx's legacy: the central conclusions of a major thinker can be rejected over time, but the assumptions that generated those conclusions can persevere.) The phrase "consciously choose" would have seemed redundant to Smith or Kant, but the adverb is often added now precisely because Freud and his successors made it possible to think about choices made not in a deliberative, rational way but under the unseen influence of unknown processes of the mind. Indeed, in a best-selling book that is critical of the recent medicalization of mental and emotional distress, *The Book of Woe: The DSM and the Unmaking of Psychiatry,* Gary Greenberg argues that the Freudian legacy, which many practicing clinical psychologists substantially subscribe to (if not to Freudian doctrines themselves), is the belief that "people might be unconsciously motivated to behave against their own best interests."[30]

It is critical to note here that if therapists argue they can help people decide what they should do and are able to help patients that way, this is the essence of self-regulation. If bureaucrats *tell* them what they *must* do, that is another matter. And so to be fair, Freud saw repressed memories and the influence of the unconscious on choice not as a factor in public policy but as a psychological condition to be treated with therapy precisely to enable patients to choose better. His work was thus not a denial of agency but an affirmation of it. If we accept that people can assess their interest and choose accordingly, the vast size of the contemporary psychotherapy industry, very little of it today centered on Freud's own specific theories, is testimony to the usefulness of this insight.[31] Freud was a product of liberal, self-regulating society, the liberation of Jews from ghetto life in Europe in particular, who because of his talents rose to become a world-changing figure. His work was dedicated to allowing patients to better understand their own behavior and therefore to choose a more fulfilling life.

But the seed of the idea that people choose poorly because of cognitive impairment, which would bear the fruit of the delegitimization of rational choice, had been planted. All kinds of socially irresponsible choices are made, the modern version has it, merely because people do not know how to think properly. They consume too much, they are selfish and insufficiently attentive to the general welfare, or they are prisoners of the general social environment, so they must be trained to think better. The argument is not just that their particular political views are reactionary but that they are impaired. Sometimes the flawed-cognition and the deterministic schools of denial of agency are combined. For example, in objecting, so far unsuccessfully, to the most recent version of the American Psychiatric Association's *Diagnostic and Statistical Manual of Mental Disorders* (DSM-5), the British Psychological Society argued that psychiatrists were mistaken to attribute the origin of mental distress "as located in individuals" while overlooking "the undeniable social causation of many such problems."[32]

The revolution that Freud launched incorporated the idea, familiar too from communist societies, that people could be sculpted as needed for the betterment of society. Behavioralist psychology, often attributed to Ivan Pavlov (1849–1936), John B. Watson (1878–1958), and B. F. Skinner (1904–1990), reduced human choice, the essence of any self-regulating system, to a mechanistic response to stimuli (following in a way both the materialist Spinoza and the blank slate of Locke). Watson took this claim of the mind as tabula rasa to one logical conclusion and claimed,

Give me a dozen healthy infants, well-formed, and my own specified world to bring them up in and I'll guarantee to take any one at random and train him to become any type of specialist I might select—doctor, lawyer, artist, merchant-chief and, yes, even beggar-man and thief, regardless of his talents, penchants, tendencies, abilities, vocations and the race of his ancestors.[33]

That human nature could and should be shaped by experts was damning enough to the idea of the self-regulating society. Parallel to this ran the idea that many of the choices people make are socially dysfunctional. The DSM, evolving from an attempt in 1917 to count varieties of "insane" people, began in 1952 to try to do for mental illness what had long been done at least informally for physiological illness: to describe and provide treatment options for people who were not functioning properly. That the first version, in 1952, was called *The Diagnostic and Statistical Manual: Mental Disorders* is revealing, because it assumes that "mental order" is the default, and presumably anytime there is cognitive "disorder," trained experts must restore order. (That word *order* again!) Just as has now long been the case for many who admire political regulation of the socioeconomy, in the mind itself, order is now often prized above all.

Table 7.1 lists the growth in the DSM over time.[34] From the initial to the current version, the number of pages and of diagnoses has grown substantially. There is nothing intrinsically wrong with this; if orthopedists diagnose new bone conditions that have long generated vague patient complaints and devise treatments for them, certainly this is medical progress. But there is a risk that as more and more of life's ordinary challenges and setbacks become medicalized, the free space for moral agency shrinks. To the extent that the medicalization of human choice blunts the useful contributions that individuals might otherwise make to self-regulating systems, it is worrisome. To be clear, this is not an argument against the idea of serious mental illness; we would not expect that, for example, people exposed to the horrors of war would always emerge from the experience psychologically unscathed. Nor is it a denial of the value of psychological therapy. But mental diagnoses have long been less reliable than other medical diagnoses, and they have been used to justify state control. For example, a diagnosis of "drapetomania," certainly outrageous if considered in the light of modern ethics, was created by Samuel A. Cartwright, a physician, to explain why a well-cared-for Southern plantation slave would do something as inexplicable as try to escape bondage.

There are other examples of the idea of erroneous thinking, with the sometimes implied and sometimes explicit corollary that rational assessment of either what the truth or one's self-interest is is impossible. Individual cognitive weakness is thus a problem that must be corrected for the benefit of the social organism. (As always, it was communist societies that here saw political regulation as imperative, with opposition to the communist authorities leading frequently to confinement in psychiatric

TABLE 7.1. *The DSM over time.*

Version	Publication Year	Pages	Number of Diagnoses
I	1952	130	128
II	1968	119	193
III	1980	494	228
IV	1994	886	383
V	2013	947	541

Source: Blashfield et al. (2014).

hospitals.) Another appallingly influential conception is the idea of false consciousness. The remark was originally made in a private letter by Engels, referring to Marx and Engels's belief that independent thought is a mirage, so that prevailing ideas are nothing but a product of the prevailing production environment. John T. Jost, in research claiming to find empirical evidence for its existence, defined it in this way:

A consciousness is "false" when it serves to perpetuate any quality by leading members of a subordinate group to believe that they are inferior, deserving of their plight, or incapable of taking action against the causes of their subordination. At the most general level, false consciousness refers to the "harboring of the false beliefs that sustain one's own oppression."[35]

In other words, if people I am trying to help reject that help or deny that they even need it, they need to be trained to think better. Note the similarity to communist educational practice.

This concept went on to play a critical role in both Marxist thinking and its totalitarian tools of personality adjustment in later decades, and it remains influential in other arenas of modern thinking, including feminist thought.[36] And so the idea that people might have different conceptions of "subordination" and its existence, let alone justice or moral conduct, is inadmissible—it is all merely defective thinking. So too then is the idea that people might (contentiously at times to be sure) reason together to better understand such matters. Undoubtedly at least part of the reason the idea of false consciousness took root among people of a socialist or communist disposition in Western countries was the unwillingness of many of the poor or working class, particularly in the United States and Canada, to play their scripted part in the Marxist historical drama. Living in societies of unprecedented opportunity by historical standards, many were unwilling to sign on to the complete direction of their societies via fascism and communism (although there were of course many exceptions, especially during the crisis-stricken 1930s).

The distance too is surely not so far between the claim of subconscious alienation that drove the earlier conception of false consciousness and, for example, the modern idea that the desire for material things is primarily the product of advertising and other deceptive persuasion by sellers of those material things rather than buyers' considered choices.

Advertisers, in other words, induce people to buy things they really wish they could be prevented from buying. Benjamin R. Barber has argued that humans are "manipulated into wanting and needing all kinds of things of which neither the body could have demanded nor the autonomous mind dreamed" and that "sales [of goods and services] depend less on autonomous choices by independent buyers than on the manipulated habits and shaped behavior of media-immersed consumers." Elsewhere he asserts that unregulated markets cause us merely to buy what we want now and fail to achieve what we "want to want"—a better society. The consumer culture that free markets generate is "infantilist," a "colonizing" force, and "addictive," not words that one would associate with agency or the ability of the socioeconomy to regulate itself.[37] The essayist Thomas Frank has rendered big business promotion of the consumption imperative as "the final triumph of the marketplace over humanity's unruly consciousness."[38]

Tim Kasser and colleagues in 2004 diagnosed a cognitive impairment they called "materialistic value orientation," which is both unhealthy for the individual and, more important from the perspective of the self-regulating society, socially damaging.[39] They summarized the research indicating that materialistic values orientation, if not rising to the level of a DSM diagnosis, is nonetheless a mental condition that hampers individuals' ability to be happy and causes them to turn away from serving society.[40] The term *oniomania*, also known as "compulsive buying disorder," frequently finds its way into the psychological literature, although it has been rejected for now for inclusion as a specific disorder in the DSM.

Certainly the Freudian echoes are clear enough in the distinction the linguist George Lakoff makes in his analysis of American political ideologies between the conservative "strict father" and the liberal "nurturant parent" worldviews. As he sees it, this difference means that conservatives prioritize "moral strength (the self-control and self-discipline to stand up to external and internal evils), respect for and obedience to authority, the setting and following of strict guidelines and behavioral norms, and so on." Liberals, in the modern American sense, believe that "moral nurturances require sympathy for others in the helping of those who need help. To help others, one must take care of oneself and nurture social ties."[41] The concern in such a view lies not in whether it is a scientifically useful description of how people come to have their political views; that is an empirical question, best left to cognitive psychologists and political scientists. But scientists are a pressure group like any other, with their own range of views about the proper extent to which society should self-regulate or be politically regulated. With a diagnosis of aberrant thought, the prescription of thought correction (in lieu of allowing self-regulating adjustment by the individual in conjunction with his socioeconomic trading partners as a way to address the problem) is tempting. For example, the risk-communication specialist Peter M. Sandman has advised governments on how to change the view of people who feel indifferent to global warming or dubious about their ability to do anything about it. He diagnoses this condition as "psychological denial," having "a strong cognitive or emotional need to avoid the issue or be on the other side."[42] Scientists frequently invoke "conspiracy theories," "denial," and other loaded language to characterize opposition to political efforts to control global warming, even when some of the questions they use to generate indexes of aberrant thinking do not measure this belief. For example, agreement with statements that the "seriousness of global warming is generally exaggerated in the media" and "[respondent] does not worry about global warming at all" is coded as "denial," even though these statements might include beliefs that humanity can, through self-regulation, accommodate such temperature changes as occur.[43] To be against a centralized, one-size-fits-all government response (given an eminently rational skepticism about the political process) in dealing with human-induced climate change is increasingly to be crazy, if (ominously) repairably so.

The most recent iteration of the claim that rational choice, hence, undirected yet well-regulated social adjustment, is a myth is the new cognitive materialism. It argues that science will soon reduce, or already has reduced, human choice to mere biochemistry—the result of an ultimately predictable sequence of chemical reactions in the brain, based on stimuli from the senses mediated by the nervous system.[44] As a general approach to the human mind, there is nothing new here; only the particulars differ. Cognition as mere material interaction can be traced at least to Spinoza in the West. But the new determinism invokes the authority of self-regulating science to argue not just that consistent anomalies in decision making can be traced to crossed wires in the brain, but that free will, and hence any ethically defensible conception of self-interest, is an illusion, the latter because what is good for the self is merely that which produces a particular response from neurons. The areas of scientific inquiry that have lent the most support to this view are cognitive psychology and behavioral economics, whose empirical results suggest that cognitive limitations mean that even given the information people have, they don't choose as well as they could. But this work is only one wing, and a much less sweeping one at that, of the cognitive-powerlessness revolution. And it, and the new materialism generally, are the continuation of a trend of thought, now over a century and a half old, that people cannot choose consistent with their true best interests.

Not all such scientists draw political implications from their findings. And when they do, they are sometimes anodyne, as in so-called libertarian paternalism. This is the idea that the choices people have, including with regard to their interaction with public programs, should be framed so that the choices they make will tend to be ones that they are subsequently glad they made.[45] But the test of whether such paternalism really improves things goes well beyond mere documentation of a cognitive misfire in a laboratory experiment. To work, the self-regulating socioeconomic process does not require that at all times people accurately assess their interest and act accordingly. Self-regulation is characterized not just by individual pursuit of interests, although for all the behavioral/cognitive hand-wringing that is surely the rule rather than the exception. (Think about how many decisions you make in a week are really plausibly not reasoned out in pursuit of your best interests as you see them.) It is also driven by competition. And the nature of economic competition is to better cater to agents' interests. It is thus not required that all sellers at any moment are able to provide to consumers what in hindsight serves them best. My university discovered that some faculty tend to postpone doing research, and in response it organized what it calls "writing boot camps." They typically last a week during the summer and require faculty who participate to meet several hours a day and write in the presence of the others. These sessions are a self-regulating way to help faculty overcome lack of focus or susceptibility to distraction so they can be more productive scholars. Such responses are common.

What matters in a cognitively constrained world is that many different experiments can be tried, and that at some point, consumers become less ignorant in this regard and agree to obtain (say, after explanation or observation) a retirement plan or other good whose benefits can be made clear despite whatever human cognitive limitations exist. These socio-economic experiments can be different framing or altered versions of the existing products—a different individual retirement plan, say—or entirely different ways of satisfying the same basic needs—a profession-based group retirement plan, paying for particular services in advance, or anything else entrepreneurs are clever enough to think of. As long as there are not government limits on entry (whether through taxation, regulation or subsidy, including subsidy of public provision), the self-regulating process can generate many options to be used by any number of agents, with any amount of precommitment, having any feasible danger/safety trade-off, and using any conceivable tactics to address buyers' cognitive frailties.

And so the trade-off must be explicitly stated. Today there are two broad "market failure" indictments of the efficacy of the self-regulating socioeconomy. The traditional ones, listed in Chapter 6, are rooted in the pursuit of self-interest properly understood; newer arguments are that the human mind is not up to the task of pursuing that interest. But it is important to avoid the fallacy of the false choice. We must decide not between a less-than-ideal self-regulating outcome and the white knight of the state, pristinely motivated, possessed of all the knowledge needed, and consisting of officials and politicians not subject to the same errors that plague the rest of us out in the self-regulating world. Instead, we must first acknowledge that regulation of an otherwise self-regulating system is done by people subject to the same cognitive flaws as the rest of us, but with much more power to limit choice and therefore experimentation. In addition, assume that information needed to make good decisions is costly to acquire, but considerably less so for on-the-scene participants motivated by at least an approximate grasp of self-interest. Then combine that with the undeniable fact that in a free socioeconomy, people's ability to experiment in meeting human purposes is limited only by the cost of doing so. The self-regulating society is then *still* superior.

The single political plan imposed to address some particular problem is likely to be vastly outperformed by the best solutions that socioeconomic experimenters can conceive. In other words, political regulation, with its unavoidable tunnel vision and need to foist a single solution on all of us, is not as flexible or creative as people competing and cooperating in a self-regulating socioeconomic system. The unexpected negative consequences of political decisions in this environment, and the invisible but nonetheless presumably substantial opportunity costs of self-regulated roads not taken, are almost never compared to the actual self-regulation outcome. Instead, the failures of political regulation call forth ever more regulation. That is a mistake. Most of the findings of the new behavioral economics are an argument for *more* competition, not for political limitation of it. The perfect is not the enemy of the good, but the worse *is* the enemy of the better.

CONCLUSION

It is important to be clear that the most catastrophic grounds for displacing self-regulation with political regulation based on this notion that "society" ought to be politically controlled have clearly been in retreat in recent decades. The Marxist theory that history proceeds inevitably and the totalitarian (including Marxist) practice of disposing of anyone who stands in the way of that are now both almost extinct, even in such nominally communist countries as China, Vietnam, or, increasingly, Cuba. (North Korea in its mad isolation is an exception.) But the question is whether the future will be as much superior to the present as it could be if there were more confidence in self-regulating processes. The evidence presented in the next chapter indicates that while naive faith in complete political regulation is seldom held, overall confidence in self-regulation in societies that have gotten the most out of it is nonetheless on the wane.

CHAPTER 8

Assessing the Decline of Confidence in Self-Regulation

"There is more than one kind of freedom," said Aunt Lydia.
"Freedom to and freedom from. In the days of anarchy, it was freedom to.
Now you are being given freedom from. Don't underrate it."
MARGARET ATWOOD (1998 [1985])

Chapters 6 and 7 presented some largely narrative evidence on the history of rejection of socioeconomic self-regulation. In this chapter, I provide more information on the changes in the ability and tendency of government to regulate otherwise self-regulating processes and then investigate how we now think about social progress. This analysis focuses first on the United States and then on the Anglosphere. I defer some speculation about what may be more promising trends in other parts of the world until the concluding chapter. The first section of this chapter investigates the economy as it is traditionally understood, and the second extends that exploration to science and freedom of communication.

THE CAPACITY TO POLITICALLY REGULATE AND ITS USE

The expansion in the U.S. federal government's capacity to regulate social activity is easy to establish. In 1789, the First U.S. Congress established four of what came to be known as cabinet departments. The country managed to survive merely with departments of State, War, Justice, and the Treasury until 1849, when the Department of the Interior was established to supervise the rapidly growing amount of land under federal control. The Department of Agriculture followed in 1862, Commerce and Labor (which split into separate departments in 1913) in 1903, Health, Education and Welfare in 1953 (splitting into the Departments of Health and Human Services and Education in 1979), Veterans Affairs in 1988, and Homeland Security in 2002. In addition to the departments that constitute the informal cabinet, many other regulatory entities not graced with the term *department* but whose heads typically have to be confirmed by the Senate have been created over the years.[1] Some of these bureaucratic accretions were congressionally authorized, some merely executive reorganizations. Some employees in many of these agencies also carry out research, although at times it is meant to explore whether further political regulation is justified. In addition, to the extent government activity is subsidized by taxpayer funds, it changes the terms under which socioeconomic actors would otherwise attempt to regulate themselves (e.g., weather forecasting by the National Weather Service, management of airport space by the Federal Aviation Administration). The vast politically regulated funding of social services such as health care and retirement benefits that occurs in most technologically advanced liberal democracies, including the United States, also displaces private saving for and provision of such services. The result is that some unknown number of private experiments to help people do these things never occurs.

In general, it is almost impossible not to assent to the proposition that the realm of activities subject to external political regulation has grown dramatically in the United States since 1789, especially since World War I. The idea that medical care or the terms of contract between business owners and their workers would be subject to substantial political regulation, let alone federal regulation, would have seemed absurd as late as 1870, but here we are.

To delineate the rise of federal regulation of previously self-regulating processes, we start with the 1887 creation of the Interstate Commerce Commission (ICC) to regulate rail transport prices. Its mission then extended to trucking and telephone rates and other terms of service. Food safety came under the purview of federal authorities after the U.S. Department of Agriculture's Division of Chemistry in the early 1880s began to research the extent of, as it were, doctored food and medicine in the country. After the enactment of the Pure Food and Drug Act in 1906, false labeling of such products was made a federal crime.[2] The federal Division of Chemistry later became the Food and Drug Administration (FDA). The ICC and FDA were the first federal agencies established as a means of using political regulation to supplement, if not displace, self-regulation. In a rare victory for self-regulation, the ICC's ability to regulate the terms of competition was gradually reduced in the 1970s and 1980s, and the agency itself was terminated in 1995.

However, the template by then had long been set. The dramatic expansion of political regulation during the Great Depression was, after an interval of Supreme Court skepticism, ratified by a series of Court decisions in the late 1930s. Now, even not directly democratically accountable political regulation (i.e., regulation that could be imposed without the need for congressional approval and a presidential signature) was allowed. The number of such "independent" regulatory agencies has expanded dramatically since, particularly since the late 1960s. The one major recently created regulatory agency as of this writing, the Consumer Finance Protection Bureau (CFPB), authorized by the Dodd-Frank Wall Street Reform and Consumer Protection Act,[3] has been layered onto the Securities and Exchange Commission, the Commodity Futures Trading Commission, the Federal Trade Commission, and numerous other existing federal entities with the authority to regulate financial exchange.

The CFPB is typical of political regulation. It was created in response to a crisis, the financial turmoil of 2007-2010, justified by supporters because the existing tangle of regulatory authority had been revealed to be insufficient to prevent any financial crisis whatsoever from happening anytime in the future. Rather than allowing financial self-regulation to increase by giving financial firms more freedom in exchange for more responsibility for the consequences of their choices, this "solution," as so many times before, was seen to be more controls and limitations troweled onto the already extensive layers of same.

Researchers have long tried to document the growth in political regulation of what would otherwise be self-regulating activities. Figure 8.1 shows two plots: the top one shows trends since 1976 in the length in pages of the Code of Federal Regulations (CFR). The second curve shows total annual pages over a longer period of time (since 1936) in the Federal Register; this includes proposed and actually promulgated regulations and a number of federal documents that are not themselves regulatory text. This curve thus imperfectly corresponds to changes over time in the scope of the federal control of otherwise self-regulating activity, Nevertheless, it has the advantage of extending back far enough to include some of the New Deal period. Both curves indicate a rise in the extent of federal con-

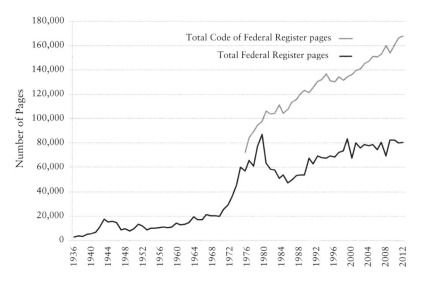

FIGURE 8.1. *Growth in political regulation.*
Source: Regulatory Studies Center, George Washington University, https://regulatorystudies.columbian
.gwu.edu/reg-stats (accessed January 10, 2017).

trol, with a particularly sharp rise during the 1970s, when the number of
agencies with the power to issue such controls grew significantly.

By these measures, the regulatory state has grown substantially since
the mid-1930s, and the Supreme Court decisions authorizing regulators
to make the functional equivalent of laws shattered whatever presumption
still remained that social problems ought to be addressed by individuals
responding as they deem proper to the environment they face. While the
data do not extend as far back in time, both the number of people whose
job it is to oversee this extralegislative lawmaking process and expendi-
tures on the operation of such agencies confirm an expansion in the scope
of political regulation of otherwise self-regulating activity.[4] Whether this
dramatic expansion is in response to public demand or self-perpetuating—
failed regulation driving not repeal of existing but production of new
regulation—is an important question, but beyond the scope of this book.

But the effect of this expansion is well within it. Estimates of the benefits and costs of regulations vary widely. As suggested earlier, because the
costs are necessarily opportunity costs, they are often difficult to estimate
with any precision. For example, it is impossible to know what kind of
medical procedures or devices would have been created and how many

of them would have been adulterated or fraudulent and would have able to withstand competitive pressure had Congress and the president not created the FDA. Most attempts to answer questions of this sort involve constructing statistical models based on mathematical and economic assumptions about the consequences of federal regulation not on social welfare as a whole but on its closest measurable proxy, gross domestic product. Tara M. Sinclair and Kathryn Vesey find that the overall size of the federal regulatory budget does not have a statistically significant effect on the rate of GDP growth or private nonfarm employment. John W. Dawson and John J. Seater measure the direct and indirect effect of the total length in pages of the CFR on GDP other than government spending. They find that the effect of regulation on this output is to lower it by a rather remarkable 72 percent between 1949 and 2005 over what it otherwise would have been had federal regulation been unchanged over that period.[5] Since political regulation in significantly market-oriented societies is often said to be motivated by results created in a self-regulating context that do not take adequate account of other things that matter but don't increase GDP (worker safety, environmental damage, businesses that are "too big," and so on), we should not be surprised that the existence of such regulation has a negative effect on whatever proxies we use to measure the outcomes of self-regulated market exchange.

The question is how big that effect is. In using whatever numerical estimations we can come up with, we must always be aware of what GDP is—an effort to measure the extent to which people can achieve their goals in life by trading the things they control by virtue of meaningful property rights with other such property owned by others. GDP, in other words, is not the goal itself. Instead, what it crudely proxies for is better housing, better opportunities to communicate with and learn from the rest of humanity, the ability to live longer, healthier lives, and so on.

HOW PEOPLE SEE SELF-REGULATION

Whether the criticism is based on things within or outside the human mind that weaken, if not eliminate, human agency, the thinking behind political regulation is that people's interactions must be controlled, directed, supervised, and channeled as the sovereign sees fit. We have seen that the degree of political control of the socioeconomy expanded throughout the twentieth century to differing degrees in different countries, and sometimes with catastrophic effects.

What about public skepticism toward self-regulation, that is, implied approval of the general form, if not the details, of political regulation? Can we detect the loss of faith in socioeconomic self-regulation in the culture? Since the rise of political invective against "trusts," "economic royalists," and the like, U.S. culture since the 1930s—films, music, social and political essays, and the like—has relatively seldom depicted entrepreneurs who succeed as heroes in the same way that people who fight for more political regulation of the socioeconomy are often presented. Outlets for such noble-minded agitators for more political regulation include increasing political regulation of labor–business owner relations, greater limits on human interaction with the natural environment, and increased political supervision of relations among ethnic groups and sexes. (A recent exception is 2015's *Joy*, the truth-based story of a woman who brings a good idea to market.)

It is true that businesspeople whose risk taking has generated the recent transformation of how we process and exchange information (high technology) are sometimes depicted very favorably. It is probably the case that the lack of political regulation of what is a still-nascent socioeconomic arena has enabled these entrepreneurs to most dramatically remake how we interact with one another. This has thus led to public admiration of such figures as Steve Jobs that is reminiscent of the widespread contemporaneous (if not universal) adulation for previous world-changing entrepreneurs such as Henry Ford and John D. Rockefeller. But in modern popular culture, the fighter against business injustices is more frequently admired than businesspeople themselves, with individual entrepreneurs the primary exception.

We can acquire more quantitative evidence thanks to Google nGrams, briefly introduced in Chapter 5. Table 8.1 depicts the year of first use and of peak use for a series of nGrams and the annual growth rate (as three-year moving averages) in the percentage of all nGrams of a given length that these strings make up. Unless otherwise noted, all nGrams are indifferent to letter case. Figures 8.2 to 8.5 also depict historical trends in proportional frequency of use for these nGrams. Again a three-year moving average, Google's default setting for an nGram search, is used. Note also that the growth rate tracks the salience of the ideas represented by the string, not necessarily whether the idea is increasingly believed or disbelieved. In addition, the creators of the database estimate that the number of English words grew by only 53,000 (to 597,000) between 1900 and 1950, but by 525,000 between 1950 and 2000.[6] By increasing the density of communication networks, the Internet from the early 1990s has increased linguistic innovation, so we might expect the share of any given nGram to decline, other things equal.

TABLE 8.1. *Trends in suggestive character strings, 1900–2008.*

String	Initial Appearance	Maximum Proportion	Average Annual Growth Rate	
			1900–2008[a]	1970–2008
Economic regulation				
"the economy"	1513	1985	1.88	−0.0099%
"macroeconomic"	1887	1995	6.91	11.37
"macroeconomic policy"	1932	1993	10.74	5.16
"supposedly efficient"	1904	1934	1.34	−0.01
Skepticism of science				
"scientific hegemony"/ "hegemony of science"[b]	1854	1999	3.53	3.92
"naturopathy"	1889	1999	6.29	4.85
"allopathy"	1824	1853	−0.0103	1.56
Individual agency				
Individual is powerless				
"myth of rational"/ "myth of the rational"	1934	2008	4.40	3.95
"Myth of the Rational"	1973	2008	—	2.86
"supposedly rational"	1898	2001	4.16	1.26
"socially constructed"	1871	1999	6.91	6.83
"socially determined"	1850	1980	2.56	−0.60
"society determines"	1823	1979	1.14	−1.57
"society forces"	1792	1974	1.44	−0.79
Individual chooses poorly				
"Consciously choose"	1844	2003	2.73	4.10
"Unconsciously choose"	1865	1990	2.66	1.04
"Irresponsible choices"	1947	2001	5.03	4.26

a. If a string's first appearance is after 1900 or 1970, average annual growth rates are calculated from that year through 2008.

b. While it appears for several years in the 1850s, "hegemony of science" first appears permanently in 1934, and the left-side average annual growth rate is calculated from 1934–2008.

Source: books.google.com/nGrams.

Note: "Scientific hegemony/hegemony of science" and "myth of rational/myth of the rational" were combined searches for either nGram.

"The Economy" Indivisible

Phrases suggestive of several kinds of objection to self-regulating processes are included (Figure 8.2). One objection is that agents acting on their own do not lead to proper functioning of the entire socioeconomy. It should thus be viewed as a large machine subject to regulation as a whole rather than an ever-changing interaction among uncountable numbers of distinct people. The term "the economy" itself is present throughout the data period, but increases in usage from the 1930s before peaking in 1985. While "macroeconomic" makes its first appearance much earlier than "macroeconomic policy," they both grow continuously starting in the early 1960s until peaking in the 1990s. Another phrase skeptical of the economy's self-regulating properties is "supposedly efficient." It exhibits dramatic swings from roughly the start of World War I through 1950, then displays steady growth until the early 1990s before falling continuously.

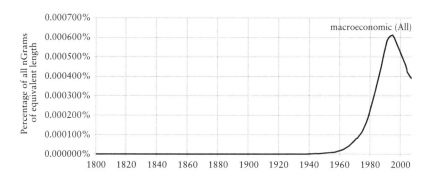

FIGURE 8.2. *Skepticism of the self-regulating economy.*
Source: books.google.com/ngrams (Search terms: "the economy," "macroeconomic," "macroeconomic policy," "supposedly efficient").

Science

Self-regulating science has benefited relatively more from benign (or perhaps inattentive) neglect from politicians (the main avenue for political regulation in the postwar years being government funding of certain scientific projects), but in recent decades has come under some skepticism from the public (Figure 8.3). In combination, "scientific hegemony" and "hegemony of science" both rise from the early 1970s. Anecdotally, one could also point to the rare but growing belief in the United States that vaccinating small children does more harm than good, part of a broader skepticism about medical claims based on experiments conducted according to the increasingly untrusted scientific method in favor of medicine that is supposedly based on tradition (herbal medicine, natural medicine more broadly, and so on). Many of these practices themselves stem from beliefs that the human body is a self-regulating system, so that illness is

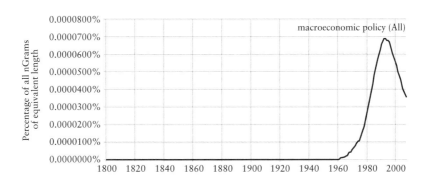

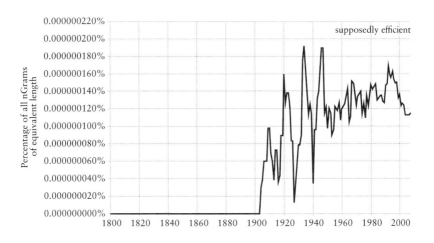

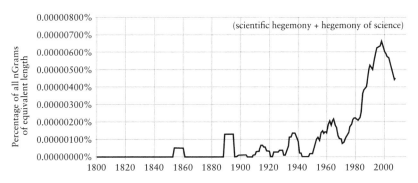

FIGURE 8.3. *Skepticism of self-regulating science.*
Source: books.google.com/ngrams (Search terms: "naturopathy," "allopathy," "scientific hegemony + hegemony of science").

a function of certain elements in that system being out of balance. (Recall from Chapter 2 that this framework has an ancient pedigree.) A cure then hinges on restoring that balance by ingesting more "natural" substances (as opposed to the "nonnatural" substances created by scientists, often working for pharmaceutical companies, combining chemicals in a new way).

The term "allopathy" refers to the practice of standard, science-based medicine. According to the *Oxford English Dictionary*, the term was most likely popularized by practitioners of homeopathy (their earliest citation is 1824) to contrast their system with the practice of using often artificially created substances ("drugs") to negate the excessive production of some other substance or mitigate or repair some bodily malfunction. Modern allopathic medicine now also includes removal or replacement of various body parts, such as inflamed appendixes or knees that have worn out, and many proponents of "natural" or "alternative" medicine are comfortable with at least some of these procedures. "Allopathy" spikes briefly in the nineteenth century and has a general upward trend from 1940.

Doctors who use so-called natural medicine based on knowledge that is generated by some process other than the scientific method are often known as "naturopaths." "Naturopathy" is essentially a twentieth-century coinage, with a rising rate of use through the late 1940s, then falling before rising again from the early 1960s. Adherents of naturopathy, both patients and practitioners, are skeptical of the entire scientific system that recommends allopathic treatment. Skeptics of climate science, to the extent that they believe the science itself is corrupted by money (as many skeptics of modern pharmaceuticals do), are similarly untrusting of the scientific method as currently practiced.[7]

Cognitive Frailty and Determinism

The final category of evidence concerns agency (Figure 8.4), the capacity of individuals to play the role they need to in any self-regulating system. Skeptical arguments derived from both cognitive weakness and the powerlessness of the individual against broader social forces will be considered together.

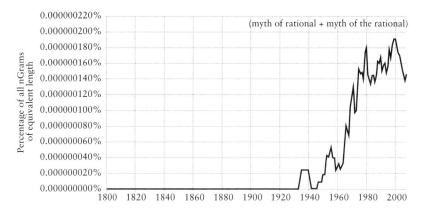

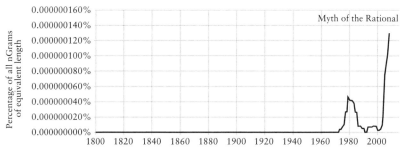

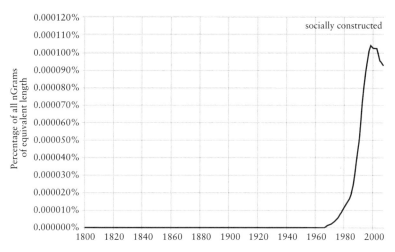

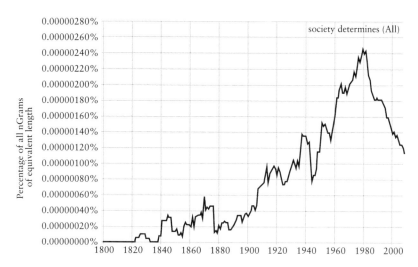

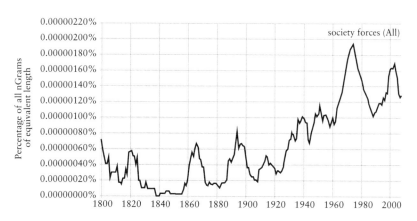

FIGURE 8.4. *Skepticism of agency (determinism).*

Source: books.google.com/ngrams (Search terms: "myth of rational + myth of the rational," "supposedly rational," "socially constructed." "socially determined," "society determines," "society forces").

The rise of such skepticism can be measured by looking at the prevalence of doubts about "rationality" as the guiding principle of the human mind. The word "rationality" is widely used and equally widely criticized. Deriving as it does from the idea of "ratio," it suggests deductive reasoning reminiscent of geometry, and thus predictability in human choice. Economists, as is their wont, express "rational" preferences mathematically. They agree that are two mathematical requirements to use the word "rational" to describe individual choice. The first is that preferences are complete, meaning that in any choice environment, for any pair of options A and B, a person must prefer A to B, prefer B to A, or be made equally happy (or unhappy) by either. In other words, there must be no pair of options that the person is unable to compare, although this does not foreclose the possibility that he ranks them equally. The second is that preferences be transitive, so that if A is preferred to B and B is preferred to C, A is preferred to C. Violations of these assumptions would mean that entrepreneurs of the malicious sort could endlessly sell goods in sequence. If A is preferred to B and B is preferred to C yet C is preferred to A, sellers can sell C, then B, then A, then C again, forever.

Given irrationality in the sense of violating at least one of these two assumptions, it is possible that political regulation that limits choices that do not involve coercion or fraud, or that changes the way in which choices are presented to consumers, can make people better off than if those laws do not exist. Of course, since the term was introduced in economic high theory, rationality (like the newer behavioral economics) has been a model only, and economic models are often less consistently useful than their equivalents in the natural sciences. In addition, to say that human behavior is imperfectly adapted to the requirements of self-regulating processes, and that is enough to negate their value, would be to commit a fundamental error; the very usefulness of such processes is that mistakes, whether deriving from cognitive imperfections or other sources, are policed through competition.

For now, we are interested in use trends. The two phrases "myth of rational" and "myth of the rational" have seen dramatically increased use in the last twenty years. A similar pattern, with a somewhat longer history of steadily increasing use, can be seen for "supposedly rational." Most striking is a search for "Myth of the Rational," which is case-specific in a way suggestive of the titles of chapters or chapter sections. It first appears in 1973 and has had a 2.86 percent growth rate since then. Since 2001 the annual growth rate has been a remarkable 164.69 percent. (Of course, we expect higher initial growth rates for ultimately successful ideas that succeed by quickly moving into broader conversation, just as with other artistic, scientific, and socioeconomic innovations.) While this pattern could be attributed to increasingly widespread citation of a few popular books with the phrase in the title, according to Worldcat, a website that lists the holdings of libraries around the world, the first such book did not appear until 2007.[8] The growth in nGrams with capitalized use indicates that over time, more authors have attached such significance to criticism of rationality that they devote significant attention to it. The records of Google Scholar further indicate that the term is used in all scholarly venues in a wide variety of contexts, including such (case-independent) phrases as "myth of the rational university," "myth of the rational male," and "myth of the rational scientist."[9] Skepticism of rationality appears to be a growing force in English-language communication.

It is also worth exploring trends in several phrases that suggest lack of individual agency or rationality (Figure 8.5). While "socially constructed" has been around since 1871, its use rate does not begin to continually grow until the early 1960s, a pattern that continues through 2008. "Socially determined," "society determines," and "society forces" (all invoking deterministic arguments for social trends) show similar patterns of growth from the period of high confidence in the self-regulating order. As for the notions of choice conceived by Freud and his descendants, both "consciously choose" and "unconsciously choose" see a sharp rise in relative use beginning at almost the same time—not around the time of Freud's work itself but in the 1960s. Arguably the rise in the use of "consciously choose" at that time is part of a larger trend that begins in the 1930s, but the long rise from the 1960s is obvious. "Irresponsible choices," suggestive of the tension between individual choices and the social good, starts later than "consciously choose" and "unconsciously choose," which is not surprising, but otherwise it displays the same pattern, albeit with more variance, then the latter two phrases.

Again, this nGram analysis cannot always say so much about the extent to which an idea wins or loses the public debate, and for each of the

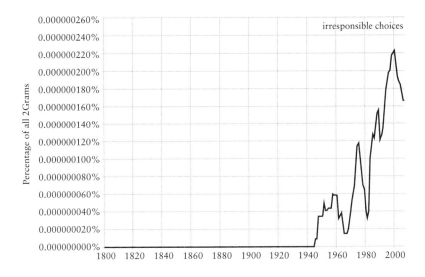

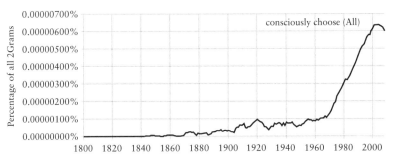

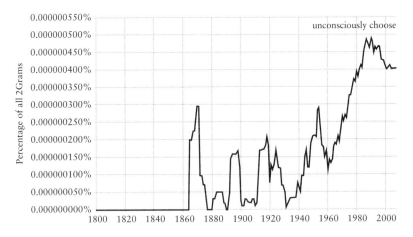

FIGURE 8.5. *Skepticism of agency (cognitive frailty).*

Source: books.google.com/ngrams (Search terms: "irresponsible choices," "consciously choose," "unconsciously choose").

Note: For "irresponsible choices" and "supposedly rational," only all-lowercase searches returned any results. For "myth of the rational" and "myth of rational" combined, case-insensitive search is unobtainable.

phrases in Table 8.1, not every use reflects the debate outlined here. But the patterns suggest a broadly developing trend of controversy over and sometimes skepticism of the autonomous agent capable of managing his own affairs. Without such a foundation, it is difficult to defend the self-regulating society.

Readers are encouraged to search for their own nGrams and send the results to me. Collectively, the findings allow the interpretation that public confidence in self-regulation has fallen for reasons of both perceived social structure and perceived individual weakness. Is that fall justified? That is, of course, a sensible question only when it is compared to the alternatives. Some overall guidance for thinking about the value of self-regulation is provided in the final chapter.

CHAPTER 9

The Best Way(s) Forward

In this respect the creative process is not unlike the processes of free
societies, which are by their nature divided, plural, even quarrelsome; they
are societies in motion, and with emotion comes tension, friction.

SALMAN RUSHDIE[1]

Frances Oldham Kelsey (1914–2015) was born and attended college in
Canada before acquiring a doctorate from the University of Chicago in
pharmacology in 1936. After working in that department for several years
as a professor, she earned a medical degree there in 1950. She moved to
Washington, D.C., in 1960, evaluating applications at the Food and Drug
Administration to allow doctors to prescribe new drugs to the public. It
was here that she exercised the legal authority she possessed in a way that
would ultimately lead her to receive one of Canada's highest awards, the
Order of Canada, a few months before her passing.

She had received a company's application for the approval of a drug
generically known as thalidomide but was unpersuaded by the data the
company submitted in support of its application. She then ordered it to
investigate the drug's safety further because of recently published research.
Company officials went over her head to try to obtain approval, but failed.
While the struggle between bureaucrat and businessmen went on, news
began to come in from Europe that pregnant women who had taken the
drug, a sedative meant to help with morning sickness, were giving birth
to babies with severe physical deformities. Only a very small number of
American children were similarly affected, and Kelsey was lauded for the
rest of her life as the paragon public servant. Even now, the example of
thalidomide is sometimes broached in response to those who argue that
the reach of political regulation is now too broad.

But it is not as simple as that. Naturally, if government regulators had
the wisdom and the desire to limit only activities that were known to cause
more damage than benefits, there would be no reason to oppose giving

them power to construct such regulations as they deemed necessary. To deprive them of that power, in fact, would be calamitous. Alas, there is no reason to think that even under present limits, bureaucratic discretion is exercised with anything like that level of providence.

The European thalidomide tragedies, occurring as they did after governments there had approved the drug but before it was approved in the United States, provided direct evidence of the consequences had Kelsey approved what turned out to be a very dangerous drug. Such evidence will always be available to consult when a drug that has already been approved turns out to be dangerous. But the other sort of error, in which political regulators choose not to approve a drug that is in fact not dangerous and would have produced great health benefits (e.g., substantially lowering the pain of a chronic injury or disease or dramatically improving the five-year survival rate for some type of cancer), is seldom actually observed because it is the road *not* taken. Meanwhile, the road taken previously, self-regulation, frequently caused these problems to be addressed to a degree that political regulation at best fails to improve on. The latter does not cause work safety or automobile travel, for example, to improve any faster than it was already improving.[2]

When we can observe, the results can be disquieting. Silver diamond fluoride has been used in Japan at least since the early 1970s to effectively prevent and treat cavities. In the United States, these are treated by dentists later, at greater expense and in a somewhat painful procedure. References to the use of similar compounds date back in the literature at least to 1917.[3] Yet only in 2014 did the FDA approve it for use in the United States. Attempts have been made to use statistical techniques to estimate the costs of such errors overall. Although they must be taken with the usual grain of salt for such exercises, a summary of such estimates indicates that they easily cost thousands of lives in the United States each year.[4]

Political regulators have poor incentives to think about this second kind of error. At least one analysis suggests that after standardizing for disease severity and prevalence, the FDA often designs its drug-testing studies with an excessive desire to avoid the first kind of error. That is the sort of effect we should expect from political regulators, civil servant or elected, who respond to short-term political incentives—to avoid blame for something bad that does happen later. But these are not the incentives faced by the people in the self-regulating socioeconomy who will make, improve, use, and improve the product as they engage in their implicit cooperative dance to figure out what works best.[5] We will see other examples as we conclude.

POLITICS AND SELF-REGULATION

This book has contended that political regulation and self-regulation work differently, and it has made the case for the latter. Of course, democratic politics surely has some features of self-regulating processes. There is at least theoretically an objective: the enactment and enforcement of government dictates supported by some sufficiently large fraction of the population. There is feedback in the form of periodic elections. Losing an election seems analogous to firms that use resources in ways that prove economically unsustainable and find themselves unable to maintain control over those resources, which is the economist's way of saying they go out of business.

So does representative democracy, perhaps in a nation in which certain basic rights are constitutionally protected, effectively convey the public will and to the greatest long-term benefit? In particular, can it outperform individuals who would otherwise compete to solve the same problems on their own? There are reasons to wonder.

Starting from the premise that we know very little of what there is to know, politics is often alarmingly deficient as a social learning process. Politicians and bureaucrats are distant, metaphorically and often literally, from the problems that people encounter. In addition, it is the nature of politics to impose single solutions on the entire polity. The periodic political appeals to vaguely "change the system" (e.g., the "health care system," the "campaign finance system," the "economic system") are instructive in this regard. Bottom-up, self-regulating systems, in contrast, allow many different solutions to simultaneously contend, and even to coexist for extended periods of time, to respond to differences in individual opportunities and desires. It would be absurd to expect that a tiny cabal of political figures could effectively plan the scientific breakthroughs or the new forms of art that *should* emerge in the next ten years. It is equally unreasonable to expect bureaucrats and legislators to be able to more effectively plan the interaction of health care suppliers and consumers, dictate the structure of bargaining over working conditions between employees and business owners, or prioritize this industry's claim over scarce resources over that one's, than individuals constantly experimenting and recombining on their own can do. Political decision makers must also be drawn from the most farsighted segments of the population if they are not to be systematically biased toward solutions that most boost their own electoral prospects, likely at the expense of long-term social welfare. The rising tide of public debt in the face of expanding social expenditure across the democratic world is the least of the evidence that this foresightedness is often lacking.

TAKING THE TWO CLASSES OF REGULATORS AS WE FIND THEM

Thinking about the performance of the two systems this way assumes that the decision makers under political regulation have the same objective as the one we properly insist on judging self-regulating systems by. When a system is regulated by politics, even in a democratic society, someone who wishes to tilt the rules to his advantage need only gain control over a few levers of power. Often these levers are both highly independent and easy to access. Among developed countries, this problem is particularly acute in the United States. There, the ability of particular interests to carve out special favors, including subsidy for themselves or restrictions on competitors, all of which by definition cement the status quo, is most apparent. To gain control of a substantial amount of the rulemaking power relevant to a particular interest, it is often not necessary to support the winning presidential candidate. Giving attention to individual bureaucrats, cabinet undersecretaries, or legislators is often sufficient to influence political regulation. (Although naturally placing your money on the winning side helps; perhaps this is why giving to both parties is so common.[6]) Admirers of the FDA might note that food regulation has sometimes been driven by special interests such as the dairy industry seeking to prevent new food products such as margarine from gaining a foothold.[7] It is much harder for such a special interest to achieve the same goal—other people's money or a limit on competition from new ideas, be they economic, philosophical, artistic, or scientific—in a self-regulating system where entry by potential competitors is low cost and customers must be satisfied.

The ability of pressure groups to manipulate political regulation to diminish even scientific competition is visible in attempts to politically regulate, and hence limit progress in, the question not just of the extent of climate change but of how humans should react to it, the implications of sociobiology (itself once dismissed as pseudoscience), or the biological component of homosexuality or intelligence. Readers can supply their own examples of supposedly "settled science," itself very unscientific language.

Self-regulating competition is remarkably vigorous. It is undoubtedly sometimes true that some businesses in the quest for ever more profit seek to gouge or defraud consumers, exploit workers, and monopolize markets. But that is an opportunity for someone else to serve individuals with their individual purposes better. So during contemplation of government action, it is necessary to compare not the hoped-for but the likely government response to both the circumstances and the potential responses of private actors to these circumstances. This comparison must be informed by the actual historical performance of both the state and participants in self-regulating systems to such challenges.

Self-regulating responses are many and simultaneous, political ones uniform and sequential at best and eternal at worst. How energetically are agents likely, when they are not politically restrained, to respond, and how (given what they can know and their own incentives) are government rule makers? Will political regulation foreclose private experiments that might bear richer fruit? Will it create new problems that call for even more controls? Is the goal of political regulators even what it ought to be? Such questions are seldom asked in public conversation in democratic societies, but they ought to be. The trade-off is not between what people have now absent government intervention and what they ought to have, but between what they have now and could have in the future under self-regulation versus what they are likely to have under political regulation.

It is lamentably common in both serious economic and ethical reasoning and ordinary political commentary to take our high school civics lessons a little too seriously and assume an ideal government reacting to a flawed society. It is wiser to assume that political officials are at best no better than the rest of us and to consider only in light of that how they are likely to affect social processes when given the chance versus how private actors are likely to behave if political regulators let them. It will not do to argue that politicians ought to do something if they are not capable of doing so, and all the more so if individuals on their own often will react in ways that promote the goals we wish to achieve. Even ignoring potentially destructive incentives that political actors might face, it is critical, given the informational and other deficiencies of political regulation, to give serious, historically informed thought to how unrestricted agents are likely to react to society's perceived problems before extending the hand of political control over already self-regulated processes.

THE PACE OF SELF-REGULATING PROGRESS OVER TIME

This book has examined three self-regulating systems: science, communication, and socioeconomic activity. It is instructive to consider the fruits in these fields when self-regulation flourishes and when it does not. I consider each of these three systems in turn. Note that better achievement of the goal of the self-regulating system can occur for several reasons—there are more participants, the conductivity of the links among them may be greater (from improved communications technology, say), and, for the socioeconomic case in particular, the conductivity may be higher because there are fewer political regulations.

Science

Casual empiricism indicates that the scope of scientific knowledge, the facilities for engaging in scientific exploration, and the communication outlets for reporting its results have grown dramatically since the end of World War II. Estimates are that the number of scientific publications now doubles about every nine years. In addition, the rate of increase in cited scientific publications can be divided into a slower stage until about 1750, one of faster growth until World War II, and a faster rate still since 1945.[8]

Of course the rate of growth in scientific publications does not necessarily match the rate of growth in scientific knowledge or its importance. Two widely available lists of unusually influential discoveries in science or technology are used to investigate this question. The first is a list of individuals who created unusually fruitful ideas in science from 700 B.C. to 1949, taken from a list of innovators there and elsewhere compiled by Charles Murray. The second is a list of great scientific and technological innovations compiled by the late writer Isaac Asimov (1920–1992), from earliest humanity through 1988.[9] The historical record is depicted in Figure 9.1, which shows

Murray achievers and Asimov achievements for each fifty-year period from 700 B.C. (The data from Asimov for the first period include breakthroughs prior to 700 B.C.) The patterns are roughly similar, as the Scientific Revolution is clearly visible in both records. Major scientific progress is obvious from the sixteenth century on in each. In the Murray data, unending growth in the absolute number of achievers per period begins at the beginning of the eighteenth century, and the Asimov data tell almost the same story. This growth coincides with the establishment and early strengthening of the scientific network, both by adding more links (people) and increasing the efficacy of feedback. The former includes the growth in both general literacy and the specialization in science, and the latter includes the still ongoing construction of the scientific system described in Chapter 3.

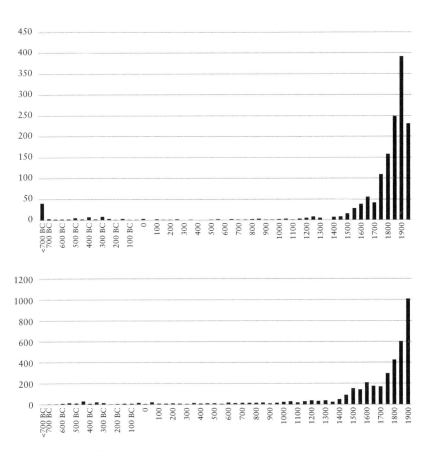

FIGURE 9.1. *World scientific achievements and achievers.*
Source: Murray (2003); Asimov (1989).

The data do not include the entire postwar period. The role of government in financing scientific research has grown dramatically during this time, and there is an argument that this has limited scientific progress. According to this view, the ever-larger role for political regulation in determining career success has made scientists, driven by the need to accumulate research dollars to advance in the academic ranks, more conservative. To get funded, one extends the existing line of research a little bit rather than trying to fundamentally break new ground.[10] To the extent that government funding tends to favor the building of expensive, parochially motivated scientific infrastructure rather than radical new thinkers, the problem is worse. Yet for science the outlook is optimistic overall and globally.

Expression

The revolution in self-regulating communication is a more recent development. Following the dramatic changes in Europe in the late eighteenth and much of the nineteenth centuries, there was retreat in the twentieth with the rise of authoritarian and totalitarian regimes. But the scope of political regulation of communication has clearly shrunk worldwide since the height of totalitarian control in the 1930s and 1940s. More recent data show that the news for freedom of communication is also optimistic overall. Freedom House rates almost every country in the world, annually now, along several dimensions of personal freedom and civil rights. Freedom of communication increased substantially from 1989 to the middle of the first decade of the 2000s, although it has slightly retreated since then. Still, the news overall is good. In the 2015 ratings, for freedom of the press, sixty-three countries were rated as "free" (as opposed to fifty-seven in 1989), seventy-one rated as "partly free" (nineteen), and sixty-five as "not free" (eighty-three).[11] If the standard of comparison is, say, 1750 or 1945, self-regulating communication is now far more common around the world than before.

Looking at communication output rather than political regulation of it, it is almost impossible to contest that the range of human expression is much greater now than it has ever been. To take one source for which some data are available, the number of books published has grown substantially over the centuries. For book titles in the English Short-Title catalogue, a list of surviving publications in libraries in Britain and its colonies from the arrival of print in 1473 to the present, Alain Veylit has indicated that even after accounting for a greater survival rate for more recent publications, the growth in books published is essentially exponential.[12]

If books are a medium for communication of ideas, an even more fundamental medium, common to all forms of communication, is words. As noted in Chapter 1, language is generally self-regulated; words are invented, disappear, and are continually recombined to make both new words and entirely new phrases. (Consider "to Google" and "infotainment.") While there have long existed some crude attempts to politically regulate the language, it was not until the modern era that governments significantly attempted to control language structure. This trend reached its height under the totalitarian regimes of the twentieth century, but as noted in Chapter 1, language generally continually evolves independent of politics.

The English language seems to have evolved more quickly in the past century. The figures on growth in the number of unique Google 1Grams in the twentieth century cited in Chapter 8 indicate a 0.19 percent rate of annual growth in the first half and a 1.08 percent rate in the second.[13] As with science, the number of agents and the ease of building links (e.g., better communications technology and increasing literacy) matter. The expanding number of people who speak English means more agents, and that combined with improved communication technology and less political regulation of communication worldwide means more feedback. A greater number of words almost certainly means a greater number of ideas that can be expressed using them. Indeed, many, if not most, new coinages denote the expression of new ideas. Word growth is both a sign of and a tool for new idea creation, which is what should be the goal of a system of communication. Self-regulating communication means more ideas, therefore more competition among ideas, therefore more progress. And in English-language works, there appear to be ever-more ideas in circulation.

Socioeconomic Innovation

For the socioeconomy, the record is more mixed. There has been tremendous innovation, the product of liberation over the centuries of self-regulating forces. But in recent years, the growing political regulation of such forces has led to slower rates of innovation.

The Economy Proper   This analysis begins by investigating the conventionally defined economy. (Other forms of artistic expression are analyzed in later sections.) The oil shock of the 1970s, in which nations angered by Western support of Israel during the 1973 Arab-Israeli War temporarily embargoed oil sales to those countries, is sometimes said to have marked the point at which postwar economic progress dramatically slowed. The economic boom of the 1980s and 1990s and the revolutionary social-economic change generated by the growth of the Internet notwithstanding, economic commentators often divide the postwar era (at least from the standpoint of western Europe, North America, and Japan) into pre-and post-1973.

Recently, more systematic research by Robert J. Gordon has provided evidence that something changed around 1970. In particular, he divides the last 150 years of American history into three portions: two, from 1870 to 1920 and from 1970 to the present, of more modest productivity surrounding a golden half-century from 1920 to 1970.[14] During this time, several major innovations, such as the discovery of new domestic oil supplies, the spread of assembly line manufacturing, and rapid electrification of homes and factories, all served to enhance what was achievable in terms of productivity growth.

Some people date the start of the slowdown in productivity growth to 1973, and others date it by decade, and refer to the 1970s as the problematic era. The oil shocks were indeed disruptive, but all of the disruption was due to government price controls on both crude oil and gasoline. (Another shock under the price control regime followed revolutionary upheaval and then revolution itself in Iran in the late 1970s.) Once those controls were swept away in early 1981, self-regulating markets adjusted easily to events such as the Iran-Iraq War and the attacks on oil tankers that it spawned, the September 11 attacks, the dramatic economic growth in oil-importing countries such as China and India throughout the 1990s and 2000s (which dramatically increased global oil demand), and the worldwide economic slump that began in 2007.

And it is a mistake to attribute the dysfunction of the 1970s primarily to oil market shocks. Robert Shackleton compiles data and confirms unusually high growth in total factor productivity (TFP) during the 1930s and 1940s, with unusually low TFP growth between 1900 and 1920, and 1973 and 1990.[15] Growth in output per hour worked, an alternative measure that also discounts for the effect of growth in the labor force on total output while not standardizing for the effect of adding more capital equipment (e.g., machines, buildings), peaks in roughly 1965. It declines steadily to almost zero growth in 1982 and then rises through the mid-1980s and then again after roughly 1995.[16]

Of course, such macroeconomic aggregates miss many details about how growth beyond GDP and lumpen "productivity" might improve the quality of life. The potential of global networked communication, orders of magnitude thicker than telephones and before that the telegraph, and based on uncountable numbers of two-way connections rather than the centralized, one-way links of radio and television, is only beginning to make its presence felt. As I write, the Internet revolution is about where manufacturing was in perhaps 1820. Yet in the United States, there are enough data to make a case that in the late 1960s, something began to go wrong. Gordon argues that the 1920–1970 era was the anomaly, characterized by a small number of fundamental, nonrepeatable technological breakthroughs and their rapid spread, boosted by the emergency commands of wartime America.[17] These events stimulated the major remaking of the U.S. economy, but only once. But it is nonetheless striking that this slowdown in economic progress in the 1970s occurred just as another significant expansion of government attempts to solve problems it had never addressed before accelerated.

For example, American mobility, particularly movement from areas with long-term economic problems, has declined for several decades. Such mobility is a key part of socioeconomic self-regulation: people move from where prospects are poor to where they are better, thus facilitating needed socioeconomic change. But several expansions in political regulation more closely tie people to where they are now. There has been dramatic growth in occupational licensing, in which state governments require permission, valid only in those states, to do particular jobs. Possession of such a license is a valuable asset, even as these license requirements limit competition. Many state income streams such as public pensions, which often require working for many years to meaningfully vest, and assistance for the poor, which varies substantially by state, similarly make it more costly to move. The rapid growth in zoning and other land use regulations makes business turnover more difficult and housing more expensive. And this is argued to explain why American mobility is at a historic low.[18]

More broadly, it is worrisome that recently Decker and colleagues have documented lower rates of dynamism in the United States, measured by the rate of new business formation and construction and less dispersal of firm revenue growth within industries, suggesting that firms increasingly resemble one another rather than being divided into rapidly growing and sharply declining firms. They also summarize others' research indicating growth in the proportion of workers working for large, mature firms and not younger, smaller ones, and declines in combined job creation and destruction. While the authors do not assess this possibility, this might be attributed partly to the tying of people to two products of political regulation: (1) health insurance provided by current employers, a clear function of the political decision to regulate health care by reliance substantially on employer-based (as opposed to independently purchased) health insurance, and (2) the comparative advantage of larger, more established firms in coping with the regulatory state, thus enabling higher compensation and more job security. People are thus more tied to a specific job. On top of this, efforts to more extensively regulate finance and both health insurance and medical services have coincided with greater concentration in these industries. Concentration makes political regulation easier, and self-regulation through competitive entry harder.[19]

In writing an obituary of Lyndon Johnson (1908–1973, president 1963–1969), who presided over what has become known as the "Great Society," the writer William F. Buckley Jr. summarized the expansion of the federal government during Johnson's presidency:

Under LBJ we got anti-poverty programs, mass transportation bills, model cities help, rent supplements, crime control, antisegregation acts, voting acts, housing acts, a communication relations act, acts on water and air pollution, on waste, roads, recreation and parks, on meat and poultry and fabrics and farm prices, on truth in lending, on fair packaging, on electronic radiation, on traffic; aid for elementary schools, for higher education, of teacher corps, aid to the poor, adult education, job opportunity training, the job corps, business aid, aid for Appalachia, an increase in the minimum wage, Medicare for the elderly, Medicaid for the non-elderly, doctors' training, nurses' training, mental health, immunization, health centers, and child help.[20]

Certainly not all of these have demonstrably gotten worse, and it is not certain that those that have improved have done so at a slower rate than had the government refrained from imposing or expanding political regulation in these areas. Water and air pollution have substantially declined. While the quality of health care for the elderly absent Medicare can only be a matter of speculation, it is in any event a program with broad public support. But concentrated urban poverty and racial segregation, and the quality of public education, can plausibly be said to have deteriorated during the period of growing political suzerainty over these areas. (With regard to the latter, the growing popularity of homeschooling, that is, the unraveling of the division of labor in the provision of education is a particularly telling indictment.)

Are we better off than we would have been had political regulation not colonized previously self-regulating socioeconomic activities? Given the decades of lower economic performance and the accompanying economic angst, interrupted only occasionally by innovations like the Internet that occur and initially grow largely beyond the reach of political regulation, a good case can be made that the answer is no.

Art, Ethics, and Philosophy   The seventeenth and eighteenth centuries saw a revolution in thinking about the value of self-regulating communication. Rising prosperity in the nineteenth century meant that more agents were materially capable of devoting their lives to art, literature, and philosophy, a process that continues today in already prosperous and rapidly developing countries; rising standards of living liberate people from the necessity of working long hours to provide basic sustenance to their families and free them to do what they wish with their lives. We would expect that the number of influential thinkers would rise when these two effects are combined, and the Murray data suggest that this is so.

Figure 9.2 depicts Murray's count of great literary achievers in both the Western and non-Western worlds. (His data do not make this distinction in science.) Figure 9.3 presents analogous data for art. The figures suggest several things. First, in terms of achievements in these areas, the relevance of the term *Dark Ages*, despite a recent reluctance of historians to use the term, is clear in the West. Second, the impact of the lower cost of building links after the invention of the printing press is clear for litera-

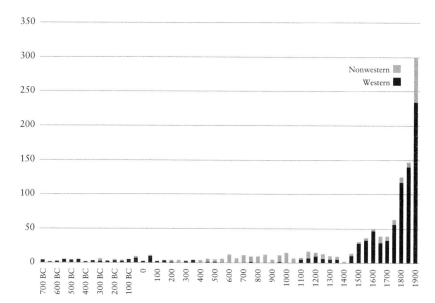

FIGURE 9.2. *World and Western literary achievers.*
Source: Murray (2003).

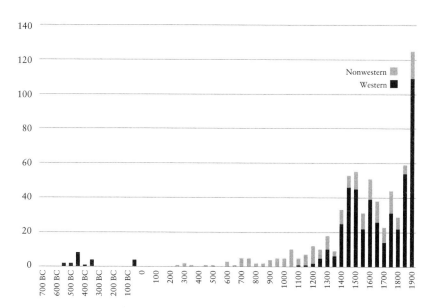

FIGURE 9.3. *World and Western artistic achievers.*
Source: Murray (2003).

ture in the West. Third, for both the West and the non-West, the impact of
the arrival of the self-regulating ideology is clear (in the twentieth century
for the latter). Finally, for Western art, there is an interim peak during the
Renaissance. The rise is choppier afterward, but it is dramatic between
1850 and 1950. Philosophy is somewhat different, as Figure 9.4 indicates.
There are great achievers and a greater representation of non-Western
figures throughout, but the rise in the last several centuries is manifest.
If we assume that each era's expression is not merely new variations on
old themes but the creation of new forms even as respect for older forms
persists, the expansion of art, literature, and philosophy across time predicted by the analysis in Chapter 5 is vivid.

Greatness, it seems, is defined more broadly as the form and substance
of human expression grow. Better preservation and sharing technology
(print, photography, the Internet), the greater ability to build links between artists and writers so that they may share ideas, and higher prosperity combine to expand human creative wealth. In the past century,
the types of artistic, literary, and philosophical human expression have
expanded with great force. Provided that there is no growth in political
regulation of such activities, the expansion of the broadly defined artistic
map should continue.

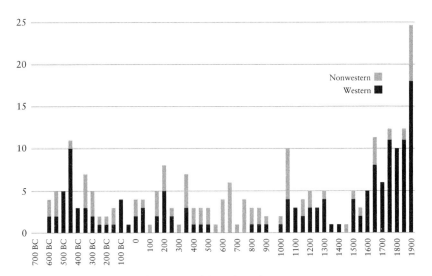

FIGURE 9.4. *World and Western philosophy achievers.*
Source: Murray (2003).

. . .

Where are we overall? The data suggest that ideas and science have grown, and to the extent that science runs into troubles, it fixes them on its own in the usual style. But the economy, at least in the United States, seems to be another story. This pattern has occurred as regulation on communication has fallen and on science has remained low, but on economic activity has increased substantially.

WHEN MIGHT SELF-REGULATION FAIL?

If asked to accept the superiority of self-regulation, especially in the socioeconomic sphere, the alert (disputatious?) reader might inquire, if socioeconomic self-regulation is so superior to political regulation, why have a state at all? The answer, of course, is that self-regulation is indeed generally superior *if the necessary conditions prevail*.

Social systems effectively self-regulate when their deficiencies are simultaneously an opportunity for other agents. This is likely to occur when it is possible that many people can propose, "You use this method [product, idea] to achieve these purposes, but use my method instead to achieve them to greater effect." *Method* and *greater effect* are immensely broad terms, in that we must work backward from human goals to the options offered by people to help achieve these goals. Competition is not just a question of having 100 producers of identical pencils instead of only 1 (the standard economics textbook account of the benefits of "competition" over a "monopoly"), so that consumers are better served by more companies producing pencils and bringing their price down. In fact, pencils are an instrument of human expression. Sometimes—as when trying to figure out a math problem that is too difficult to do in one's head but not difficult enough to justify getting the calculator—they are the just-so tool for the task. But we wish to give people reasons to offer new and better ways to create human expression, live longer, solicit the money and effort of people to help the poor, and so on—in other words, to improve lives. The things people propose to achieve with pencils and other tools of expression, and not merely a greater number of businesses producing a soulless, identical product, are the essence of competition.

But for the socioeconomy to self-regulate effectively, those who want to do things (or who are open to suggestions for new ways to do them) must be linked (or linkable) with those who can provide a proposed means. I have contended throughout that for most human purposes, the self-regulating society full of ever-alert idea entrepreneurs is far superior to its politically regulated alternative. But perhaps not always. Consider air pollution, a severe problem decades earlier in the industrialized world and a rapidly growing problem now in some developing countries. Self-regulating forces can certainly induce people to provide protection against such pollution, from face coverings of varying degrees of severity to home air filters to the construction of houses far away from the polluted city center. But given that the person damaged by pollution has no potential of a direct commercial relationship with the person generating it (Who in particular dumped the particular particles into the air you breathed just now?), there is no direct channel to communicate one's desire that the amount of pollution produced by that second person should fall. In addition, if a firm introduced a way to produce the same product with less pollution, society as a whole would surely benefit, but even though some individuals have a general desire to live a greener lifestyle, no specific individuals could be known to have benefited because of the firm's selling of that product to *other* specific yet unknown people.

Over the centuries, pollution has sometimes fallen because of forces within the self-regulating economy: the desire of profit-seeking firms to save resource expenses. But it is difficult to deny the significant effect of environmental political regulation on air and water quality since the early 1970s. We may thus state as a general principle that where individuals find it extremely difficult to communicate their particular desires to particular potential experimenters and experimenters find it similarly hard to provide benefits to those particular individuals, self-regulating forces will be weak.

Having said that, while the economic concepts of public goods and externalities described in Chapter 6 capture this idea, there is a natural tendency to underestimate not just the ability of people affected by the circumstances to negotiate among themselves but of innovators to rearrange the socioeconomy so that this inability to directly communicate vanishes.[21] Nonetheless, when large numbers of people are affected anonymously, negatively, and substantially by large numbers of equally anonymous others (large-scale environmental damage is the classic case), we may rightly be suspicious of the efficacy of self-regulation.

Historically, the common law of torts has served to substitute for private negotiation when strangers incapable of negotiating in advance are unexpectedly thrown together, as in the adjudication of fault in auto accidents. That the common law is evolutionary is an argument in its favor as a supplement to self-regulating socioeconomic forces and a substitute for majoritarian selection of ill-thought-out, possibly corruptly motivated and possibly permanent political controls. Also in the common law's favor is that the truth in individual cases is built through the adversarial process, which may be more conducive to the generation of information than the inquisitorial system that prevails in other countries, in which the court decides which information it needs. If one accepts Richard Posner's view that the common law's structure and evolution are in agreement with what is required to maximize the ability of people to create wealth given technological and other social change, its useful role is enhanced. This is particularly so compared to uniform legislative dictates, which are generally hostile to self-regulation.[22]

In addition to the problem of ineffective feedback because of the lack of direct links in some socioeconomic transactions, what economists call entry barriers may also limit the effectiveness of self-regulation. As natural, impervious barriers, these forces are vastly overestimated in the socioeconomy as a whole. Microsoft's "monopoly" of desktop computer operating systems in the 1990s proved ephemeral, as has every other one not the result of legal privilege before it. But there is significant evidence of an increase recently of nonpolitical barriers, sometimes mental (i.e., self-censorship) and sometimes institutional, to freedom of communication.

In the United States, these attempts now draw the greatest attention when they occur on college campuses, ironically so given the important role universities have long played in promoting free inquiry. In the past two decades, there have been a growing number of attempts on campuses both elite and ordinary to limit what students and faculty may say, in the interests of avoiding the taking of offense, "marginalization," "microaggressions," and so on. Recently, for example at the University of California and Middlebury College, people who use violence to shut down expression have bizarrely characterized that expression itself as violence. We should be concerned when numerous aggrieved interests—students, faculty, administrators, off-campus troublemakers, or elected officials—seek to limit participation in communication networks by limiting the choice of speakers students may hear or the things professors are allowed to teach them. Every speaker shouted down or disinvited, every professor intimidated, every section purged from syllabuses increases our ignorance. The quality of ideas rises in tandem with the vigor of the competition they face or have faced; that universities themselves often invoke pursuit of truth as one of their missions (the motto of Harvard has long been "Veritas") makes any failure by university personnel to recognize this strength of self-regulating communication tragic.

Fortunately, while many scholars who view themselves as defenders of the Western tradition are fighting (as they should) practices that limit freedom of communication on campus, whether imposed university-wide by administrators or in individual courses by professors, the full range of responses capable of being made to people who wish to sample a more robust spectrum of ideas must be considered. Increasingly education need not be obtained only by spending large amounts of money to park oneself for four or more years on a residential campus. Instead, people may seek education online. And leaders in more traditional venues may, as the dean of students at the University of Chicago, John Ellison, did in 2016 in a letter to incoming students, proclaim support for robust freedom to communicate. Almost certainly this is better preparation for a world in which respect for political correctness is likely to be in short supply; if so, schools that boast of this commitment will do well. In contrast, the University of Missouri is suffering declines in applications and enrollment after incidents in 2015 led, among other things, to being perceived as being hostile to such freedom.

While advocates of making some kinds of expression unspeakable in public are free to offer education subject to that rule, that option is no more likely to dominate the market for the exchange and acquisition of ideas than, in hindsight, nineteenth-century mail-order giants such as Sears, Roebuck and Montgomery Ward were likely to dominate the market for broad-spectrum retail middlemen. All that is needed is a desire to hear different points of view and that it be possible to provide at low cost an environment in which such views can be easily exchanged and refined. The problem of so-called political correctness, the latest chapter in the long-standing debate about the sorts of language considered a manifestation of ethical progress on the one hand and obscurantist on the other, will be

best worked out by free give-and-take among ideas, not by selective repression of some of them.[23]

As usual, we will have to work it out, one social experiment at a time.
As long as there are no entry barriers to opposing ideas, including ideas
that advocate new terminology for old things, competition among ideas
will yield the best outcome. This may work to the detriment of universities that become hostile to freedom of communication. Given the long historical record of higher education in conceiving new ideas, such a change
would be unfortunate; we will have to see. In the meantime, we owe it to
future generations to maintain the right to speak and, equally important,
the right to listen on campus.

NEW TECHNOLOGY AND SELF-REGULATION

This book has taken a long-term perspective on the human project as a
whole. As I write, the Internet has been a major public phenomenon for only
a quarter-century. But readers who remember using the Web for the first time
will also remember being struck by how transformative it seemed. And so it
is important to consider its impact on the strength of self-regulating forces.
In doing so, it is worth remembering that the high technology that has done
so much to enhance social evolution—by moving from large mainframes
that had to be continuously kept cool at great expense, to "personal" computers that relied on cassette tapes to store data, to hardware and software
that allowed users of desktop machines to access content on server computers around the world, to portable devices that allow users to carry that
access to content with them everywhere, to whatever will come next—has
happened almost entirely spontaneously. Among current industries in the
United States, high technology is distinctive in having been left largely unmolested politically for most of its history. No one reading this can hope to
accurately predict the nature of technology ten years from now as long as
it remains self-regulated; all we can be confident of is that it will be much
better at enabling human possibilities than the technology of today. Looked
at from the point of view of the power of self-regulation, this technology is
currently both its most vivid example and greatest enabler.

Admittedly, other things being equal, the computing revolution does
strengthen the ability of political actors to control in their own interest
social forces that otherwise tend toward self-regulation. The Internet might

enable rulers to better monitor and punish citizens who do things they dislike, and undoubtedly there will be continuing attempts to use advanced technology to keep out "socially disruptive" (read: politically threatening) ideas from abroad. By monitoring citizens with an eye to punishing them for what they say, new technology could cause self-regulation to decline. But the ongoing evolution of the Internet makes the case for reliance on self-regulation even more compelling and its likely scope greater.

All self-regulating social systems require that people be connected so that they can acquire and respond to information. In the early days of the Scientific Revolution, a small cadre of people who had come to consider themselves part-time scientists exchanged information in a leisurely way at the speed of the seventeenth century. By the twentieth century, the well-established scientific network could rely on modern transportation to take people to scientific conferences and on modern publishing to print an ever-larger number of scientific journals and books to be delivered by mail or online. The Internet has served as a tremendous multiplying force in this respect. People can more easily exchange data, conduct experiments and report on the results, and generate and debate new ideas.

Beyond science, they can also on their own use the technology to create new art, broadly defined, and new forms of art. In addition, people can and do take advantage of the expanding possibilities generated by the Internet to come up with new ways to address old human problems and to give them opportunities to tackle challenges that it never even occurred to them that they had. The extent to which the world's most desperately poor people are using rapidly evolving communications technology to escape poverty by linking to networks and then creating is breathtaking. Instead of waiting five years and perhaps paying bribes on top of that to get a government landline installed, one need only get an entry-level cell phone and begin hooking up with customers. This dynamism, powered by ever more participants in socioeconomic networks, should manifest not just as improved technology and new market structures but in all arenas of creativity. Imagine if all of the bile spent over the last several decades in arguing over how to alter political regulation of the provision of health care had instead been spent as energy improving it from below. With as much freedom to dynamically self-regulate as high technology has enjoyed, how much more progress would we have had?

The greater vibrancy of information exchange means that the examples that our high school textbooks used to teach us about the opportunities for business to abuse its workers and customers are all obsolete (if they were accurately rendered in the first place). The company town, which made it time cheap but monetarily expensive for workers to purchase goods anywhere except the company store, has been replaced by amazon.com and its ilk. The Better Business Bureau and Consumers Union, long the examples relied on in paper textbooks that chose to emphasize competition, now merely supplement the vast amount of available feedback. And this feedback is increasingly two-way—not just of sellers by buyers but buyers by sellers at websites with essentially infinite storage capacities for assessments of either side by the other. Airbnb is a vivid current example of such a setup.[24] Businesses also rely on such tools to compare suppliers and evaluate potential markets for what they sell. In addition, people who rely on eBay to pick up an old phonograph or sell something they found in a box at the back of the garage might view that as its main function; in fact, it provides a space for suppliers or product buyers to easily bid against one another, increasing the speed at which prices move down to the lowest level the overall market can support, enhancing static self-regulation.

Political regulation not only harvests such feedback much less effectively than self-regulation; it is more subject to corruption. Companies such as Uber have used the Internet, especially its incorporation into mobile "telephones" (since the word suggests transmission merely of sounds, I place it in quotation marks), to provide new ways for people with their own cars to make money by providing transportation to people who need it. Special interest groups that benefit from the existing system, built on a limited number of government-authorized taxis, have protested the entry of this new form of competition, sometimes vandalizing property in the process and sometimes drawing the sympathetic ear of politicians who have long supported the political regulation of labor markets.[25] These incumbents argue that the existing taxi companies have to play by the rules—specifically government limitations on self-regulating flexibility in the provision of transportation—so the new competitors should as well. The regulations, the incumbents say, are necessary in any event, citing passenger safety concerns in particular.

What is not generally appreciated is that the goals that people who drive for companies such as Uber have in deciding to sign up are limitless. Some of them, like many traditional taxi drivers, view it as a full-time job. Some of them view it as a temporary job to earn a little extra money, allowing them to concentrate on other life projects that they expect to be more fulfilling in the long run. Some of them enjoy the interaction with passengers, some not having to answer to a boss. What none of them have to do is accumulate money to cover the high cost of obtaining a piece of paper certifying they have political regulators' permission to run a taxi service. Finding a ride in this new way is frequently cheaper and more convenient for ride buyers and less burdensome for ride sellers. What is more, the new technology allows for spontaneously directed (in the sense of responding to both cost of provision and consumer willingness to pay) evolution in the provision of transportation, whether surge pricing (increased prices when demand is expected to be high or supply costlier, say because of a snowstorm) or self-driving cars. The regimented urban transportation alternative, even if we heroically assume that regulators simply wish to promote the public good, cannot perform with the same level of flexibility.

In this example, along with such other looming markets as health care tailored to individual data and needs[26] and the provision of short- or long-term housing, political regulation emphatically does not perform in the way that self-regulation does. "They should obey the rules, shouldn't they?" is often not the right question. "Should there be such rules?" is. Even such arguments in favor of political regulation as customer safety neglect that such regulation is inferior to the ability to monitor the quality of drivers *and* passengers delivered (as it were) by the new technology. Drivers whom passengers find undesirable—due to cars that are not clean, unsafe driving habits, being too chatty, not being chatty enough, general creepiness, any other reason at all—will be penalized either by drivers directly or by the companies that hire them. This is the very essence of a self-regulating process: participants are incented to find problems and address them, so that the overall system works better.

The struggle between the people who want to be allowed to try new ways to tackle new and old problems and those who benefit from the existing system in which political influence is the coin of the realm is the most important determinant of how much the Internet will improve human welfare. Its rapid improvement is surely related to the fact that its surprising emergence, along with that of computers generally, caught political regulators by surprise; hence, they were initially unable to impose much control on this self-regulating vibrancy. If the claims in this book are correct, the imposition of political regulation on it would have substantial negative consequences for human welfare.

Thus, the lower cost of generating information due to the Internet enhances the relative advantage of self-regulation. The cost of packaging and transmitting information is now so low that the human mind's ability to conceive and arrange it is the main limit to its expansion. On account of the Internet—the "net" part is for "network," after all—the channels of information and their conductivity are now increasing at a faster rate than ever before. If information is a key input to human progress and requires combining it with other information (supportive or critical) to unlock its potential, naturally the Internet will enhance the relative value of self-regulation as a generator of economic, ethical, artistic, and scientific progress.

Humans have always been able to combine and recombine in all manner of new personal networks, and in this way they remake society. But the pace at which they could do so was agonizingly slow before recorded history, and still glacial even after the invention of writing. A farmer or slave in ancient Egypt at the time of the building of the first pyramids (roughly 2600 B.C.), had he been transported to the time of Ramses II (1303 B.C.-1213 B.C.), would have recognized much that he saw around him in terms of social structure and the division of society into slaves and farmers, on the one hand, and scribes, merchants, and the ruling class, on the other. But a French peasant in 1770 would have been far more disoriented by the Paris of 1850, with its factories, coffee shops, opera houses, and civic participation. And a factory worker from the New York of 1950 transported into the Los Angeles of 2016 might be even more baffled by the dizzying array of languages, ethnicities, religions, technologies, housing, families, types of work, and social arrangements in general on display.

Treating the sick, educating the young (and enhancing the education of the middle-aged and older), quenching the human thirst for community, and tending to our fellows' minds and souls are all done much differently now. If the peasant-laden agricultural estate was the dominant form of economic organization in the West in the seventeenth century, and the mass production factory and skyscraper played that role in the nineteenth and twentieth, spontaneously generated communities of commercial and social partners and atomistic, individualized instead of centralized trading arrangements are increasingly playing that role in the twenty-first.

SELF-REGULATION GLOBALLY

This book has been dominated by discussion of the West. But the fruits of self-regulatory processes are certainly not confined to Western societies, and as these societies become less attached to self-regulation, other countries may more than make up the slack. The data largely support the most common recent accounts of market forces around the world—that they are expanding and leading to greater prosperity.

The Fraser Institute tracks economic freedom, a concept that includes the economic size of the state (taxes and spending), protection of property rights, sound money, barriers to trading with people in other countries, and the extent of regulation of commercial activity. The index is subjective, but it is consistent, and can be used for intertemporal comparisons. Figure 9.5 depicts unweighted country averages for the institute's rating from 1970 to 2013. While annual data are not available before 2000, the pattern suggests that freedom declined during the 1970s, rose dramatically after the Soviet collapse, stabilized in the early 2000s, fell noticeably after

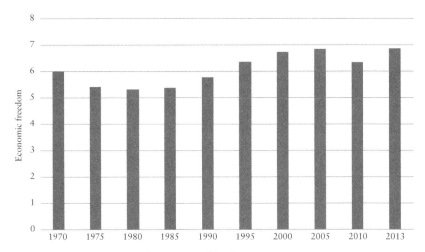

FIGURE 9.5. *Economic freedom worldwide, 1970–2013.*
Source: Fraser Institute (various years).

the 2007 global financial crash, and then returned to its prior level. The difference in the global mean country value since 1980, when it was 5.3, perhaps the global low-water mark of trust in self-regulation during this time, is not small—more than 1 standard deviation.[27]

There is a long way to go, but many of the world's people have come a long way. Only a handful of countries can be said to have gone dramatically against the tide in the past fifteen years in the direction of political control of the socioeconomy, while many, including the vast countries of India, China, and Brazil, have gone in the other direction. The peoples of these countries would be the first to testify to its liberating power. From a historic point of view, the turn of many substantially politically regulated societies toward socioeconomic self-regulation will be one of the most important stories of late twentieth- and early twenty-first-century history. More participants in the global self-regulating socioeconomy will everywhere mean more feedback, more experiments, and therefore more progress for all of us, no matter where we live. Indeed, the primary risk to socioeconomic self-regulation as I write is occurring in wealthy democratic countries, many of whose voters and citizens vote their discontent with it into law and shut self-regulating communication networks down through intimidation.

The globalization of science tells much the same story. The prestigious science journal *Nature* in 2012 published an index of international scientific collaboration and specialization, and several years ago described the spread of scientific productivity.[28] The general finding was that more people in more countries are doing more kinds of science. While it might have been easy a century or so after the founding of the Royal Society to imagine that most of the science that could be done had already been done, the scientific system seems to resemble art or the socioeconomy overall. Just as there is an unlimited supply of human problems for entrepreneurs to work on (and today's approaches, if successful, generate tomorrow's problems, which yesterday's people would have loved to have had), new methods to address existing problems and completely new discoveries expand rather than contract the scope of undiscovered science. When we consider the extent to which human expression too has continuously expanded, so that some ideas are abandoned but the new ones created give idea producers even more things to think about, it is clear that another strength of self-regulating systems is the way they continuously induce human exploration.

The news for freedom of communication is also optimistic overall, but the optimism here is tempered. Freedom House also rates almost every country in the world annually along several dimensions of personal freedom and civil rights. Whatever may be currently happening on American college campuses, global freedom of communication increased substantially from 1989 to the middle of the first decade of the 2000s, although it has slightly retreated since then. Still, the long-term news is good. In the 2015 ratings, for freedom of the press, sixty-three countries were rated as "free" (as opposed to fifty-seven in 1989), seventy-one rated as "partly free" (nineteen), and sixty-five as "not free" (eighty-three).[29] Since free communication is usually thought to threaten political authorities around the world, the contrast between increasing scientific cooperation (public funding's strictures aside) and a recent decrease in freedom of communication is not too surprising. Still, if the standard of comparison is, say, 1750 or 1945, self-regulating communication is now far more common around the world than before. Overall, even if the tendency as a whole since the late nineteenth century has been toward less reliance on self-regulating processes (especially socioeconomic ones) in the West, the news worldwide is on balance optimistic after several disastrous detours. The networking power of the Internet not only makes it harder for politics to suppress the exchange of information, it dramatically increases the extent of global links between people. The resultant spread of self-regulating processes is good news for the advancement of human progress on all fronts.

HOW TO LIVE IN A SELF-REGULATING WORLD

Self-regulation generates both effective adjustment to short-term surprises and long-term progress in many social systems. Thinking about what kind of society is best positioned to reap its benefits, and without neglecting the contributions of others documented here, two Brits had it about right: Adam Smith for static and John Stuart Mill for dynamic self-regulation. Smith emphasized the importance of easy entry, without which sellers could use the competitive limits political regulation bestowed on them to artificially prosper at the hands of consumers and investors in other potential socioeconomic experiments. Mill stressed the role social experimentation plays in human progress. In both cases, the citizen who is persuaded of the value of self-regulation should seek a politics that avoids limiting the energy of experiments carried out under competition. Several implications emerge from this framework.

First, think in degrees, and not in a binary way. Life is not usually one or zero, all or nothing, and a political regulator who speaks in terms of "solving" problems is usually talking nonsense. Health, opportunity, equality, and the other nominally virtuous purposes of politics are not things the lack of which needs to be solved. They are continuous and evolutionary, adjustable by degree and not present or absent because some political regulators have done (or failed to do) something, or that some political regulators and not others hold power. It is far better to speak in terms of improving health care in as many ways and for as many as possible than of "guaranteeing access" to "health care," or speaking of it as a right. So too with Internet access, education, compensation for work, and just about every other issue likely to preoccupy political regulators. That they *do* talk in these good/evil, success/failure binary terms suggests how effective such language is with the public.

Second, remember that figuring out how to do things is hard. If you don't believe it, try handling from your desk one that oil companies, gas station owners, and buyers address with great effectiveness every day in many places around the world: how much gasoline should go to each selling location, and how can it be done so that no gasoline is thrown away, even as customers never show up at the gas pump with no gasoline available for them to buy. Remarkably, in many societies, this problem is continuously solved despite the constant flow of disruptions to deal with. Remember that all problem solving is of this constantly fluctuating, evolving type—people move, countries become more prosperous, new engine technology is invented, other uses for crude oil are conceived, and so on—yet all these changes are quickly accommodated. Try to think about the fundamental economic problems as how to continuously reconcile all the ever-changing goals people have and limits they face, and not as maximizing the crude aggregate known as GDP or achieving some particular level of uniformity in whatever "income" we can measure, or providing a "right" to "health care," "education," a "living wage," and so on. Thinking of economic activity as improvement, and not as solving some social engineering problem, leads one to appreciate more the virtues of the self-regulating society. Competition is the most effective way to lower our collective ignorance. Respect it.

Third, give thought to why certain social results prevail. The distribution of anything that we care about is probably not adventitious; it is the result of social processes playing out. To upset those forces will have repercussions elsewhere, and almost certainly unfortunate ones. Society at any moment is what it is for a reason; to change it because it is by some arbitrary standard inferior is to foreclose many future paths to address problems, each competing against the others. Had contemporary society lamented the unfairness of Renaissance-era financial innovation or the instability brought about by sweeping away the stranglehold of the guilds and thus blocked them (let alone technologies like the printing press), much would have been lost later. It was only by exercising and then expanding the right to try experiments (the literal translation of laissez-faire is "let do," after all) that the progress that we enjoy happened. Again, the rapid global transformation both of and brought about by the Internet is instructive in this regard.

Fourth, there has been much talk in recent decades, especially in the wealthiest countries, of the benefits of "diversity." The hypothesis of dynamic self-regulation indeed supports the value of diverse experiments, provided that people are free to try any experiment they like. But politicians tend to concentrate on a small number of characteristics whose alleged importance citizens can be easily persuaded of—ethnoreligious and gender traits in particular. Never mind that the definition of race (and very recently gender) is fluid and that religions evolve, merge, and disappear.[30] Politicians Platonify the way people are now and are driven to divide us into permanent, rigid human categories. This is a mistake. It should be up to nonpolitical social experimentation to determine how we differ and how much those differences matter. What is needed is a society that is open to experimentation, combined with a willingness to accept whatever diversities (plural, note) are likely to facilitate experimentation.

Diversity can indeed contribute to more experiments because of a greater variety of life experiences—Millsian experiments. But what kind of diversity? When political regulators and their suitors seek to specify it, quantify it, and then manipulate it with rules, it immediately becomes a thing to be managed along whatever lines these people prescribe, and therefore loses most of its power to promote social improvement. Seen this way, universities, for example, might not wish to reify "race" in their hiring and admissions decisions, and choose instead to promote any diversity that makes the generation and exchange of ideas more fruitful.

Finally, the welfare state is a seemingly permanent feature of modern life. It is certainly true that the self-regulating socioeconomy produces significant nonuniformity (a better word than the normatively presumptive *inequality*) in contemporary monetary incomes and material wealth. If we take public programs to address such nonuniformity as given (and reasonable arguments can be made for them), it is better to leave as much freedom to choose as possible in the hands of providers and users. Such approaches will help poorer people cope with a lack of resources while minimizing destructive disruptions of self-regulation. Thus, politically mediated income transfers either as the mere means to purchase goods in general or (more specifically and therefore more dangerously) to promote the purchases of specific goods such as health care and housing by people of modest means can be justified. But it is worth remembering that the more such transfers are specifically regimented by political authorities— as in the United States, at least, health care and insurance in particular are—the less effective they are likely to be in achieving their goals, and the more substantially they will destroy the self-regulating experiments that would arise otherwise. In short, cash transfers are relatively inoffensive; vast, detailed government programs are more dangerous.

SOME FINAL IMPLICATIONS

When I was a child in the early 1970s, I asked my mother what a "conservative" and "liberal" (in the American sense) were, since these terms always seemed to be in the papers and on the network television news that my parents watched faithfully each night. She gave me an answer that still holds up pretty well after all these years: "conservatives want things to stay the way they are, and liberals want change." She could have added that such change was assumed by liberals in the modern sense to be achievable only by government direction. But there is a third possibility: society can and should change, but not all change is wise, so it is best to give individuals the maximum freedom to make things (including systems and institutions) and to break them, to try as many social experiments as possible.

Politics is different. When scientists, moralists, or others have a definitive view about how society "ought" to be and they merge these normative views with assumptions about how people subject to their commands *will* act, so as to create an ideology about the lawmaking process, bad things happen. If society cannot regulate itself, this view has it, the state must fill that vacuum. A widespread belief at least since the French Revolution has been that if people are imperfectly constituted, then they should be forced to behave perfectly. But that individuals are made or choose imperfectly in no way implies that the state shaping their choices, including by shaping people themselves, yields a better outcome. Even (naively) ignoring special-interest agitation as a primary determinant of political regulation, with a few well-defined exceptions there is little historical reason to think that centrally, coercively policing what is seen as socially costly conduct in the name of promoting better decision making will lead to something better than what would have been achieved otherwise. If the old objection to Keynesian economics was that public borrowing would crowd out private investments, now we ought to be concerned that politically regulated activity is crowding out self-regulated experiments.

And so when an expansion of government intervention is contemplated in the construction and destruction of social networks, several questions should be asked that seldom are. In the past, they went unasked because they didn't need to be (self-regulating progress being so obvious), and now because asking them never occurs to political regulators or others (many voters among them) who devote their lives to government's "solving problems." Granting the existence of some problem, is it a problem of modern vintage that people in previous decades or centuries would not have had the luxury of facing (e.g., how to "equalize" access to Internet communication), because self-regulating processes had not yet solved the even more pressing problems they contemporaneously faced? Given the interests (whether "merely" monetary or thoroughly benevolent) of individuals, how effectively is this problem likely to be addressed through self-regulation? (Note that we cannot say precisely how.)

Now suppose that politicians start from the premise of possessing moral and judgmental superiority in comparison to the entire self-regulated community. Then note the assistance that parliamentary procedures tend to give to short-term, us-against-them thinking and to decision-making inflexibility. Finally, add on a more realistic accounting of the sundry other less savory incentives political decision makers face and their inability to harvest the local knowledge that is the most important for effective decision making. Given this, how are political regulators likely to address this problem? Is the very act of addressing it through politics, let alone through some particular political solution, really wise? Perhaps it is best to always think in terms of enabling improvement in the overall human condition rather than solving particular problems now. In this way, the superiority of self-regulation is much clearer. No scientist ever wants to "complete" science, nor do we ever expect to "solve" art or ideas. The temptation of political regulators to succumb to the Platonic fallacy—follow the single ideal recipe to achieve paradise on earth—is clear, as is its weakness.

We owe the concept of the self-regulating socioeconomy primarily to English writers and, in its purely economic aspects, to Spanish and French writers as well. It is a product of pre-Enlightenment, Enlightenment, and early modern era thought and action. It is certainly fair to debate, as it is fair to debate any idea, whether the flexibility and turmoil that are necessary to effective self-regulation transfer well to other societies where social hierarchy is more deeply ingrained in the culture. As we have seen, the spontaneously constructed system to weed out the bad science and preserve and build on the good science, a process that extends to ideas generally, has yielded astonishing results. It is precisely because of the freedom of communication that scientific, ethical, artistic, and other expression has progressed so remarkably. Since commercial and social experimentation are characterized by the same lack of knowledge as these kinds of inquiry (and, as noted, competition is in some sense inquiry itself), these kinds of experimentation ought to be governed by the same commitment to openness to experimentation and a willingness to accept competition's verdict.

The spread of the self-regulating socioeconomy beyond the West has already begun to produce new scientific, ethical, artistic, commercial, and social entrepreneurs. People who live in such societies will benefit immensely, but so too will those of us in the rest of the world, because it is a question of numbers. The spread of the freedom to try, fail, and succeed means more experimenters, which inevitably means more success, which means more human progress. The architect Raymond Hood had it about right when he said in the 1930s that "congestion is good. . . . New York is the first place in the world where a man can work within a 10-minute walk of a quarter of a million people. . . . Think how this expands the field from which we can choose our friends, our coworkers and contacts, how easy it is to develop a constant interchange of thought."[31] His only error was not to complete the thought and appreciate how important "congestion"—lots of experimenters per problem—is in any self-regulating social process and how such processes improve humanity's possibilities.

Overall, as the economist Vernon Smith has noted, the law is limited enough as a tool to prevent us from actively harming others. As a tool to prevent us from harming ourselves, let alone as a tool to force us to help others, it is far less effective and indeed more destructive than the ordinary inducements that arise naturally from what it means to be human—the instinct toward benevolence, plus the desire to succeed, in other words. It is true that humans, as the simplistic overreduction of economic thinking often asserts, can sometimes pursue a very narrow conception of self-interest—money, power, and so on. But in a society that allows (nonviolent) competition among humans to proceed on all fronts, there is a natural tendency for humans to be able to get ahead by improving the lives of others too. The increase in doubt of the strength of this tendency in Western democracies in general and the United States in particular will have unfortunate consequences for future generations if it is not reined in. Most human progress has resulted from liberalization of the restraints imposed by political regulators on subjects and citizens, so that they may go out and try to do better. If enough try, improvement is guaranteed.

The evolutionary desires for hierarchy in general and to be on top of it in particular, once expressed in the language of divinity, then divine right, is now dressed up in the masquerade of the state as the bearer of both centralized expertise and the conjured public will. These two things are, the recent religion has it, the primary ingredients of all kinds of progress. The dynamics of self-regulating processes are fundamentally different; they impel (sometimes explicitly by design and sometimes merely as a natural effect) not merely growth in complexity but actual progress, a critical difference. While self-regulating processes inevitably throw up no small number of errors, the errors are quickly purged and the successes duplicated. They are simply collectively smarter than politically regulated ones. We should learn, or rather remember how, to trust them.

Notes

PREFACE AND ACKNOWLEDGMENTS

1. Graham (2016).

CHAPTER 1

1. Baines. (1848), 40.
2. Velasquez-Manoff (2012).
3. See, for example, Pommerau (2008).
4. The economist Peter Boettke in a lecture once discussed the almost complete unfamiliarity of contemporary English speakers with the word *ruth* in its adjective form (as opposed to as a proper noun). Only when they hear the word *ruthless* can they infer this older, and largely vanished, meaning. Some political regulation of language does exist, with the Académie Française policing the use of loan words in French and the Chinese government introducing simplified characters in 1956 as two notable examples.
5. Yang (2013).
6. Morehouse (2015).
7. Today many argue that human-induced extinctions *are* immoral, in contrast to the many extinctions that took place before the emergence of the human species. The truth of that assertion is beyond the scope of this book
8. See the many examples in Ostrom (1990).
9. Polanyi (1962); Rauch (2014).

CHAPTER 2

1. Baudin (1961), 200–201.
2. Psalms 8:5 (King James Version).
3. On chimpanzees, see Boehm (1999) and Johnson and Earle (1987). On bonobos, the results of more recent research on them and the controversy it has generated, see Parker (2007).
4. Humphrey (1976); Alexander (1990).
5. Service (1962).
6. See, for example, Service (1975), especially chap. 3.
7. Reyes-Centenoa et al. (2014).
8. Wurz (2012).
9. Renfrew (1974).
10. Keeley (1996).
11. Wright (2009).
12. Boorstin (1999), 5.
13. James (1982), 53.
14. Fukuyama (2011), 55; Boserup (1981), 40–42.
15. Crone (2015), 40.
16. Translations vary. This one is from http://avalon.law.yale.edu/ancient/hamframe.asp.
17. The Chinese characters for God in the monotheistic sense are *shàng dì* (上帝), which have the meaning of "highest god" or "above God." According to Google nGrams, a tool for tracking language trends discussed in Chapter 5, this term did not appear in Chinese texts until 1617, thirty-five years after the arrival of Jesuit missionaries in China.
18. Boorstin (1993), 18.

19. Keay (2012).
20. Tainter (1988), 6.
21. Sharer (2009), 132.
22. Hughes (1975), 152.
23. Chatterjee (1985).
24. Laudan (2013), 50.
25. Leeming (2010).
26. Translation from O'Flaherty (1973), 62.
27. "Critias" (1989), 305.
28. Thucydides (1960), 191.
29. Polybius in particular admired the Roman system for its ability to harness the various social classes when the Roman need was compelling.
30. Diamond (1999).
31. Thompson (1973), 105.
32. Bernstein (2013), 6.
33. A notable non-European work during this time was that of Japan's Yukichi Fukuzawa, published in 1875 and available in English translation from the Japanese (Fukuzawa, 2009).
34. Montesquieu (1949 [1748]).
35. Baron de Montesquieu (1949), 111 ("well-regulated"), 112 ("the power"), 113 ("the perils"), 56 ("who live," "have nothing").
36. Ibid., 150 ("power should"), 155 ("separate views"), 163 ("so perfect"),
37. Ibid., 25.
38. Hegel (1949).
39. Hegel (1964), 81–82.
40. Hegel (1965), x.
41. Hegel (1965), 110.
42. Houlgate (2015), 302.
43. Fox (2005), 135.
44. Bigelow (1895), 209.
45. Ibid.
46. Ibid., 206.
47. Osterhammer (2014), 711.

CHAPTER 3

1. Ponnamperuma (1984), 14.
2. Schick (1920).
3. Lepeschkin (1931), 568. For a favorable press write-up of Lepeschkin's evidence in favor of the "radiation release" hypothesis, see Lepeschkin (1932), 168. There was a story on, and then a debate on, the menotoxin hypothesis in letters to *The Lancet* as recently as 1977. Bryant, Heathcote, and Pickles (1977), 753.
4. For a recounting of many such stories, see Gratzer (2000). The account of "menotoxins" and emissions of ultraviolet radiation at death in particular is found in 44–46.
5. This distinction between science and not science is associated with Karl R. Popper's book, first published in German in 1934 and then translated into English by Popper himself in Popper (1959).
6. Kwa (2011), 15.
7. In McKeon (2001), 185–186.
8. Some argue that that even now, real-world practitioners often discover knowledge through trial and (extensive) error, while professors of science, engineering, finance, and others look back in time, mathematically specify what the practitioners are doing, and take credit for discovering the knowledge (Taleb, 2012; Rosenberg, 1986). But other times, as with the hypothesis of electromagnetism by James Clerk Maxwell (1831–1879) in 1873, the science came first.

9. P. Watson (2006), 482.

10. Fara (2009), 82–83.

11. Cited in Bowen (1963), 35.

12. Descartes (1962 [1637]).

13. Ibid., 80.

14. Fara (2009), 133–134.

15. A Mersenne prime is a prime number that is one less than a whole-number power of two (e.g., 31 or 7).

16. Boorstin (1985).

17. For example, it is the title of a chapter about the new mode of inquiry that emerged then. Barzun (2000), 191–235.

18. Montes (2008).

19. A. Alexander (2014), 250.

20. Cited in Caton (1988), 199.

21. Nakayama (1985), cited in Osterhammer (2014), 809.

22. J. D. Michaelis, Raisonnement Über die Protestantischen Universitäten in Deutschland [Reasonings over the Protestant universities in Germany] (1768), cited in Hofstetter (2001), 7.

23. Ibid., 12.

24. Paulsen (1906), 228.

25. Lévy (2003).

26. Spier (2002).

27. Crombie (1995).

28. Wolchover (2015); Dawid (2013).

29. Sokal (1996), 231. The broader indictment, after Sokal revealed the day the article came out that it was an elaborate compilation of gibberish, was originally published in French and then in English as Sokal and Bricmont (1998). A rejoinder to the indictment conveyed by the original article was originally published by Jacques Derrida (1930–2004) in *Le Monde* and can be found in a collection of his essays: Derrida (2005).

30. Ross (1996), 4. The skepticism of putatively "objective" knowledge did not extend to failing to include an objective table of contents to tell readers where to find the articles they wished to read, the academic affiliations of the authors, and other information.

31. The latter was fraud exposed not by criminal justice but by the sleuthing of scientists themselves. *Scientific American* once referred to the case as a "scientific crime"(De Groote, 2016).

CHAPTER 4

1. Gordon (1737), 96.

2. Bernstein (2013), 10.

3. To be fair, it was common for authors of work being contemplated for inclusion on the list to have the chance to defend it before Church authorities before the decision was taken.

4. These events are related in Osborne (2009).

5. Fevre and Martin (2010).

6. John Milton, "Areopagitica," in Milton (1991), 252 ("hee who," "for reason"), 255 ("writes," "summons up").

7. Ibid., 260–261.

8. Bernstein (2013), 200.

9. Chartier and Martin (1990).

10. Israel (2011).

11. Rousseau (1997 [1762]), 53.

12. The letter was published as Diderot (1937).

13. Laursen (2005), 105–106.

14. Helvétius (1801), 196. Note that here, "censure" means only criticism, not state censorship. Viziers were the chief bureaucrats of Ottoman sultans.

15. Zamoyski (2015).

16. Ibid., 439.

17. Hall (1793), 4.

18. Cited in Kennedy (2013), 16.

19. Mill, like his father James Mill before him, spent a number of years at the British East India Company but never went to India. The East India Company, which governed India until the company itself was terminated after the great rebellion of 1857, certainly did not govern in utilitarian fashion while he was there, although his task was merely to analyze dispatches sent from the territory. It is certainly possible that his beliefs about the legitimacy of nondemocratic rule when "dealing with barbarians, provided the end be their improvement, and the means justified by actually affecting that end" (*On Liberty*, I.10) were influenced by this experience (Mill, 1963 [1859]), 16.

20. Ibid., 83.

21. Ibid., 28.

22. "Continental Congress to the Inhabitants of the Province of Québec" (1987 [1774]), 442.

23. Debs v. United States, 249 U.S. 211 (1919); Schenck v. United States, 249 U.S. 47 (1917).

24. Abrams v. United States, 250 U.S. 616, 630 (1919).

25. Whitney v. California, 274 U.S. 357 (1927), 374.

26. Ibid., 375–377. The case involved Anita Whitney, who was convicted under California's Criminal Syndicalism Act of participating in a public meeting to establish the Communist Labor Party of America. The controlling opinion held that banning organizations like the party was a legitimate exercise of the public power.

27. New York Times Co. v. Sullivan, 376 U.S. 254 (1964).

28. In order, the cases are Simon & Schuster v. Members of New York State Crime Victims Board, 502 U.S. 105 (1991); Rosenberger v. Rector and Visitors of University of Virginia, 515 U.S. 819 (1995); R.A.V. v. City of St. Paul, 505 U.S. 377 (1992); United States v. Eichman, 496 U.S. 310 (1990).

29. Article 11, sections 1–2.

CHAPTER 5

1. Brigham (ed., 1982), 72–73.2. Leonard (2016), 79.

3. "Kautilya's Arthashastra" (1915), 17.

4. Peter Watson claims that for China in particular, such beliefs prevented the Chinese from developing "modern business methods or modern science." Watson (2006), 322–323.

5. *Politics* Book 10, in McKeon (2001), 1141. Skepticism of merchants has a long pedigree too in Chinese thought and its offshoots. It has been reported that during the Japanese Tokugawa era (1603–1867) a common saying translated into English was, "The offspring of a toad is a toad; the offspring of a merchant is a merchant" (Sheldon 1983, 478).

6. A possible exception to this framework is Hesiod, whose *Works and Days* is said to invoke the now-fundamental economic ideas of scarcity of resources, humans' competing ends, the virtues of competition, and the idea that hard work will at least partly achieve some of these ends (Gordon, 1963).

7. See Ambirijan (1997).

8. Klaar (2010), 893.

9. Rothbard (2009).

10. Roover (1958).

11. Watson (2006), 540.

12. Cantillon (2000), 21.

13. Hayek (1985 [1931]).

14. The table was a drawing. For a discussion of the changes Quesnay made to it over time, see Charles (2003).

15. Use of the term *intervention* admittedly supposes that self-regulating commerce is the natural order of things.

16. Locke (1965 [1690]), 26–27.

17. Locke never used "blank slate," speaking instead of humans coming into the world like "white paper, void of all characters, without any *Ideas*." Locke (1975 [1681]), 104.

18. Ibid., 10.

19. Mandeville (1997 [1723]), 23 ("Tyranny," "Wild," "Power"), 28 ("The root").

20. De la Rivière (2001), 46–47.

21. Turgot (2011 [1766]), 107.

22. Young (1996).

23. Smith (1976 [1776]), 17.

24. Ibid., 18.

25. Ibid., 113 ("exposed").

26. Ibid., 144.

27. Ibid., 172.

28. Godwin (2013). For the prominence of liberal thinking in English and French political thought during the later Enlightenment generally, see Rosenvallion (1979).

29. On refrigeration, see Goodwin, Grennes and Craig (2002).

30. For a collection of papers on the background and effects of translations of TWON into ten different languages, see the papers in Lai (2000).

31. In recent decades so-called "economic imperialism," the expansion of economic reasoning into what was previously the exclusive domain of other social scientists, has become more common. Turnabout being fair play, economists too have seen their traditional areas of inquiry become the subject of interest of such "harder" scientists as cognitive psychologists and even physicists.

32. Good summaries include Gleditsch (2008) and, with a focus on the minority of literature that is skeptical, Schneider, Barbieri and Gleditsch (2003).

33. Montesquieu, *The Spirit of the Laws* (1949), 316 ("cure"), 367 ("refined").

34. Voltaire (2007 [1733]).

35. Kant (1983 [1795]), 18 (emphasis in original).

36. Ibid., 25.

37. McCloskey (2007).

38. Pinker (2011), especially chap. 4.

39. A useful introduction to Rorty's theses is Rorty (2009).

40. "Herbert Spencer" (1903).

41. Spencer (1864), 444, 453, 457, 468, 474.

42. "Herbert Spencer" (1903).

43. Spencer (1897), vii. "That time" refers to Spencer's text *Social Statics*, published in 1850.

44. The entire quote here, indicating that moral evolution would cull hypercompetitive business practices, is from Bannister (2010), 78. The inner quotes are the exact words Spencer spoke at a lecture in New York on November 9, 1882. Also directly quoted by Bannister were Spencer's remarks that "the process of evolution throughout the organic world at large, brings an increasing surplus of energies that are not absorbed in fulfilling material needs, and points to a still larger surplus for the humanity of the future" (ibid.)

45. Sumner (1919), 480.

46. Leonard (2009).

47. "William Graham Sumner, Yale Professor, Dead" (1910).

48. "Death of Charles Darwin" (1882).

49. Google nGrams is a tool that searches all books that Google has digitized for a word phrase of any length. Any single word is a "1Gram," "survival of the fittest" is a "4Gram," and so on. The chart indicates the percentage of all "2Grams" found in books in Google's collection during the years displayed in the chart that are "social Darwinism." For

an exercise such as this, the phenomenon of interest is not so much the absolute proportion of a particular nGram as much as the change over time. I use the tool again in Chapters 6 and 8. For an introduction see Michel et al. (2011).

50. Leonard (2009).

51. Ridley (2011), 86.

52. Lord Kilbracken (1931), 83–84.

53. Partridge (2003), 75–76.

54. It would be remiss to not mention that in two dimensions, Gladstone was not libertarian by modern standards. He had a long history of partiality in matters of religion (although he worked, ultimately successfully, to end funding of the Church of England in Ireland), and as he got older he supported public pensions for the poor at the end of their lives. On this latter point and self-regulation, see Chapter 9.

55. Clark (2006), 328. The inner quotation is taken directly from the Prussian imperial post-Jena October Edict of 1807.

56. Mokyr (2012). For the rise of objective measures, see Allen (2012).

57. For discussion of Wayland, see Heyne (2008). For Perry, see Leonard (2016), 12–13.

58. While achieved largely nonviolently, abolition was delayed until 1886 in Cuba and 1888 in Brazil.

59. Osterhammer (2014), 454.

60. According to a significant body of historical analysis, Luddism was not simply targeted at machines that threatened to replace human workers, but at a refusal by the mill owners who installed them to adhere to the traditional apprentice system (Conniff, 2011). From the point of view of making reasonably priced clothing available to more people, such a reversion would have been equally problematic.

61. For documentation of increasing social segregation among white Americans in particular, see Murray (2012).

62. McCloskey (2010).

63. Osterhammer (2014), 771.

CHAPTER 6

1. Montesquieu (1949), 398.

2. For evidence regarding the long pedigree of financial instability, see Reinhart and Rogoff (2011).

3. On the latter, see Moore (2014).

4. Summarized in Barzun (2000), 117–143.

5. Watson (2006), 567.

6. Quoted as a response given to Tupy (2016).

7. Finland suffered one between 1866 and 1868, and in the twentieth century, there were the catastrophic communist-induced famines in the Soviet Union—both the well-known catastrophe in Ukraine in the early 1930s and the largely unknown one that killed at least 1 million people in Ukraine and Russia in 1921–1922.

8. Marshall (1961 [1920]), 4 ("excessive"); 593 ("mean sun," emphasis in original); 662–663 (movement of fluids); 526 (forces and system of balls).

9. Ibid., 41 ("to increase"), 502 ("evils"), 560–563 (poverty because of lack of parental resources).

10. Pigou (1912, 1920); Mill (1871). The last chapter of Mill's text, Chapter XI of book V, is titled "Of the Grounds and Limits of the Laisser-Faire or Non-Interference Principle."

11. Hardin (2016).

12. Sidgwick (1883).

13. Samuelson (1954).

14. The idea of equating quantities at the margin is critical in modern economic thinking. One wishes to look at marginal rather than total values. For example, while it is true that the average basketball player makes much more than the average teacher in the United

States, the number of teachers that Americans hire is far greater than the number of professional basketball players. In each case, we hope that we continue to hire people to do these tasks as long as the marginal value of hiring one more in each activity exceeds the marginal opportunity cost that worker doing that task faces. We spend far more in total on education than on professional basketball, but at the margin, teachers earn far less because there are far more people willing and able to do teaching, and teaching often must be done face-to-face rather than simultaneously broadcast to millions of students, as basketball is to viewers.

15. Marchovec (1997).

16. Coase (1960.)

17. For ways in which people create their own systems for managing the production in the sharing of ideas, distinct from formal intellectual property rules, see Raustiak and Sigman (2012).

18. Bartolini (2000). Note that radical alternatives were supported in part because the so-called roaring twenties were a distinctively American event. In Western Europe, numerous countries had difficulties with readjusting under fixed exchange rates to the postwar economic environment and, in Germany's case, to the onerous reparations mandated by the Treaty of Versailles.

19. This point is raised in Goldberg (2007), 36.

20. Sherman Antitrust Act (Sherman Act, 26 Stat. 209, 15 U.S.C. §§ 1–7).

21. Wilson (1908), 70.

22. His entire paragraph reads: "There will be a wrong done, not if we govern and govern as we will, govern with a strong hand that will brook no resistance, and according to principles of might gathered from our own experience, not from theirs, which has never yet touched the vital matter we are concerned with; but only if we govern in the spirit of autocrats and of those who serve themselves, not their subjects. The whole solution lies less in our methods than in our temper. We must govern as those who learn it and they must obey as those who are in tutelage. They are children and we are men in these deep matters of government and justice." Wilson (1902), 731.

23. Clayton Antitrust Act of 1914, 15 U.S.C. §§ 12–27, 29 U.S.C. §§ 52–53).

24. Rule, Cointet, and Bearman (2015).

25. For details on this explanation of "macroeconomic" instability, see Osborne (2001).

26. Theodore Roosevelt was of course already famous as someone who would interfere with self-regulation if it qualified as "trust busting." He had to be persuaded to let J. P. Morgan, who was already well known for privately organizing financing to prevent a U.S. default during an earlier panic of 1893, engineer a steel company merger to try to end the 1907 financial panic.

27. Shlaes (2007), especially chap. 3.

28. That the New Deal worsened the Depression is supported by evidence in Cole and Ohanian (2004). The judicial decision that declared the NRA unconstitutional was *Schechter Poultry Corp. v. United States*, 295 U.S. 495 (1935).

29. Grossman (2014). Grossman urges readers not to confuse the laws concerning income taxation with the overall "CCH Standard Federal Tax Reporter," which includes those laws, related court cases, Treasury regulations, and other content that is relevant to but is not the same as the law itself. This latter figure has grown to roughly 70,000 pages, which is arguably another measure of the degree to which Congress has used tax law to insert itself into previously self-regulating processes.

CHAPTER 7

1. Ely (1896), 162–163.

2. Marx and Engels (2012 [1850, German version 1848]), 35.

3. Marx (1904 [German version 1859]), 11.

4. Marx (1963).

5. Hayek (1945), 521.

6. Cheng (2009).

7. Among the more influential works are Hardt and Negri (2000) and Wallerstein (1974).

8. Foucault (1972 [French version 1969]).

9. Said (1978).

10. Rousseau (1979 [1762]); Helvétius 1810 [1777]), 17.

11. Chernyshevsky (2014 [1861]); Gorky (1992 [1907]). Other examples are provided in Cheng (2009).

12. Rose (2007).

13. Galton (1883), 25.

14. Rose (2007), 60.

15. Shaw (1904), 21.

16. Ely (1906), 171.

17. Ely (1896), 781.

18. Leonard (2016).

19. Seager (1913), 10.

20. Although he emphasizes the impropriety of the firing rather than the occasion for it, the details of Ross' dismissal are found in Samuels (1991).

21. Buck v. Bell, 274 U.S. 200 (1927). (Internal citations deleted.) The decision was 8–1, with Justices William Howard Taft, Willis Van Henry Rogers Seager, James C. McReynolds, Louis Brandeis, George Sutherland, Pierce Butler, Edward T. Sanford, and Harlan F. Stone joining. Not all of these justices are regarded by historians as progressives. McReynolds in particular is sometimes credited by modern libertarians with being a holdout in the 1930s against the New Deal's expansion of federal power.

22. Adkins v. Children's Hospital, 261 U.S. 525 (1923). Discussion of the effort by eugenicists to keep women where the future of the race demanded they be is discussed in Leonard (2016), esp. chap. 10.

23. Kline (2001), 107.

24. The eugenically motivated Nazi efforts were directed not just against Jews, who in the Nazi ideology were a devious, sinister threat, but against the mentally and physically handicapped and ethnic "subhumans," Slavs in particular (Snyder, 2011).

25. Rose (2007), 61.

26. For evidence on such increasing class-based stratification in the United States, see Murray (2012).

27. It has also been noted that "sustainability," like "public health" or "justice," is something that on its own no sensible person could be against. To advocate it as a goal by itself, without rigorous definition or consideration of the trade-offs, is thus completely unhelpful (Boudreaux, 2014).

28. See, e.g., Dahlberg and Mercy (2009).

29. Freud (2010 [1899]).

30. Greenberg (2013), 144. Note that Greenberg makes this remark in the context of being no particular fan of the self-regulating socioeconomy, which he believes is dominated by the rich and powerful, to society's detriment. In particular, he argues that mental illness is often "the suffering inflicted by our own peculiar institutions, the depression and anxiety sponsored by the displacements of late capitalism and postmodernity" (6), refers to such personality types as "thieves, rapists, and hedge fund managers" (148), and to "the capitalist imperative to turn all need into markets" (350).

31. For a different view about the entire concept of mental dysfunction, see the papers contained in Szasz (1984).

32. British Psychological Society (2011), 2.

33. Watson (1930), 82. To be sure, this argument was raised to establish that genes are everything, an idea discussed above.

34. Blashfield at al. (2014). For a view disputing the premise that counting diagnoses is even all that meaningful, and arguing that, using a consistent definition, the listed "Num-

ber of psychiatric disorders" decreased between DSM IV and DSM 5 from 172 to 152, see McCarron (2013).

35. Jost (1995), 400. The embedded quotation is from Cunningham (1987), 255.

36. For example, Cris Mayo (2013) says that "false consciousness implies that someone may be blinded by ideology and not realize the truth about herself or her situation" (244).

37. Barber (1995), 37 ("manipulated"); Barber (1998), 37–38 ("sales"). Barber (2007) *passim* ("want to want," "infantilist" "colonizing," "addictive").

38. Frank (1997), 272.

39. Kasser et al. (2004).

40. Kasser (2011).

41. Lakoff (2002), 35.

42. Sandman (2009).

43. McCright and Dunlap (2011); Grimes (2016).

44. Will ere long reduce: Wilson (1999). Has reduced: Harris (2012). For a more sophisticated, arguably optimistic view on the human consciousness and agency, see Gelernter (2016).

45. Thaler and Sunstein (2003).

CHAPTER 8

1. The Constitution makes no mention either of a cabinet or any distinction between departments and mere agencies. Presidents sometimes accord particular agency heads or other government officials (e.g., the U.N. ambassador) honorary cabinet status, but while this allows them to attend the occasional meetings of the entire cabinet, it does not give them any other power or responsibility. By legislation rather than the Constitution, cabinet secretaries are part of the presidential order of succession. This order has long been the same as that in which their departments were created.

2. Federal Food and Drugs Act of 1906 (34 Stat. 768 (1906)).

3. Pub.L. 111–203, H.R. 4173

4. For regulatory budgets, see data compiled by the Regulatory Studies Center at George Washington University, at http://regulatorystudies.columbian.gwu.edu/reg-stats.

5. Sinclair and Vesey (2012); Dawson and Seater (2013).

6. Michel et al. (2011).

7. It is important to distinguish between three concepts: disagreement over what to do about the implications of climate science, evidence-or logic-based (i.e., scientific) criticism of existing climate science, and the belief that the climate-science process itself is corrupt.

8. Caplan (2007). A best-seller with the phrase is Fox (2009).

9. Search conducted on *scholar.google.com* on August 16, 2015.

CHAPTER 9

1. Rushdie (1993), 122.

2. Ridley (2011), 107 (workplace safety); Murray (1997), 47–56 (auto safety). Murray argues that much political regulation fails this trend-line test.

3. The history and literature of the use of these compounds are summarized in Shah et al. (2014).

4. Klein and Tabarrok (2016).

5. For evidence of excessive attention to the first type of error (in statistics a type 2 error) in the design of FDA studies, see Montazerhodjat and Lo (2015). For evidence of such a tendency in FDA decision making more generally, see Tabarrok (2000).

6. This special-interest-struggle view of government policymaking is part of the economic field known as public choice. Two landmark papers are Tullock (1967) and Krueger (1974).

7. Juma (2016).

8. Bornmann and Mutz (2015).

9. Murray (2003); Asimov (1989).

10. Ness (2014).

11. Freedom House (2015).

12. Veylit (n.d.).

13. Michel et al. (2011).

14. Gordon (2016). Total factor productivity stipulates a particular mathematical relationship between output and, usually, two inputs—labor and capital. Statistical analysis can reveal how GDP growth is distributed among growth in the two inputs, plus growth in the overall effectiveness of using them, that is, growth in total factor productivity.

15. Shackleton (2013).

16. Hamilton and Chinn (2014).

17. For an optimistic interpretation of recent decades in the United States, especially along the ethical/moral dimension, see McCloskey (2016).

18. Schleicher (forthcoming).

19. Decker et al. (2016).

20. Buckley Jr. (2016), 26–7.

21. That people can negotiate the resolution of negative externalities among themselves is an argument made famous in Coase (1960).

22. See Posner (2014), especially chap. 20, for the argument and several asserted examples.

23. Consistent with the discussion in Chapter 5 of the moral improvement a self-regulating socioeconomy can generate, many speech patterns that were not just acceptable but common a century ago—racial slurs, for example—have all but disappeared in modern society. Such a purging of speech, far from amounting to censorship (here, meaning government suppression of individual speech), has both led to and been led by growing inter-ethnic harmony. That many in modern industrial societies view the current situation as one of growing ethnoreligious intolerance strongly suggests the need to take a long-term point of view on such questions.

24. Note that such services include information on the amiability (or absence thereof) of the landlord, safety of the neighborhood, ease of bringing luggage into the room, and a host of other considerations that are important to travelers and always have been. These were largely unknowable until someone at the companies offering the ratings websites, perhaps based on feedback from reviewers, decided to allow largely unrestricted buyer assessment of sellers.

25. One such violent protest in France is described in Rubin and Scott (2015).

26. Increasingly, individuals are able to wear devices that constantly collect data useful in diagnosing the current state of their health to be stored in the cloud, and to use computer power to analyze it, not always with the direct involvement of such human intermediaries as doctors.

27. Fraser Institute (various years).

28. "Global Mobility: Science Mapped Out" (2012).

29. Freedom House (2015).

30. The definition of the "white" "race" changed over time from northwestern Europeans to Christian Europeans generally to including Jews. Even now, people in other parts of the world (I have had experience with Japan and Taiwan in particular) view Arabs and Persians as "white," even as many "whites" do not. The idea of the Latino (or is it Hispanic?) identity, while of recent vintage, has become more emphasized in political circles as a racial category even as south of the Rio Grande there is no such thing as a "Latino." And this is without even wading through various conceptions of "mixed race."

31. Quoted in Boorstin (1993), 547–548.

References

Alexander, Amir. *Infinitesimal: How a Dangerous Mathematical Theory Shaped the Modern World.* New York: Scientific American/Farrar, Strauss and Giroux, 2014.

Alexander, Richard. *How Did Humans Evolve? Reflections on the Uniquely Unique Species.* Ann Arbor: University of Michigan Press, 1990.

Allen, Douglas W. *The Institutional Revolution: Measurement and the Economic Emergence of the Modern World.* Chicago: University of Chicago Press, 2012.

Ambirijan, S. "The Concepts of Happiness, Ethics, and Economic Growth in Ancient Economic Thought." In B. B. Price, ed., *Ancient Economic Thought*, 19–42. London: Routledge, 1997.

Asimov, Isaac. *Asimov's Chronology of Science and Discovery.* New York: Harper, 1989.

Baines, Edward Jr. *Crosby-Hall Lectures in Education.* London: John Snow, 1848.

Bannister, Robert C. *Social Darwinism: Science and Myth in Anglo-American Social Thought.* Philadelphia: Temple University Press, 2010.

Barber, Benjamin R. *Jihad vs. Mcworld: How Globalism and Tribalism Are Reshaping the World.* New York: Times Books, 1995.

———. "Democracy at Risk: American Culture in a Global Culture." *World Policy Journal* 15, no. 2 (1998): 29–41.

———. *Consumed: How Markets Corrupt Children, Infantilize Adults, and Swallow Citizens Whole.* New York: Norton, 2007.

Bartolini, Stefano. *The Political Mobilization of the European Left, 1860–1980: The Class Cleavage.* Cambridge: Cambridge University Press, 2000.

Barzun, Jacques. *From Dawn to Decadence, 1500 to the Present: 500 Years of Western Cultural Life.* New York: HarperCollins, 2000.

Baudin, Louis. *A Socialist Empire: The Incas of Peru.* Edited by Arthur Goddard. Translated by Katherine Woods. Princeton, NJ: D. Van Nostrand, 1961.

Berlin, Isaiah. "Two Concepts of Liberty." In Isaiah Berlin, *Liberty*, 1–54. Oxford: Oxford University Press, 2004.

Bergmann, Barbara. "A Threat Ahead from Word Processors." *New York Times*, May 30, 1982.

Bernstein, William. *Masters of the Word: How Media Shaped History.* New York: Grove/Atlantic, 2013.

Bigelow, Poultney. "The German Struggle for Liberty." *Harper's New Monthly Magazine* 91, no. 542 (1895): 202–219.

Blashfield, Roger K., Jared W. Keeley, Elizabeth H. Flanagan, and Shannon R. Miles. "The Cycle of Classification: DSM-I through DSM-5." *Annual Review of Clinical Psychology* 10 (2014): 25–51.

Boehm, Christopher. *Hierarchy in the Forest: The Evolution of Egalitarian Behavior.* Cambridge, MA: Harvard University Press, 1999.

Boorstin, Daniel R. *The Creators: A History of Creators of the Imagination.* New York: Vintage Books, 1993.

———. *The Seekers: The Story of Man's Continuing Quest to Understand His World.* New York: Vintage Books, 1999.

———. *The Discoverers: A History of Man's Search to Know his World and Himself.* New York: Vintage, 1983.

Bornmann, Lutz, and Rüdiger Mutz. "Growth Rates of Modern Science: A Bibliometric

Analysis Based on the Number of Publications and Cited References." *Journal for the Association of Information Science and Technology* 66 (2015): 2215–2222.

Boserup, Ester. *Population and Technological Change*. Chicago: University of Chicago Press, 1981.

Boudreaux, Donald J. "Unsustainable Platitudes." *Pittsburgh Tribune-Review*, August 12, 2014. http://triblive.com/opinion/donaldboudreaux/6556379–74/petroleum-sustainability -policies#axzz3fFSC8nZJ.

Bowen, Catherine Drinker. *Francis Bacon: The Temper of a Man*. Boston: Little, Brown, 1963.

Brigham, C., ed. *Wit and Wisdom: A Public Affairs Miscellany*. Melbourne: Melbourne University Press, 1982.

British Psychological Society. "Response to the American Psychiatric Association: DSM-5 Development." 2011. http://apps.bps.org.uk/_publicationfiles/consultation-responses/ DSM-5%202011%20-%20BPS%20response.pdf.

Bryant, J. A., D. J. Heathcote, and V. R. Pickles. "The Search for 'Menotoxin.'" *Lancet* 309, no. 8014 (1977): 753.

Buckley, William F. Jr. *A Torch Kept Lit: Great Lives of the Twentieth Century*. Edited by James Rosen. New York: Crown Forum, 2016.

Cantillon, Richard. *An Essay on Economic Theory: An English Translation* [Essai sur la nature du commerce en générale]. Translated by Chantal Saucier. Edited by Mark Thorton. Auburn, AL: Ludwig von Mises Institute, 2000.

Caplan, Bryan. *The Myth of the Rational Voter: Why Democracies Choose Bad Policies*. Princeton, NJ: Princeton University Press, 2007.

Caton, Hiram. *The Politics of Progress: The Origins and Development of the Commercial Republic, 1600–1835*. Gainesville: University of Florida Press, 1988.

Charles, Loïc. "The Visual History of the *Tableau économique*." *European Journal of the History of Economic Thought* 10(2003): 527–550.

Chartier, Roger, and Henri-Jean Martin, *Histoire de l'édition Française*, vol. 2: *Le livre triomphant (1660–1830)*, Paris: Fayard, 1990.

Chatterjee, Meera. "The Food of Healing." *India International Centre Quarterly* 12, no. 2 (1985): 129–140.

Cheng, Yinghong. *Creating the New Man: From Enlightenment Ideals to Socialist Realities*. Honolulu: University of Hawai'i Press, 2009.

Chernyshevsky, Gavrilovich. *What Is to Be Done? The Story about the New Man*. Translated by Michael R. Katz. Edited by William G. Wagner. Ithaca, NY: Cornell University Press, 2014 [1861].

Clark, Christopher. *Iron Kingdom: The Rise and Downfall of Prussia, 1600–1947*. Cambridge, MA: Belknap Press, 2006.

Clive, John. *Macaulay: The Shaping of the Historian*. New York: Knopf, 1973.

Coase, Ronald H. "The Problem of Social Cost." *Journal of Law and Economics* 3 (1960): 1–44.

Cole, Harold L., and Lee E. Ohanian. "New Deal Policies and the Persistence of the Great Depression: A General Equilibrium Analysis." *Journal of Political Economy* 112, no. 4 (2004): 779–816.

Conniff, Richard. "King Ludd's War." *Smithsonian* 41, no. 11 (2011): 82–94.

"Continental Congress to the Inhabitants of the Province of Québec." 1774. In *The Founders' Constitution*, edited by Philip B. Kurland and Ralph Lerner, 441–444. Indianapolis: Liberty Fund, 1987.

"Critias." In *Plato in Twelve Volumes*, vol. 9: *Timaeus, Critias, Cleitophon, Menexenus, Epistles*. Translated and edited by R. G. Bury. Cambridge, MA: Harvard University Press, 1989.

Crombie, Alastair. *Styles of Scientific Thinking in the European Tradition: The History of Argument and Explanation Especially in the Mathematical and Biomedical Sciences and Arts*. London: Gerald Duckworth & Company, 1995.

Crone, Patricia. *Pre-Industrial Societies: Anatomy of the Pre-Modern World*. New York: Blackwell, 2015 [1989].

Cunningham, F. *Democratic Theory and Socialism*. Cambridge: Cambridge University Press, 1987.

Dahlberg, L. L., and J. A. Mercy. "The History of Violence as a Public Health Issue." *AMA Virtual Mentor* 11, no. 2 (2009): 167–172.

Dawid, Richard. *String Theory and the Scientific Method*. Cambridge: Cambridge University Press, 2013.

Dawson, John W., and John J. Seater. "Federal Regulation and Aggregate Economic Growth." *Journal of Economic Growth* 18, no. 2 (2013): 137–177.

De la Rivière, Pierre Paul Mercier. *L'ordre naturel et essentiel des sociétés politiques* [The natural and essential order of political societies]. Paris: Fayard, 2001.

De Roover, Raymond. "The Concept of the Just Price: Theory and Economic Policy." *Journal of Economic History* 18, no. 4 (1958): 418–434.

"Death of Charles Darwin." *New York Times*, April 25, 1882.

Decker, Ryan A., John Haltiwanger, Ron S. Jarmin, and Javier Miranda. "Declining Business Dynamism: Implications for Productivity?" Brookings Institution, August 2016, https://www.brookings.edu/wp-content/uploads/2016/08/haltiwanger_conference_draft.pdf.

Derrida, Jacques. *Paper Machine (Cultural Memory in the Present)*. Translated by Rachel Bowlby. Stanford: Stanford University Press, 2005.

Descartes, René. *Discourse on Method*. Translated by John Veitch. Chicago: Open Court, 1962 [1637].

Diamond, Jared. *Guns, Germs and Steel: The Fates of Human Societies*. New York: Norton, 1999.

Diderot, Denis. *Pages inédites contre un tyran*. Paris: GLM, 1937.

Earle, Timothy, and Allen W Johnson. *The Evolution of Human Societies: From Foraging Group to Agrarian State*. Stanford: Stanford University Press, 1987.

Einstein, Albert. *The Albert Einstein Reader*. New York: Citadel, 2006.

Ely, Richard T. *The Social Law of Service*. New York: Eaton & Mains, 1896.

———. "Fraternity vs. Paternalism in Government." *Century Magazine* 55, no. 5 (1898): 780–784.

———. *Studies in the Evolution of Industrial Society*. New York: Macmillan, 1906.

Fara, Patricia. *Science: A Four Thousand Year History*. Oxford: Oxford University Press, 2009.

Fevre, Lucien, and Jean-Henri Martin. *The Coming of the Book: The Impact of Printing, 1450–1800*. London: Verso, 2010.

Foucault, Michel. *The Archaeology of Knowledge*. Translated by Alan Sheridan. London: Routledge 1972.

Fox, Justin. *The Myth of the Rational Market: A History of Risk, Reward, and Delusion on Wall Street*. New York: New York Times Company, 2009.

Fox, Michael Allen. *The Accessible Hegel*. Amherst, NY: Humanity Books, 2005.

Frank, Thomas. "Dark Ages." In *Commodify Your Dissent: Salvos from the Baffler*, edited by Thomas Frank and Matt Weiland, 255–274. New York: Norton, 1997.

Fraser Institute. *Economic Freedom of the World: Annual Report*. Vancouver: Fraser Institute, various years.

Freedom House. *Freedom in the World*. New York: Freedom House, 2015.

Freud, Sigmund. *The Interpretation of Dreams*. Translated by James Strachey. New York: Basic Books, 2010 [1899].

Fukuyama, Francis. *The Origins of Political Order: From Prehuman Times to the French Revolution*. New York: Farrar, Strauss and Giroux, 2011.

Galton, Francis. *Inquiries into Human Faculty and its Development*. London: Macmillan, 1883.

Gelernter, David. *The Tides of Mind: Uncovering the Spectrum of Consciousness*. New York: Liveright, 2016.

Gleditsch, Nils Petter. "The Liberal Moment Fifteen Years On." *International Studies Quarterly* 52, no. 4 (2008): 691–712.

"Global Mobility: Science Mapped Out." *Nature* 490, no. 7420 (2012), 325–338.

Godwin, William. *Enquiry Concerning Political Justice.* Oxford: Oxford University Press, 2013.

Goldberg, Jonah. *Liberal Fascism: The Secret History of the American Left from Mussolini to the Politics of Meaning.* New York: Doubleday, 2007.

Goodwin, Barry K., Thomas Grennes, and Lee A. Craig. "Mechanical Refrigeration and the Integration of Perishable Commodity Markets." *Explorations in Economic History* 39, no. 2 (2002): 154–182.

Gordon, Barry. "Aristotle and Hesiod: The Economic Problem in Greek Thought," *Review of Social Economy* 21, no. 2 (1963): 147–156.

Gordon, Robert J. *The Rise and Fall of American Growth: The U.S. Standard of Living since the Civil War.* Princeton: Princeton University Press, 2016.

Gordon, Thomas. "Of Freedom of Speech. That the Same Is Inseparable from Publick Liberty." In *Cato's Letters; or, Essays on Liberty, Civil and Religious, and Other Important Subjects*, vol. 1. Edited by John Trenchard and Thomas Gordon. London: W. Wilkins, T. Woodward, J. Walthof and J. J. Peele, 1737.

Gorky, Maxim. *Mother: The Great Revolutionary Novel.* New York: Citadel, 1992 [1907].

Graham, David. "The Private Sector Is Now Providing Basic Services to Flint." *Atlantic*, January 26, 2016. http://www.theatlantic.com/politics/archive/2016/01/flint-water-crisis-walmart/427062/.

Gratzer, Walter. *The Undergrowth of Science: Delusion, Self-Deception and Human Frailty.* Oxford: Oxford University Press, 2000.

Greenberg, Gary. *The Book of Woe: The DSM and the Unmaking of Psychiatry.* New York: Blue Rider Press, 2013.

Grimes, David Robert. "On the Viability of Conspiratorial Beliefs." *PLoS One* 11, no. 3(2016): e0151003. http://journals.plos.org/plosone/article?id=10.1371/journal.pone.0147905.

De Groote, Isabelle. "Solving the Piltdown Man Scientific Fraud." *Scientific American*, August 10, 2016, https://www.scientificamerican.com/article/solving-the-piltdown-man-scientific-fraud/.

Grossman, Andrew L. "Is the Tax Code Really 70,000 Pages Long? No, Not Even Close." *Slate*, April 14, 2014. http://www.slate.com/articles/news_and_politics/politics/2014/04/how_long_is_the_tax_code_it_is_far_shorter_than_70_000_pages.html.

Hall, Robert. "An Apology for Freedom of the Press, and the General Liberty." London: GGJ and J. Robinson, 1793.

Hamilton, James D., and Menzie Chinn. "Pessimism about U.S. Growth Rates." *Econbrowser: Analysis of Current Economic Conditions and Policy*, September 15, 2014, http://econbrowser.com/archives/2014/09/pessimism-about-u-s-growth-rates.

Hardin, Garrett. "Tragedy of the Commons." In Liberty Fund, *The Concise Encyclopedia of Economics.* February 19, 2016. http://www.econlib.org/library/Enc/TragedyoftheCommons.html.

Hardt, Michael, and Antonio Negri. *Empire.* Cambridge, MA: Harvard University Press, 2000.

Harris, Sam. *Free Will.* New York: Free Press, 2012.

Hayek, F. A. "The Use of Knowledge in Society." *American Economic Review* 35, no. 4 (1945): 519–530.

———. "Richard Cantillon," Translated by Micheál Ó Suilleabháin. *Journal of Libertarian Studies* 7, no. 2 ([1931] 1985): 217–247.

———. *The Fatal Conceit: The Errors of Socialism.* Chicago: University of Chicago Press, 1988.

Hegel, Georg Wilhelm Friedrich. *The Phenomenology of Mind.* London: Allen & Unwin, 1949.

———. *The Phenomenology of Spirit*, Edited and translated by J. B. Baille. London: George Allen and Unwin, 1964.

———. *Philosophy of Right.* Frome, UK: D. R. Hillman & Sons, 1965.

Helvétius, Claude-Adrien. *A Treatise on Man: His Intellectual Faculties and His Education.* Translated by W. Hooper. London: Werner, Hoose and Sharpe, 1810 [1777].

Helvétius, Claude-Adrien. *De l'esprit* [Essays on the mind and its several faculties]. London: Albion Press, 1801.

"Herbert Spencer." *New York Times*, December 9, 1903.

Heyne, Paul. *Are Economists Basically Immoral? And Other Essays on Economics, Ethics and Religion*. Indianapolis: Liberty Fund, 2008.

Hofstetter, Michael J. *The Romantic Idea of a University: England and Germany, 1770–1850*. Basingstoke, UK: Palgrave, 2001.

Houlgate, Stephen. *A Companion to Hegel*. Hoboken, NJ: Wiley, 2015.

Hughes, J. Donald. *Ecology in Ancient Civilizations*. Albuquerque: University of New Mexico Press, 1975.

Humphrey, N. K. "The Social Function of Intellect." In *Growing Points in Ethology*, edited by P. P. G. Bateson and R. A. Hinde. Cambridge: Cambridge University Press, 1976.

Israel, Jonathan. "Libertas Philosophandi in the Eighteenth Century: Radical Enlightenment versus Moderate Enlightenment" In *Freedom of Speech: The History of an Idea*, edited by Elizabeth Powers, 1–18. Lewisburg, PA: Bucknell University Press, 2011.

James, William. *The Varieties of Religious Experience*. New York: Penguin, 1982.

Jost, John T. "Negative Illusions: Conceptual Clarification and Psychological Evidence Concerning False Consciousness." *Political Psychology* 16, no. 2 (1995): 397–424.

Juma, Calestous. *Innovation and Its Enemies: Why People Resist New Technologies*. Oxford: Oxford University Press, 2016.

Kant, Immanuel. *To Perpetual Peace: A Philosophical Sketch*. Translated by Ted Humphrey. Indianapolis: Hackett, 1983.

Kasser, Tim. "Materialistic Value Orientation." In *The Palgrave Handbook of Spirituality in Business*, edited by Luk Bouckaert and Laszlo Zsolnai, 204–211. New York: Palgrave Macmillan, 2011.

Kasser, Tim, Richard M. Ryan, Charles E. Couchman, and Kennon Sheldon. "Materialistic Values: Their Causes and Consequences." In *Psychology and Consumer Culture: The Struggle for a Good Life in a Materialistic World*, edited by Tim Kasser and A. D. Kenne, 11–28. Washington, DC: American Psychological Association, 2004.

Kautilya's Arthashastra. Translated by David McKay. 1915. https://ia802703.us.archive.org/13/items/Arthasastra_English_Translation/Arthashastra_of_Chanakya_-_English.pdf.

Keay, John. *India: A History*, rev. and updated. New York: Grove Press, 2012.

Keeley, Lawrence H. *War before Civilization*. New York: Oxford University Press, 1996.

Kennedy, Catriona. *The Palgrave Macmillan Narratives of the Revolutionary and the Napoleonic Wars: Military and Civilian Experience in Britain and Ireland*. New York: Palgrave Macmillan, 2013.

Kilbracken, Lord. *Reminiscences of Lord Kilbracken*. London: Macmillan, 1931.

Kwa, Chunglin. *Styles of Knowing: A New History of Science from Ancient Times to the Present*. Translated by David McKay. Pittsburgh: University of Pittsburgh Press, 2011.

Klaar, Victor V. "Ethics and Economics." In *21st Century Economics: A Reference Handbook*, edited by Rhona C. Free, 891–900. Thousand Oaks, CA: Sage, 2010.

Klein, Daniel B., and Alexander Tabarrok. "Theory, Evidence and Examples of FDA Harm." In *FDAReview.org*: A Project of the Independent Institute. 2016. http://www.fdareview.org/05_harm.php.

Kline, Wendy. *Building a Better Race*. Berkeley: University of California Press, 2001.

Knox, T. M. "Translator's Foreword." In G. W. F. Hegel, *Hegel's Philosophy of Right*. Frome, UK: D. R. Hillman & Sons, 1965.

Krueger, Anne O. "The Political Economy of the Rent-Seeking Society." *American Economic Review* 64 (1974): 291–303.

Lai, Cheng-Chung, ed. *Adam Smith across Nations: Translations and Receptions of The Wealth of Nations*. Oxford: Oxford University Press, 2000.

Lakoff, George. *Moral Politics: How Liberals and Conservatives Think*. Chicago: University of Chicago Press, 2002.

Laudan, Rachel. *Cuisine and Empire: Cooking in World History*. Berkeley: University of California Press, 2013.

Laursen, John Christian "Censorship in the Nordic Countries, ca. 1750–1890: Transformations in Law, Theory, and Practice." *Journal of Modern European History* 3, no. 1, (2005): 100–116.

Leeming, David Adams. *Creation Myths of the World: An Encyclopedia*. Santa Barbara, CA: ABC-Clio Press, 2010.

Leonard, Thomas C. "Origins of the Myth of Social Darwinism: The Ambiguous Legacy of Richard Hofstadter's Social Darwinism in American Thought." *Journal of Economic Behavior and Organization 71*, no. 1 (2009): 37–51.

———. *Illiberal Reformers: Race, Eugenics, and American Economics in the Progressive Era*. Princeton: Princeton University Press, 2016.

Lepeschkin, W. W. "The Effect of Sunlight on Human Blood Cells." *Science* 73, no. 1899 (1931): 568.

———. "Necrobiotic Rays." *Science* 76, no. 1964 (1932): 168.

Lévy, Pierre. "Education et Cyberculture." Promotheus 21, October 3, 2003. http://www .ub.edu/prometheus21/articulos/obsciberprome/levy2.pdf.

Locke, John. *An Essay Concerning the True, Original Extent and End of Civil Government [Second Treatise of Government]*. Edited by Charles L. Sherman. New York: Appleton Century Crofts, 1965 [1690].

———. *An Essay Concerning Human Understanding*. Edited by Peter H. Nidditch. Oxford: Clarendon Press, 1975 [1681].

Mandeville, Bernard. *The Fable of the Bees and Other Writings*. Indianapolis: Hackett, 1997 [1723].

Marchovec, Frank M. *Perfect Competition and the Transformation of Economics*. London: Rutledge, 1997.

Marshall, Alfred. *Principles of Economics*, 8th ed. Cambridge: Macmillan, 1961 [1920].

Marx, Karl. *Contribution to the Critique of Political Economy*. Translated by N. I. Stone. Chicago: Charles H. Kerr & Co., 1904 [1859].

———. *The Eighteenth Brumaire of Louis Bonaparte*. New York: International Publishers, 1963.

Marx, Karl, and Frederick Engels. *Manifesto of the Communist Party: A Modern Edition*. London: Verso, 2012 [1850].

Mayo, Cris. "Gender Disidentification: The Perils of the Post-Gender Condition." In *Education Feminism: Classic and Contemporary Readings*, edited by Barbara J. Thayer-Bacon, Lynda Stone, and Katharine M. Sprecher, 243–252. Albany, NY: SUNY-Albany Press, 2013.

McCarron, Robert M. "The DSM-5 and the Art of Medicine: Certainly Uncertain." *Annals of Internal Medicine* 159, no. 5 (2013): 360–361.

McCloskey, Deirdre N. *The Bourgeois Virtues: Ethics for an Age of Commerce*. Chicago: University of Chicago Press, 2007.

———. *Bourgeois Equality: How Ideas, Not Capital or Institutions, Enriched the World*. Chicago: University of Chicago Press, 2016.

———. *Bourgeois Dignity: Why Economics Can't Explain the Modern World*. Chicago: University of Chicago Press, 2010.

McCright, Aaron, and Riley E. Dunlap, "Cool Dudes: The Denial of Climate Change among Conservative White Males in the U.S." *Global Environmental Change* 21, no. 4 (2011): 1163–1172.

McKeon, Richard, ed. *The Basic Works of Aristotle*. New York: Modern Library, 2001.

Michaelis, J. D. *Raisonnement Über die Protestantischen Universitäten in Deutschland. Reasonings over the Protestant Universities in Germany*. Frankfurt and Leipzig: Privately printed, 1768.

Michel, Jean-Baptiste, Yuan Kai Shen, Aviva Presser Aiden, Adrian Veres, Matthew K. Gray,

Google Books Team, Joseph P. Pickett, et al. "Quantitative Analysis of Culture Using Millions of Digitized Books." *Science* 331, no. 6014 (2011): 176–182.

Mill, John Stuart. *On Liberty, Representative Government, and The Subjection of Women: Three Essays by John Stuart Mill, with an Introduction by Millicent Garrett Fawcett.* London: Oxford University Press, 1963.

———. *Principles of Political Economy.* London: Longmans, Green, Reader & Dyer, 1871.

Milton, John. "Areopagitica." In *John Milton: The Major Works, Including "Paradise Lost."* Edited by Stephen Orgel and Jonathan Goldberg, 236–272. Oxford: Oxford University Press, 1991.Mokyr, Joel. *The Enlightened Economy: An Economic History of Britain, 1700–1850.* New Haven, CT: Yale University Press, 2012.

Montazerhodjat, Vahid, and Andrew W. Lo. "Is the FDA Too Conservative or Too Aggressive? A Bayesian Decision Analysis of Clinical Trial Design." Social Science Research Network Paper 2641547, January 26, 2016. Accessed November 12, 2016, at http://papers.ssrn.com/sol3/papers.cfm?abstract_id=2641547.

Montes, Leonidas. "Newton's Real Influence on Adam Smith and Its Context." *Cambridge Journal of Economics* 32, no. 4 (2008), 555–576.

Montesquieu, Baron de. *The Spirit of the Laws.* Translated by Thomas Nugent. New York: Hafner, 1949.

Moore, Malcolm. "Young Chinese Maoists Set Up Hippie Commune." *Daily Telegraph*, April 24, 2014. http://www.telegraph.co.uk/news/worldnews/asia/china/10785505/Young-Chinese-Maoists-set-up-hippy-commune.html.

Morehouse, Lisa. "Head to the US-Mexico Border and Find a Chinese Food Scene Like None Other." *PRI World*, April 14, 2015. http://kuow.org/post/head-us-mexico-border-and-find-chinese-food-scene-none-other.

Murray, Charles. *What It Means to be a Libertarian: A Personal Interpretation.* New York: Broadway Books, 1997.

———. *Human Accomplishment: The Pursuit of Excellence in the Arts and Sciences, 800 BC to 1950.* New York: HarperCollins, 2003.

———. *Coming Apart: The State of White America, 1960–2010.* New York: Crown Forum, 2012.

Nakayama, Shigeru. *Academic and Scientific Traditions in China, Japan and the West.* Tokyo: University of Tokyo press, 1985.

Ness, Roberta. *The Creativity Crisis: Reinventing Science to Unleash Possibility.* New York: Oxford University Press, 2014.

O'Flaherty, Wendy Doniger. "The Origin of Heresy in the Hindu Mythology." Ph.D. diss., Oxford University, Linacre College, 1973.Osborne, Evan. "Financial Crashes in the Globalization Era." *Independent Review* 6, no. 2 (2001): 165–184.

———. *The Rise of the Anti-Corporate Movement: Corporations and the People Who Hate Them.* Stanford: Stanford University Press, 2009.

Osterhammer, Jürgen. *The Transformation of the World: A Global History of the Nineteenth Century.* Translated by Patrick Camiller. Princeton: Princeton University Press, 2014.

Ostrom, Elinor. *Governing the Commons: The Evolution of Institutions for Collective Action.* Cambridge: Cambridge University Press, 1990.

Parker, Ian. "Swingers: Bonobos Are Celebrated as Peace-Loving, Matriarchal, and Sexually Liberated. Are They?" *New Yorker*, July 30, 2007, 48–61.

Partridge, Michael. *Gladstone.* London: Routledge, 2003.

Paulsen, Friedrich. *The German Universities and University Study.* Translated by Frank Thilly and William L. Elwang. New York: Scribner, 1906.

Pigou, A. C. *Wealth and Welfare.* London: Macmillan, 1912.

———. *The Economics of Welfare.* London: Macmillan, 1920.

Pinker, Steven. *The Better Angels of Our Nature: Why Violence Has Declined.* New York: Viking Press, 2011.

Polanyi, Michael. "The Republic of Science: Its Political and Economic Theory." *Minerva* 1, no. 1 (1962): 54–73.

de Pommereau, Isabelle. "Are Towns Really Safer without Traffic Lights?" *Christian Science Monitor*, September 12, 2008.

Ponnamperuma, Cyril. "Seeds of Life." In *The Omni Interviews*, edited by Pamela Weintraub, 1–19. New York: Ticknor & Fields, 1984.

Popper, Karl. *The Logic of Scientific Discovery*. New York: Basic Books, 1959.

Posner, Richard A. *Economic Analysis of Law*, 9th ed. New York: Wolters Kluwer, 2014.

Raustiak, Kal, and Christopher Sigman. *The Knockoff Economy: How Imitation Spurs Innovation*. New York: Oxford University Press, 2012.

Rauch Jonathan. *Kindly Inquisitors: The New Attacks on Free Thought*, exp. ed. Chicago: University of Chicago Press, 2014.

Reinhart, Carmen M., and Kenneth Rogoff. *This Time It's Different: Eight Centuries of Financial Folly*. Princeton: Princeton University Press, 2011.

Renfrew, Colin. "Beyond a Subsistence Economy: The Evolution of Social Organization in Prehistoric Europe." In Colin Renfrew, Ian Todd, and Ruth Tringham, eds., *Bulletin of the American Schools of Oriental Research, Supplementary Studies*, 1974, 69–95.

Reyes-Centenoa, Hugo, Silvia Ghirottob, Florent Détroit, Dominique Grimaud-Hervéc, Guido Barbujanib, and Katerina Harvatia. "Genomic and Cranial Phenotype Data Support Multiple Modern Human Dispersals from Africa and a Southern Route into Asia." *Proceedings of the National Academy of Sciences* 111, no. 20 (2014): 7163–7164.

Ridley, Matt. *The Rational Optimist: How Prosperity Evolves*. New York: Harper Perennial, 2011.

Rorty, Richard. *Contingency, Irony and Solidarity*. Cambridge: Cambridge University Press, 2009.

Rose, Nikolas. *The Politics of Life Itself: Biomedicine, Power and Subjectivity in the Twenty-First Century*. Princeton: Princeton University Press, 2007.

Rosenberg, Nathan. *Inside the Black Box: Technology and Economics*. Cambridge: Cambridge University Press, 1986.

Rosenvallion, Pierre. *Le capitalism utopique: Critique de l'idéologie économique*. Paris: Editions du Seuil, 1979.

Ross, Andrew. "Introduction." *Social Text* no. 46/47 (1996): 1–13.

Rothbard, Murray, "The World of Salamanca," *Mises Daily*, October 27, 2009. http://mises .org/library/world-salamanca.

Rousseau, Jean-Jacques. *Emile: Or on Education*. Translated by Allan Bloom. New York: Basic Books, 1979 [1762].

———. "On the Social Contract." *The Social Contract and Later Political Writings*. Edited and translated by Victor Gourevitch. Cambridge: Cambridge University Press, 1997.

Rubin, Alyssa J., and Mark Scott. "Clashes Erupt across France as Taxi Drivers Protest Uber." *New York Times*, June 26, 2015.

Rule, Alix, Jean-Philippe Cointet, and Peter S. Bearman. "Lexical Shifts, Substantive Changes, and Continuity in State of the Union Discourse, 1790–2014." *Proceedings of the National Academy of Sciences* 112, no. 35 (2015): 10837–10844. doi:10.1073/pnas.1512221112, http://www.pnas.org/content/112/35/10837.full.

Rushdie, Salman. *The Rushdie Letters: Freedom to Speak, Freedom to Write*. Edited by Stephen MacDonough and Article 19. Lincoln: University of Nebraska Press, 1993.

Said, Edward. *Orientalism*. New York: Pantheon Books, 1978.

Samuels, Warren A. "The Firing of E. A. Ross from Stanford University: Injustice Compounded by Deception." *Journal of Economic Education* 22, no. 2 (1991): 183–190.

Samuelson, Paul A. "The Pure Theory of Public Expenditure." *Review of Economics and Statistics* 36, no. 4 (1954): 387–389.

Sandman, Peter M. "Climate Change Risk Communication: The Problem of Psychological Denial." 2009. http://www.psandman.com/col/climate.htm.

Schick, Béla. "Das Menstruationsgift." *Wiener Klinische Wochenschrift* 33 (1920): 395–397.

Schleicher, David. "Stuck! The Law and Economics of Residential Stability." *Yale Law Journal* (forthcoming). https://papers.ssrn.com/sol3/papers.cfm?abstract_id=2896309.

Schneider, Gerald, Katherine Barbieri, and Nils Petter Gleditsch. "Does Globalization Contribute to Peace? A Critical Survey of the Literature." In *Globalization and Armed Conflict*, edited by Gerald Schneider, Katherine Barbieri, and Nils Petter Gleditsch, 3–30. Lanham, MD: Rowman and Littlefield, 2003.

Seager, Henry Rogers. "The Minimum Wage as Part of a Program for Social Reform." *Annals of the American Academy of Political Science* 48, no. 10 (1913): 3–12.

Service, Elman Rogers. *Primitive Social Organization: An Evolutionary Perspective*. New York: Random House, 1962.

———. *Origins of the State and Civilization: The Process of Cultural Evolution*. New York: Norton, 1975.

Shackleton, Robert. "Total Factor Productivity Growth in Historical Perspective," Congressional Budget Office Working Paper, 2013–01. 2013. https://www.cbo.gov/sites/default/files/cbofiles/attachments/44002_TFP_Growth_03-18-2013.pdf.

Shah, Shalin, Vijay Bhaskar, Karthik Venkatraghavan, Prashant Choudhary, M. Ganesh, and Krishna Trivedi. "Silver Diamine Fluoride: A Review and Current Applications." *Journal of Advanced Oral Research*, 5, no. 2 (2014): 25–35.

Sharer, Robert. *Daily Life in Maya Civilization*. Westport, CT: Greenwood Press, 2009.

Shaw, George Bernard. "Discussion." *American Journal of Sociology* 10, no. 1 (1904): 21–23.

Sheldon, Charles D. "Merchants and Society in Tokugawa Japan." *Modern Asian Studies* 17 (1983): 477–478.

Shlaes, Amity. *The Forgotten Man: A New History of the Great Depression*. New York: HarperCollins, 2007.

Sidgwick, Henry. *The Principles of Political Economy*. London: Macmillan, 1883.

Sinclair, Tara M., and Kathryn Vesey. "Regulation, Jobs, and Economic Growth: An Empirical Analysis." George Washington University Regulatory Studies Center Working Paper, 2012.

Smith, Adam. *An Inquiry into the Nature and Causes of the Wealth of Nations*. Chicago: University of Chicago Press, 1976 [1766].

Snyder, Timothy. *Bloodlands: Europe between Hitler and Stalin*. New York: Basic Books, 2011.

Sokal, Alan. "Transgressing the Boundaries: Towards a Transformative Hermeneutics of Quantum Gravity." *Social Text* no. 46/47 (1996): 217–252.

Sokal, Alan, and Jean Bricmont. *Fashionable Nonsense: Postmodern Intellectuals' Abuse of Science*. London: Profile Books, 1998.

Spencer, Herbert. *Principles of Biology*. London: Williams and Norgate, 1864.

———. *The Principles of Ethics*, vol. 1. New York: D. Appleton, 1897.

Spier, Ray. "The History of the Peer-Review Process." *Trends in Biotechnology* 20, no. 8 (2002): 357–358.

Stewart, Dugald. "Account of the Life and Writings of Adam Smith," In Adam Smith and Dugald Stewart, *Essays on Philosophical Subjects*. London: T. Cadell Jun and W. Davies, 1795.

Sumner, William Graham. *The Forgotten Man and Other Essays*, edited by Albert Galloway Keller. New Haven, CT: Yale University Press, 1919.

Szasz, Thomas. *The Therapeutic State: Psychiatry in the Mirror of Current Events*. Amherst, NY: Prometheus Books, 1984.

Tabarrok, Alexander T. "Assessing the FDA via the Anomaly of Off-Label Drug Prescribing." *Independent Review* 5, no. 1 (2000): 25–53.

Tainter, Joseph A. *The Collapse of Complex Societies*. Cambridge: Cambridge University Press, 1988.

Taleb, Nassim Nicholas. *Antifragile: Things That Gain from Disorder*. New York: Random House, 2012.

Thaler, Richard H., and Cass R. Sunstein, "Behavioral Economics, Public Policy, and Paternalism." *American Economic Review* 93, no. 2 (2003): 175–179.

Thompson, Allen. *The Dynamics of the Industrial Revolution*. New York: St. Martin's Press, 1973.

Thucydides. *The History of the Peloponnesian War*. New York: Galaxy, 1960.

Tullock, Gordon. "The Welfare Costs of Tariffs, Monopolies and Theft." *Western Economic Journal* 5, no. 3 (1967): 224–232.

Turgot, Anne Robert Jacques. "In Praise of Gournay." In *The Turgot Collection: Writings, Speeches and Letters of Anne Robert Jacques Turgot, Baron de Laune*, edited by David Gordo,99–127. Auburn, AL: Ludwig von Mises Institute, 2011.

Tupy, Marian. "Hong Kong and the Power of Economic Freedom." *Reason Online*, March 8, 2016. http://reason.com/archives/2016/03/08/hong-kong-and-the-power-of-economic-free.

Velasquez-Manoff, Moisés. *An Epidemic of Absence: A New Way of Understanding Allergies and Autoimmune Diseases*. New York: Simon and Schuster, 2012.

Veylit, Alain. "Some Statistics on the Number of Surviving Printed Titles for Great Britain." N.d. Accessed November 12, 2016, at *http://estc.ucr.edu/ESTCStatistics.html*.

Voltaire. *Philosophical Letters, or, Letters Regarding the English Nation*. Edited by John Leigh. Translated by Prudence L. Steiner. Indianapolis: Hackett, 2007 [1733].

Wallerstein, Immanuel. "The Rise and Future Demise of the World Capitalist System: Concepts for Comparative Analysis." *Comparative Studies in Society and History* 16, no. 4 (1974): 387–415.

Watson, John B. *Behaviorism*. Chicago: University of Chicago Press, 1930.

Watson, Peter. *Ideas: A History of Thought and Invention, from Fire to Freud*. New York: Harper Perennial, 2006.

"William Graham Sumner, Yale Professor, Dead." *New York Times*, April 23, 1910.

Wilson, Edward O. *Consilience: The Unity of Knowledge*. New York: Vintage, 1999.

Wilson, Woodrow. *Constitutional Government in the United States*. New York: Columbia University Press, 1908.

———. "The Ideals of America." *Atlantic* 90 (December 1902): 721–734.

Wolchover, Natalie. "A Fight for the Soul of Science." *Quanta*. 2015. https://www.quanta magazine.org/20151216–physicists-and-philosophers-debate-the-boundaries-of-science/.

Wright, Robert. *The Evolution of God*. New York: Little, Brown, 2009.

Wurz, S. "The Transition to Modern Behavior." *Nature Education Knowledge* 3, no. 10 (2012). https://www.nature.com/scitable/knowledge/library/the-transition-to-modern -behavior-86614339.

Yang, Jisheng. *Tombstone: The Great Chinese Famine, 1958–1962*, edited by Edward Friedman. Edited and translated by Stacy Mosher and Jian Guo. New York: Farrar, Straus and Giroux, 2013.

Young, Leslie. "The Tao of Markets: Sima Qian and the Invisible Hand." *Pacific Economic Review* 1, no. 2 (1996): 137–145.

Zamoyski, Adam. *Phantom Terror: Political Paranoia and the Creation of the Modern State, 1789–1848*. New York: Basic Books, 2015.

Index